CYCLING IN THE HEBRIDES

About the Author

After years of road running and mountaineering had wreaked havoc with his knees, Richard Barrett returned to long-distance cycling in his fifties, when he bought himself one of the classic British-made touring bikes that he always intended to buy with the money he made from his newspaper round, but never did. Combined with sea kayaking, it allows him to continue his love affair with the Hebrides, which he first visited as a teenager.

His career was spent in marketing in a number of multinational organisations in the UK and abroad, but he now lives in North Harris where he runs a guest house with his wife.

Other Cicerone guides by the author
Walking on Harris and Lewis

Dedication

A bike was an essential form of transport for my late father, Dick, who cycled to work throughout his life and continued to ride into his mid-80s.

Today bikes are a passion for our son, Joe, a bike mechanic and downhill instructor, who makes his living on the back of the explosion in leisure cycling – something my dad could never quite fathom.

This book is dedicated to you both.

CYCLING IN THE HEBRIDES

ISLAND TOURING AND DAY RIDES

by Richard Barrett

2 POLICE SQUARE, MILNTHORPE, CUMBRIA LA7 7PY
www.cicerone.co.uk

Printed in China on behalf of Latitude Press Ltd
A catalogue record for this book is available from the British Library.
All photographs are by the author unless otherwise stated.

This product includes mapping data licensed from Ordnance Survey® with the permission of the Controller of Her Majesty's Stationery Office. © Crown copyright 2012. All rights reserved. Licence number PU100012932

Base maps for routes by Lovell Johns Ltd www.lovelljohns.com

Acknowledgements

My thanks go to the people who accompanied me on these rides – especially those who kept their cool when asked to go back and ride into camera shot for a second or third time. They include Nick Cloake, Kieran Ryan and Simon Wheeler and my wife Cindy. I should also thank the riders we met along the way for their companionship, help and advice. Jonathan, Lois, James and the team at Cicerone were a delight to work with and their sound guidance notes made delivering the manuscript and accompanying photographs a pleasure.

Advice to Readers

While every effort is made by our authors to ensure the accuracy of guidebooks as they go to print, changes can occur during the lifetime of an edition. If we know of any, there will be an Updates tab on this book's page on the Cicerone website (www.cicerone.co.uk), so please check before planning your trip. We also advise that you check information about such things as transport, accommodation and shops locally. Even rights of way can be altered over time. We are always grateful for information about any discrepancies between a guidebook and the facts on the ground, sent by email to info@cicerone.co.uk or by post to Cicerone, 2 Police Square, Milnthorpe LA7 7PY, United Kingdom.

Front cover: Passing a traditional *tigh gael* at Malacleit, North Uist (Route 5D)

CONTENTS

Route symbols on map extracts

~ route

alternative route

▷ route direction

🚲 start / finish point

☕🔧 refreshments, cycle shop

🚲 £ cycle hire, cash point

⇌ railway station

castle

Route map scale 1:250 000 (1cm = 2.5km)

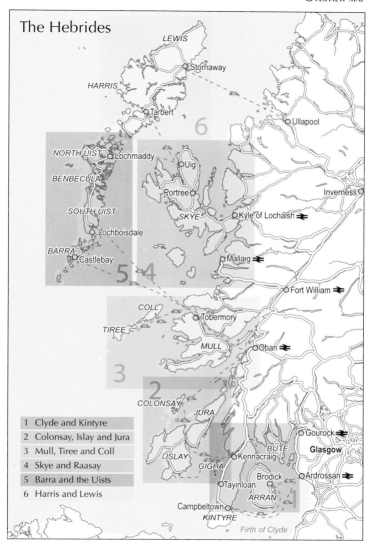

The Hebrides

1 Clyde and Kintyre
2 Colonsay, Islay and Jura
3 Mull, Tiree and Coll
4 Skye and Raasay
5 Barra and the Uists
6 Harris and Lewis

LEWIS
Stornaway
HARRIS
Tarbert
Ullapool
NORTH UIST Lochmaddy
BENBECULA
Uig
SOUTH UIST
Portree
Inverness
SKYE
Lochboisdale
Kyle of Lochalsh
BARRA
Castlebay
Mallaig
Fort William
COLL
Tobermory
TIREE
MULL
Oban
COLONSAY
JURA
Gourock
BUTE
Glasgow
ISLAY
Kennacraig
Brodick
GIGHA
Ardrossan
Tayinloan
ARRAN
Campbeltown
KINTYRE
Firth of Clyde

Loaded mountain bike on Tiree (Part 3)

INTRODUCTION

*It is by riding a bicycle that you learn
the contours of a country best, since
you have to sweat up the hills and coast
down them... you remember them as
they actually are.*
Ernest Hemingway

Travelling by boat heightens the physical senses and the spirit of adventure. People stand on deck in all weathers, lungs bursting with fresh air, looking back as their point of departure fades into a haze then staring at the indefinite line on the horizon that marks their destination, slowly crystallising into landmarks they are eager to explore. Unrestrained by seat belts and liberated from sanitised air

conditioning, they revel in the freedom to move around, watch the mercurial changes in the light and soak up the atmosphere. This is travel as it should be and there is nowhere better to enjoy it than island-hopping in the Hebrides. Use a bicycle to get around for part if not all of your holiday and you can enjoy the thrill of travelling under your own steam for days on end.

Strictly speaking the Hebrides run from Islay in the south to Lewis in the north. However Arran and the other islands in the Firth of Clyde are included here to maximise island-hopping possibilities. As a result this guidebook includes routes on all the

Kiloran Beach – said to be the prettiest in the Hebrides (Route 2.6)

Looking across to Eigg and Rum (Route 3D)

major islands served from the ferry ports on the west coast of Scotland, from Ardrossan in the south to Ullapool in the north. In total there are 147 islands with an area of 40 hectares (100 acres) or more within this enlarged region, although only 54 of these are inhabited today.

The Isle of Lewis has the largest population, with about 18,000 residents even without the benefit of the further 2000 folk on its conjoined neighbour, the Isle of Harris. At the other extreme, both Sanda, off the tip of Kintyre, and Shuna, one of the Slate Islands south of Oban, are recorded in the 2001 Census as having a full-time population of one. Of those islands that were populated at the time of the 1961 Census, 22 were uninhabited by 2001, although the total population of the region has remained fairly constant throughout this period: some

islands, such as Arran, Mull and Skye, have enjoyed steady growth while others have seen a gradual decline. Not that you will ever feel overrun with people. Great Cumbrae, which is the most densely populated Scottish Island, only has 500 residents per square mile – about two thirds of the average for the whole of the UK.

Despite proximity to each other, many of the islands have an atmosphere distinctly their own. Sometimes this is due to topology, fertility and industry, sometimes to the presence of a safe deep water harbour as a base for fishing, and occasionally the tenure of a past or present owner. As a result, neighbouring islands such as Islay, Jura and Colonsay can all seem very different. Islay is fertile and comparatively prosperous; Jura is wild and empty; and Colonsay transports one back to the country estates of the

Edwardian era. Such variety means that cycling in the Hebrides is always interesting with the landscape, the people and even the weather continually changing, so that no two days are the same.

The rides described in this guidebook are similarly varied, ranging from a 12-mile (19km) day ride to a 600-mile (970km) tour, while visitors to a compact island like Great Cumbrae will find a surprising variety of cycling in a small area. So this book caters not just for those who are cycle touring but also for those who simply want to get in a few rides while they are on holiday in the Hebrides.

TERRAIN

The Hebrides and the islands in the Forth of Clyde are geologically diverse, and this gives a range of riding conditions that vary from the steep hills of islands as far apart as Arran and Skye to the windswept peat moors of the Western Isles. The area lies to the north and west of the Highland Boundary Fault, which splits Arran in two and runs northeast to Stonehaven. Most of the region's rocks date back to the Cambrian and Precambrian eras and have been gouged by ice and rounded by wind and water, making for gentle hills and easier riding. But mixed in with these older rocks are younger intrusions of igneous rocks, such as the gabbro of the jagged Black Cuillin, that result in steeper inclines and harder riding.

Such diversity means there is little pattern to the difficulty of the rides. Riding in the north of Arran is certainly harder than riding on the other side

Ord Beach, Sleat (Route 4.1)

of the Highland Boundary Fault in the south of the island. Similarly Coll and Tiree barely rise above sea level and are easy rides as long as there is little wind, whereas rides on neighbouring Mull are challenging whatever the weather.

We think of the Hebrides as being a wilderness at the very edge of Europe, but other than the higher ground, the land bears the scars of human activity not least in the absence of woodland and scrub which would have covered 50–60 per cent of the area. The trees gradually disappeared over millennia, partly due to the onset of a colder and wetter climate and partly due to clearance for building and fuel. The large populations of sheep and deer that were first introduced in high numbers in the 19th century preclude natural regeneration and mean that today woody vegetation is only found in inaccessible ravines or on steeper cliffs. However there are a number

of community initiatives on islands such as Eigg and Harris to reestablish woodlands for commercial, ecological and recreational purposes.

WILDLIFE AND PLANTS

Lack of biodiversity means that the region is home to fewer birds and mammals than the rest of Britain. But what it lacks in numbers, it certainly makes up for in quality. Bird life includes rarities such as the elusive corncrake, the red-necked phalarope and the yellow-billed diver, which only ever appears for a few brief weeks on the extreme north of Lewis; crowd-pleasing favourites such as the puffin and the clownish, red-billed chough; and the magnificent golden eagle and white-tailed sea eagle. The latter was re-introduced to Rum in 1975 and has successfully spread to neighbouring islands, particularly Mull, where it is a major tourist attraction.

Red deer hinds (photo: Robin Reid)

(Left to right) Starry saxifrage; Hebridean spotted orchid (photos: Robin Reid)

Red deer are common on the hills, but the only other large mammal is the hare. The Duke of Argyll introduced the brown hare to Tiree in 1827 and it has since thrived to the extent that it is impossible to miss. But you need to venture into the high hills to see the smaller and more furtive mountain hare, of which there are large numbers on Harris and Lewis. There have been inconclusive sightings of the rare Scottish wildcat on the Trotternish Peninsula of Skye and on Mull, and although the pine marten is still common on the Scottish mainland, it is considered to be entirely absent from the islands.

Hedgehogs introduced to North Uist to control garden slugs are thought to have upset the breeding of waders and an initiative to trap and remove them has been underway in recent years.

Offshore, the grey seal and common seal are found all the way up the western seaboard in internationally important numbers, with colonies of the former on Oronsay and the Treshnish Isles. On longer ferry crossings, porpoises, dolphins, basking sharks and, if you are really lucky, minke whales can occasionally be seen.

Although there is a great diversity of wild flowers across the islands, other than the prominent yellow flag irises and the spectacle of the machair in early summer, when the fertile pasture that runs down the Atlantic shore of the Western Isles is a carpet of colour, a passing cyclist will be oblivious to the gems beyond the verge. Rare orchids abound in the right spots and other late-flowering wild flowers can be found on the fertile coastal plains. But the attractions for the avid botanist are the apparently insignificant mosses and liverworts that thrive in this maritime climate.

HISTORY AND CULTURE

Our modern sensibilities and enslavement to the car lead us to think of the region as remote and inaccessible.

15

But before roads were pushed into the region in the 18th and 19th centuries, sea was the main form of transport and travelling through the Hebrides would have been considered far easier than venturing across the Highlands. The Hebrides have many of the most recent roads in the UK – such as the road to the village of Reinigeadal on Harris which was only built in 1989.

The standing stones at Callanish on Lewis are evidence of a sophisticated community during the Neolithic period and other finds show that the area was well populated before 6000BC. Written records for the region begin in the 6th century AD when the kingdom of Dal Riata was founded, encompassing the southern islands with parts of mainland Scotland and Northern Ireland, from where Columba set out to found the monastery on Iona; a first step that would lead to monasteries being established on Oronsay and Lismore as Christianity spread across northern Britain.

Picts dominated the northern and outer isles until the Vikings occupied them in the 8th century. Although only their place names and a few artefacts, such as the Lewis chessmen, remain, they stayed for four centuries before relinquishing control to the Scottish crown in 1266. Five centuries of clan rivalry followed, with territories changing hands numerous times. In an attempt to restore the Stuart crown, many island clans put aside their quarrels and rallied to the support of the Old Pretender at the 1715 uprising and then Bonnie Prince Charlie, the Young Pretender, in 1745. Their defeat at the Battle of Culloden lead to the demise of the clans and allowed English-speaking landlords to take over many of their estates. This brought lasting peace to the region, but not an end to the islanders' strife.

While the early 19th century saw the growth of industries such as slate quarrying and kelp burning, that lead to improvements to roads and quays and a surge in the population, by the middle of the century the boom was over. Industries failed, the population could not feed itself and many landlords were financially ruined. Many people from across the Hebrides were either given financial help to emigrate or forcibly evicted, and the land was given over to sheep or deer. Numerous local uprisings against the lack of access to land, such as the 'Battle of the Braes' on Skye and the Bernera Riots on Lewis, eventually led to the Crofters Act of 1886.

While crofting, cattle rearing, fishing and tourism gave many people employment, others emigrated or entered military service and the population continued to dwindle throughout most of the 20th century. Today, the populations of the more accessible islands such as Bute, Arran and Skye are recovering with an influx of retired people. But the smaller and more remote Western Isles struggle to stem a decline in their population that first started well over a century ago. For many, this fragility is all part of the romance.

THOMAS TELFORD 1757–1834

*The quay at Portree (Route 4B),
one of many in the Hebrides designed by Thomas Telford*

When you are cycling in the Highlands and Islands, sooner or later you will find yourself on one of Telford's roads or disembarking from one of his quays. He will have determined its position and overseen its construction – and yet his considerable achievements largely go unnoticed. Despite humble beginnings as a stonemason in the Borders of Scotland, Telford's prodigious appetite for work lead to the early patronage of Sir William Pulteney and this allowed him to build an illustrious career as a civil engineer. He never married and was itinerant for most of his life, surveying, designing and overseeing massive construction projects that were run by an army of assistants, many of whom followed him from job to job. Today he is most often remembered for his pioneering bridges across the Menai and the Conway in North Wales and for the Caledonian Canal. But perhaps his greatest achievement was the road network he built across Scotland between 1803 and 1825.

After the clans had been routed at Culloden in 1745 the British Government ignored the Highlands for half a century. Between 1725 and 1737, General Wade had constructed 250 miles of military roads across the Highlands that linked the main garrisons, but these were needlessly steep and had no bridges so were largely abandoned by the local population. By the late 18th century the Highland population was dwindling due to emigration and the Government was concerned enough to fund a regeneration project in which building new roads and harbours formed a major part. In 1801 Telford was commissioned to produce a report and subsequently to oversee the construction of 920 miles (1480km) of roads, over 1000 bridges and numerous quays. The Church of Scotland had been petitioning for new churches, and in 1823 the Government funded the construction of 32 new 'Parliamentary' churches and 41 manses, which were built to designs chosen by Telford. The stipulation that expenditure was not to exceed £1500 at any one site means they are simple and unadorned – and occasionally austere.

Telford managed this mammoth task by establishing six districts, each headed by one of his faithful assistants. This meant he had time to get involved in numerous other projects all over the United Kingdom and as far afield as Sweden, where he oversaw the construction of the Gotha Canal. But he visited the Highlands and Islands regularly for the next 30 years, monitoring progress and dealing with construction issues as they arose. The list below, which is far from exhaustive, highlights just some of his projects along the west coast and through the Hebrides:

- **Roads**
  Fort William–Arisaig, Ardgour–Acharacle, Glen Shiel, Dingwall–Lochcarron and Shieldaig, Kyleakin–Uig, the 'String Road' across Arran

- **Harbours**
  Ardrossan, Craighouse, Portree, Tayvallich, Tobermory and Ullapool

- **Churches**
  Acharacle, Berneray, Hallin, Iona, Kinlochspelvie, Kilmeny, Plockton, Poolewe, Portnahaven, Steinscholl, Strontian, Timsgarry, Tobermory, Ullapool and Ulva

In 1819 the Lakeland poet Robert Southey accompanied Telford on one of his routine inspection tours of the various construction projects across the Highlands and subsequently wrote that he was the 'Colossus of Roads', a nickname that has stuck with him. The two became lifelong friends to the extent that Telford left Southey a sizeable legacy in his will.

MV Hebridean Isles passing below the Paps of Jura (Part 2)

GETTING THERE

Last time I was on Berneray I met a man who had ridden all the way to the Western Isles from his home in Yorkshire, covering a distance of 380 miles (610km) in four days. Like many hardened touring cyclists, using any other form of transportation as part of a touring holiday was an anathema to him. If you plan to cycle all the way you should consider the National Cycle Network, which now extends as far as Oban and Inverness and is steadily penetrating further into the region. However, most of us simply want to start our proper holiday as soon as possible and will resort to whatever form of transport fits our needs.

By road

Getting to the Hebrides is a major undertaking. The distance from London to Skye is roughly 650 miles (1000km), making it about the same as a trip to the French Alps. For most people, that probably means a two-day drive with an overnight stop. Others may prefer to drive through the night and with two people driving you can take advantage of the relatively empty roads and make good progress. Just bear in mind that once you leave the main motorway network between Glasgow and Edinburgh, there are few 24 hour filling stations other than Fort William and Inverness, so keep an eye on the fuel gauge.

LONG-STAY PARKING

Ardrossan
Long-stay parking is available at the ferry terminal – daily charges apply.

Gourock
Long-stay parking for up to 24 hours is available at the railway station – daily charges apply. Otherwise it's a matter of parking in a quiet back street.

Kennacraig
Free long-stay parking is available at the ferry terminal.

Largs
Long-stay parking for up to 24 hours is available at the Seafront car park located next to the Escape Amusement Complex – charges apply. Free long-stay parking is available just south of the town at Largs Marina. Otherwise it's a matter of parking in a quiet back street.

Mallaig
Free long-stay parking is available at the large open car park near the railway station.

Oban
Free long-stay parking is available at open car parks at Lochavullin Road and Longsdale Road. Secure long-stay parking and storage is provided by Hazelbank Motors – tel 01631 566476 – and Timbertech – tel 01631 566660.

Uig
Free long-stay parking is available at the ferry terminal.

Ullapool
Free long-stay parking is available at open car parks in the town.

Wemyss Bay
Parking for up to 24 hours is available at the railway station – daily charges apply. Otherwise it's a matter of parking in a quiet back street.

By air
There are airports at Stornoway, Benbecula, Barra, Colonsay, Tiree, Islay, Oban and Campbeltown, with most services linking into the national and international air network through the main Scottish airports of Glasgow, Edinburgh, Inverness and Aberdeen.

See Highland and Islands Airports at www.hial.co.uk for details.

If you are planning to fly with your bike, you should contact your airline and make a reservation when you book your seat. They will charge you for carrying your bike and will ask that you follow their packing instructions. These typically include turning and locking the handlebars parallel with the frame, removing the pedals and front wheel and attaching them to the frame and deflating the tyres before placing the bike in a carrying bag or transit box. If you are planning to tour, you will need to organise somewhere to store the transit material ready for collection on your return.

By rail

Ardrossan, Largs, Wemyss Bay, Gourock, Oban, Mallaig and Kyle of Lochalsh are all on the rail network so it is possible to have a low-carbon, car-free holiday. Ullapool is the only major mainland ferry port not on the network, and although the train operator provides a bus service from Inverness station this does not carry cycles. You could take the train as far as Garve and then cycle the 32 miles (51km) to Ullapool. An easier alternative is to book a place on the D&E Coaches service, as that pulls a bike trailer. It runs from Inverness station to Ullapool between May and September, but needs to be pre-booked. See www.decoaches.co.uk/services.asp or tel 01463 222444.

If you are planning to carry your bike by rail, you will need to make a reservation with each train operator you will be using and ensure you follow their individual procedures. This typically involves picking up a bike tag at the ticket office and placing your bike in the dedicated stowage area. It's always worth asking platform staff where this is located before you get on. ScotRail operates 95 per cent of passenger train services within Scotland and you will almost certainly be using them for the final step of your journey no matter where you started from. Cycles are carried free of charge on ScotRail services, although reservations are required on longer distance ScotRail routes. For further information contact ScotRail on 0845 601 5929 or see www.scotrail.co.uk for details.

ScotRail also operate the Caledonian Sleeper. This is an overnight train service with twin berth cabins that runs from London Euston up the UK's west coast main line to Scotland six nights a week, enabling you to complete most of your journey in deep slumber and awake totally refreshed. See www.scotrail.co.uk/caledoniansleeper/index.html.

By bus

National Express, Britain's only scheduled coach network, explicitly states that they do not carry non-folding bicycles, which eliminates the possibility of getting into the region by bus. Some major Scottish bus operators, such as Citylink, carry bicycles but ask that they are in a box or bag and typically qualify their terms and conditions with clauses such as 'subject to space being available' or 'at the driver's discretion'. As this gives cyclists no reassurance that their bike will actually be carried, let alone any advice what to do with the transit box when they want to start cycling: they may as well just say 'No'. Others are more flexible. For instance West Coast Motors, which operates services across Argyll and all of the coaches that serve the major routes through the Western Isles, have space for a couple of bikes in their cargo hold if they are not already taken. However you still have no guarantee of a ride. So take advantage of them when the opportunity arises – but always be prepared to get back in the saddle and pedal.

GETTING AROUND

No matter whether you are cycle touring, staying put at a single location or visiting a number of islands in the course of your holiday, you will need to refer to the Caledonian MacBrayne ('CalMac') timetables, which can be viewed and downloaded from their website (www.calmac.co.uk) or tel 0800 066 5000. The summer timetable starts at the end of March and runs through to the end of October, but even in the tourist season services to the more remote and less populated islands are still infrequent.

If you are planning to tour either by bike or by vehicle, you should try to take advantage of one of the many Island Hopscotch tickets. These are pre-planned routes that take in a number of islands and offer a saving over the normal tariff. To make your planning

Approaching Tarbert, Isle of Harris (Part 6)

easier, in this book the islands are grouped following the format of Island Hopscotch tickets. However it is always advisable to reserve your accommodation first, as bed spaces are limited in the peak season. Similarly, you may be able to save a few pounds by purchasing an 8 or 15-day Island Rover ticket.

To save the disappointment of being left on the quayside, reservations for vehicles are recommended, especially during the summer months. This is not necessary for foot passengers and cyclists, although large groups are asked to contact the office at the port of departure before the day of travel so space can be reserved for you. If there is a ticket office at the terminal, simply turn up at least half an hour before departure so you have plenty of time to purchase a ticket and fill out a boarding pass.

Ticket prices for foot passengers are still modest and bikes are carried free of charge, so cycle touring in the Hebrides can be a cheap holiday,

especially if you are hostelling or camping. Make your way to the head of the queue of waiting vehicles, where a crew member will tell you when to board and where to put your bike. Take care when riding down the ramp as they can be slippery. Where there is no shore-based ticketing office, you pay onboard. So wait in the queue with other vehicles until a crew member invites you to board.

Because the longer crossings can be rough, it is always advisable to secure your bike with the ropes available in the designated stowage area rather than risk it being thrown around. Once at sea, there is no further access to the car deck and hence no need to take your panniers into the passenger areas. Simply take your valuables in your handlebar bag. If you have been rough camping and haven't had the opportunity for a shower for a few days, you might want to take your toiletries and towels with you as some of the ships on

MAKING USE OF THE CLASSIC PLEASURE STEAMERS

The pleasure steamers, the Balmoral and the Waverley, the latter the last seagoing paddle steamer in the world, sail a changing itinerary around the Clyde and occasionally further up the west coast between May and September. Both ships were built in the 1940s and were acquired and authentically refurbished by The Paddle Steamer Preservation Society, which now runs a full programme of cruises during the summer months. They carry bikes for a nominal charge and single fares are available which means they are a memorable but still practical alternative to a scheduled CalMac service. Many cruises start and finish at Glasgow Science Park, which is particularly convenient for those arriving by rail. See www.waverleyexcursions.co.uk for details.

the longer routes have showers – as do certain terminal buildings.

It is advisable to carry a printout of all the routes you might possibly use by downloading the timetable from the CalMac website. The only routes you will be missing are an alternative service between Gourock and Dunoon operated by Western Ferries – see www.western-ferries.co.uk – and the ferry to Kerrera – see www.kerrera-ferry.co.uk.

THE WEATHER AND WHEN TO GO

A failed attempt to berth at Coll in bad weather (Part 3)

The best time to go touring in the Hebrides is between April and October, when the days are longer and the weather is at its best. But even then, you will undoubtedly get wet and blustery days, so be prepared for them. As a general rule always plan your route so that you are riding south to north with the prevailing southwesterly winds. The majority of the routes in this guide are designed to take account of the wind. However check the weather forecast before you set out each day and be prepared to amend your plans when and where you can to take account of the poor weather.

The Hebrides consists of small landmasses in a large maritime environment, so it pays to check shipping forecasts and coastal waters forecasts as these will give you the outlook for wind speeds and visibility. These can be heard on BBC Radio 4 on 198 kHz long wave at 0048hrs, 0520hrs, 1201hrs and 1754hrs, can be accessed through the BBC Weather pages on the internet or obtained from the local tourist information offices. That way you will lessen the risk of getting caught out in a gale or having to ride in a thick mist.

Wind deserves respect in the Hebrides, especially in the Western Isles, and even in summer it is worth carrying a cycling balaclava or buff that fits underneath your cycling helmet. In January 2005 the islands experienced the worst gales for 50 years, with a lorry driver in Lewis reporting a sheep being blown across his windscreen! Sadly a family of five was killed during the same storm when their car was blown off the South Ford causeway linking Benbecula and

A fine bunkhouse at Leverburgh, Harris (Part 6)

South Uist. If in doubt, abandon the day's ride until tomorrow and find something else to do today!

WHERE TO STAY

The area offers a range of hotels, guest houses, B&Bs and hostels, so there is something to suit most pockets. The cheapest option is a tent and this also gives the flexibility to change plans at short notice. Although the right to roam means you can camp anywhere in Scotland, if you want amenities such as toilets and showers then you will need to use proper campsites and may need to book in advance. Staying in hostels is also a relatively cheap option. The Scottish Youth Hostel Association – www.syha.org.uk – has a number of hostels in the Hebrides and along the western seaboard, but you will need to make reservations in advance during peak holiday periods and it is cheaper if you become a member. There are also a number of independent hostels – www.hostels-scotland.co.uk – scattered across the region and although these are open to all comers, you still need to book in advance at many of them. All but the most basic hostels provide bedding but you may wish to carry your own sleeping bag liner.

Many of VisitScotland's star-graded B&Bs, guest houses and hotels have enrolled with 'Cyclists Welcome' scheme, and these are worth seeking out. Having this accreditation means that the property has been assessed by VisitScotland and meets their criteria for being biker-friendly. These include:

- having a dedicated space for drying outdoor clothing and a lockable covered shed for bike storage
- providing dinner up until 2000hrs if there are no other places to eat nearby
- providing an early breakfast option from 0700hrs, or a breakfast tray for very early starters,
- filling your flask and offering a packed lunch should you request it
- having the weather forecast and maps available.

Whatever you choose, if you want to arrive early, to drop off your bike and go sightseeing, or anticipate arriving late due to unforeseen delay, it's only courteous to ring ahead and let them know. You should also remember that accommodation is in short supply and in the peak season even campsites can get full, so it is advisable to make a reservation before you arrive on the islands. Whatever your needs, a good place to start looking for accommodation is on the Visit Scotland website: www.visitscotland.com.

Of course camping is another option. The Scottish Land Reform Act 2003 confirmed a long-held presumption of access to all land unless there is a very good reason for the public to be excluded. So the public now have a statutory right of access to all land, except for areas such as railway land, quarries, harbours, airfields and defence land where they are excluded by law. Access rights extend to wild camping and this means that as long as you do not have motorised transport, small numbers of people using lightweight tents can camp as long as their stay is short-term, generally reckoned to be no more than 3 or 4 nights in any one spot.

Slate miners' cottages at Toberonochy (Route 3.1)

PREPARING YOUR BIKE

It is not a good idea to buy a new bike immediately before setting out on a touring holiday as new brake and gear cables will undoubtedly stretch and require fine-tuning and you need time to become accustomed to the bike. Because you will be riding for extended periods of time, it is important that you adjust the bike to your size: for more on setting up your bike to fit you see the 'Riding comfortably' section below.

Folding bikes on Colonsay (Part 2)

What type of bike?

Without wanting to offend the fans of tandems, tricycles, and folding and recumbent cycles, there are broadly three types of bike and all are suitable for the routes in this book. However, there are some things that you can do to make your rides more comfortable.

Road bikes

Touring bikes are usually made out of steel and have a longer frame than a normal road bike. This makes them springy and allows you to stretch out more. But there is nothing wrong with using a road bike for touring and all you really need to do is add a rack and fit the widest tyres that your wheel rims and frame clearance will allow. Most 'roadies' ride on 23mm tyres but moving up to 25mm or 28mm tyres will give that extra bit of comfort and leave you less prone to punctures.

If your bike does not have threaded braze-ons, you will need to use a rack that clamps on to an alloy seat post. This is entirely adequate for lightweight 'credit-card' touring, but if you are riding a bike with a carbon

Loaded and ready for the ferry at Uig, Skye (Part 4)

frame, you are probably best to try to go ultra-lightweight and limit yourself to a single rack bag. And don't even think about clamping a rack to a carbon seat post. Buy a cheap alloy one instead.

City bikes

The only difference between road bikes and city bikes is normally the quality of the fittings and that most city bikes have flat handlebars. So in addition to fitting wider tyres, many people fit bar ends or even butterfly bars to give more choice in resting tired hands.

Mountain bikes

It is also worth considering fitting bar ends or butterfly bars to a mountain bike – and if your bike has full suspension you may need to fit the type of rack that clamps on to the seat tube. You might want to consider changing the knobbly tyres for lower profile urban tyres which have less rolling resistance giving a far quieter ride. Locking off the suspension will also waste less energy when riding on good tarmac roads.

Locking out the suspension
on a mountain bike

Tyres

Cycle tyres are classified by their diameter measured in centimeters, ranging from the skinny 23mm tyres used on racing bikes, through the 30–40mm tyres preferred by cycle tourists, to the larger diameters used on mountain bikes. My personal preference for riding and light-weight touring in the Hebrides are puncture-resistant touring tyres, with a 25mm on the front and a 28mm on the rear.

Urban slicks – better on a mountain bike than knobbly tyres

Unless the gears on your bike are suitable for the terrain you will be riding, you will find yourself struggling up any hills. It is always better to have a low gear in reserve than a high gear you never use and typically this means having a back sprocket with the same number of teeth as the front largest chain ring. If you explain where you are going to the folk at your local bike shop and tell them about the biggest climb you are likely to encounter, they will be able to fit any gears you need.

It is always advisable to have your bike serviced a couple of weeks before your trip, allowing sufficient time for any worn parts to be replaced and run-in before your departure. Some people will have the knowledge and tools to do this themselves, otherwise your local bike shop will be happy to do this for you.

Pre-trip bike check

- Wheels should run smoothly and show no signs of buckling. Check to see if there is any side-to-side play in the hubs or any missing or slack spokes.
- Tyres should be in good condition with plenty of tread left on them and no signs of weathering or weaknesses in the walls. They should also be inflated to the pressure recommended by the manufacturer as the less rubber there is in contact with the road, the easier it will be to pedal.
- Brakes should be effective with plenty of wear left on the brake blocks and room remaining for adjustment in the tension of the cables, which should move smoothly and not show any signs of kinking or undue wear.

- Pedals and crankshaft should turn smoothly without any play in the axle.
- Gears should change smoothly and silently without the chain overriding the chain rings or sprockets when selecting high or low gears.
- All fixing nuts and bolts on mudguards and carriers should all be tight.

Even if there is nothing obviously wrong with your bike, apply oil to the chain and gears, check for loose spokes and excess play in brake and gear cables and have a short ride to make a final check that it's in tip-top condition before you leave home.

PREPARING YOURSELF

You'll need some tools and spare parts but unless you know how to use them, all the tools or spares you pack will be useless. So it pays to have at least one person in your party who can carry out the most common roadside repairs and do makeshift remedies for more major problems that will get you to the nearest cycle shop (marked on the maps as ⚒). Pack a small cycle maintenance manual as a backstop, but consider attending a cycle maintenance course as this will give you the hands-on skills you will be eternally grateful for when you find yourself fiddling with faulty gears in dwindling daylight and perhaps a force seven gale.

If you do not currently hold a license for driving a vehicle of any kind, you should ensure that you are thoroughly familiar with the requirements of the Highway Code and consider attending one of the approved cycle training courses listed on the Cycle Touring Club website – www.ctc.org.uk. No matter where you go, you will find yourself having to ride along stretches of busy main roads and through town centres, where it is essential for both your own safety, and that of others, that you observe the Highway Code.

To enjoy your tour and prevent each day from becoming too much of a personal challenge, you should ensure that you attain a level of fitness that enables you to complete each day without becoming exhausted. This may mean starting a personal fitness programme three or four months before your departure to give you sufficient time to build up stamina so you can complete the required distances comfortably. Start off with a ride that is just within your current fitness level and ride it a few times until you can ride it comfortably on two consecutive days. Then double the distance until you can ride the average daily distance needed for your planned tour without feeling unduly tired at the end of each day.

If you are going to encounter steep hills, practise 'feathering' the brakes – gently applying and releasing pressure on alternate levers – to control your speed on descents.

Carrying luggage, particularly a full set of panniers laden with camping gear, will slow you down dramatically. The accepted rule of thumb is that riding with a full load halves your average speed and comfortable daily range. So you should either do some training runs with fully-laden panniers until you can achieve the distances needed for the tour or you should aim for training runs that are twice as long as you will cover on the tour. The first of these is perhaps the best choice, as your bike will handle very differently when weighed down with a full set of luggage and it is better to get accustomed to this on quiet back roads before riding in heavy traffic.

PLANNING YOUR TRIP

Your average cycling speed will depend on: your general fitness; your bike and the luggage you are carrying; the terrain; and other factors such as the wind and the road surface. No matter how fast you ride on your daily commute or weekend run into the country, cycling with luggage is going to slow you down considerably, so temper your enthusiasm for clocking up the miles, give yourself more time to soak up the surroundings and sightsee, plan shorter days – and enjoy yourself.

Generally 8–9mph (15kph) is recognised as a good average touring speed for a reasonably fit person over rolling terrain although fitter, more experienced riders will achieve 12mph (20kph) and above. That means in a typical day, with five to six hours of riding, you could cover anything between 45 miles (75km) and 75 miles (120km), depending

Checking the GPS near Leverburgh, Harris (Route 6A and 6B)

on your fitness, the terrain and the weather conditions. The only way to assess your own capability is to load up the bike and do some test runs to see what speed and distance you can comfortably sustain over consecutive days. Allow extra time for cycling into a headwind as it will slow you down and sap your strength. Times given for the routes in this book assume an average speed of 9mph/15kph.

If these speeds seem unattainable for you, don't worry, you are not alone. There are many cyclists who have been riding for years who never go much faster than 6–7mph (10–12kph). Speed only becomes an issue if you set yourself unattainable distances to cover each day and you end up too exhausted to enjoy the holiday and consistently late at your pre-booked accommodation. So set yourself modest goals each day; allow time to take in the visitor attractions and take a break every hour even if you don't think you need one.

On routes that involve ferry crossings, you will need to add the ferry time – see Appendix C – to the suggested riding time as well as making an allowance for sightseeing, refreshment breaks and waiting at slipways. You will need to pay attention to ferry times, especially if you are visiting an island for a day trip, as you risk getting stranded. So it is better to arrive early at the slipway rather than watching the boat disappear into the distance. On days when the sea is particularly rough ferries

can be cancelled, or islands where berthing would be difficult are omitted from the schedule, sometimes for days at a time. Similarly, ferries occasionally develop technical problems that result in service disruptions. So pay attention to weather forecasts, look out for announcements both on board and at terminals and be prepared to change your plans. On a more positive note, it does not get dark until very late in the north of Scotland during the summer months so there is plenty of opportunity to catch up on lost time.

WHAT AND HOW TO PACK

What you need to pack is dictated by the type of trip you are undertaking and where you plan to stay. If you are planning to camp, you will need to carry a full load with tent, sleeping bag, cooking gear and everything else you need for outdoor living. This will probably mean having a full set of panniers or a trailer. If you are going to stay overnight at hotels, B&Bs or hostels you can get away with just a set of rear panniers, although you may still need to carry a sleeping bag if you are staying in the more basic hostels. If you are simply riding for a day, then you can take much less as all you will need to carry is waterproofs, tools, some food to keep you going and any personal belongings such as your phone and camera.

Clip-on pannier rack suitable for a mountain bike with rear suspension

Not wanting to struggle with a heavy load, my personal preference is to travel as light as possible so I tend to avoid camping and alternate between hostels and hotels or B&Bs to keep spending in check. However this does mean some prior booking during the peak tourist months of June, July and August and this can limit flexibility. Whichever option you choose, there are some key rules.

- **Keep kit to a minimum** – Give priority to the essentials listed below and avoid the tendency to take more than you use, particularly when it comes to clothing for wearing in the evenings. If you choose clothing that can be easily washed out and dried overnight, you can actually get away with surprisingly little. Check with your fellow riders that you are not duplicating tools and first aid kits and have a good sort after the first few days and post any unused bits and pieces home.

- **Keep it light** – Carry a light down-filled sleeping bag rather than a heavier synthetic one and invest in an ultra lightweight tent. They may cost more, but they are certainly worth it and will give many years of good service. Transfer essentials such as shampoo and foodstuffs to smaller plastic containers and only take sufficient for your trip.

KIT LIST

Bike

- Bike lock
- Pannier racks
- Panniers
- Rack bag or handlebar bag
- Bungee cords – useful for securing bikes on ferries
- Front and rear lights and spare batteries or charger
- Water bottles
- Cable ties and strong elastic bands
- Insulation tape
- Spare gear and brake cables
- Spare brake blocks or pads
- Tool kit: tyre levers, puncture repair outfit, multi-tool, small adjustable spanner, Allen keys, spoke key and a few spokes, chain tool and a few powerlinks
- Two spare inner tubes
- Pump
- Folded spare tyre
- Oil and/or grease
- Disposable gloves
- Wipes

Clothing

- Cycling top – long or short sleeved cycling jersey
- Cycling shorts – either lycra or loose-fitting
- Cycling bottoms for colder weather
- Socks and change of socks
- Underwear
- Cycling shoes and over-shoes
- Warm base layer or fleece
- Two pairs of cycling gloves
- Cycling helmet
- Cycling glasses or sunglasses
- Thin balaclava, buff or hat
- Waterproof jacket and over-trousers
- Long-sleeved top and long trousers for evenings
- Light footwear
- Night clothes

Toiletries

- Shampoo
- Comb
- Toothbrush and small toothpaste
- High factor sun block
- Moisturising cream
- Deodorant
- Lip salve
- Insect repellent and antihistamine cream
- Earplugs (for both preventing wind-induced ear ache – and blocking out the noise of companions who snore)
- Compact first aid kit
- Sterilizing tablets
- Quick drying towel
- Toilet tissue or wet wipes

General

- Maps and ferry timetables
- Compass and/or Global Positioning System (GPS)
- Guidebooks

- Itinerary and accommodation list with phone numbers
- Headtorch
- Pencil or pen
- Emergency phone numbers
- Cash and credit card
- Tickets
- House key
- Watch
- Spectacles or contact lenses and spares
- Camera with spare films or memory card
- Spare camera batteries or charger
- Plug adaptor for any electrics
- Mobile phone and charger
- Small sewing kit for repairs
- Emergency rations such as dried fruit or energy bars
- Strong plastic bags for washing and vulnerable items

Optional extras
- Leisure reading
- MP3 player and charger
- Personal radio

Loaded for camping

How to pack

If you are new to cycle touring one of the best ways to get to grips with packing is to pile everything you need to take in the middle of the floor, assess whether anything can be made smaller or lighter and then try out a few different ways of packing, remembering to keep items you might need when you are riding easily accessible at the top of the kerbside pannier and heavier items lower down wherever possible.

Panniers come at a wide range of prices. When properly fastened, the more expensive ones should be totally waterproof. Others may come with integral rain covers, but if this isn't the case, then you will need to pack everything in dry bags or strong plastic liners. Fragile items such as phones, cameras and maps need their own waterproof containers or bags and are best carried in a detachable handlebar bag, where they will be easily accessible. Likewise money, credit cards and other valuables are best carried in a handlebar bag or a secure pocket in your clothing and should never be left unattended on the bike.

35

Your bike will handle better if you pack the smaller, heavier items in the front panniers and the bulkier lighter items in the rear panniers, so that roughly 40 per cent of the total weight is at the front and 60 per cent at the rear. At the same time, check that the weight of left and right hand side panniers is roughly equal, as an imbalance will make your bike difficult to control.

Avoid having to ride with a rucksack or even a small water reservoir on your back as it will soon become uncomfortable and tiring. If you think you need to carry a rucksack then you've probably packed too much gear, so empty it all out and start again, looking to eliminate the non-essentials.

RIDING COMFORTABLY

Because you will be riding for extended periods of time, it is important that you adjust the bike to your size. The saddle is at the right height when there is still a slight bend in your knee with the pedal at the bottom of the stroke. The way to check this is to place your heel flat on the pedal when it is at the bottom of the stroke and set the saddle height to this. Then, when you put your foot on the pedal in a normal riding position with the ball of the foot centred on the pedal you should find your leg is still slightly bent. The handlebars should be level with, or just below, the height

of your saddle but try a couple of positions until you feel comfortable.

Riding for long periods can result in cramps in the hand, so consider adding bar-ends to flat handlebars and changing hand positions frequently. Having padded bars and cycling gloves with gel inserts in the palms all adds to comfort, but remember to take each hand off the bars from time to time to flex and stretch the fingers too. One of the commonest aches suffered by riding for long periods of time is across the shoulders and occasionally in the lower back. The best way to prevent these is to pay attention to your posture, try to keep your upper body relaxed and to ride with your arms slightly flexed rather than locked onto the handlebars.

Riding in the wrong gear will soon start to cause aches and pain, particularly in the knees. The recommended cadence (the rate at which you turn the pedals) is in the range 70–90 revolutions per minute. You should try to maintain this rate all the time, constantly adjusting the gears to take account of the changing terrain. Pedalling in a gear that is too low is tiring and pushing against a gear that is too high is a primary cause of knee problems and one of the main reasons people abandon trips. If you start to feel any twinges in the joints stop riding, check out your saddle height and riding position and pay particular attention to your cadence when you resume.

Similarly, try to avoid standing up on the pedals when you encounter hills and change down a gear or two until you are comfortable. If you have engaged your lowest gear and still find yourself needing to stand up to climb hills, it may be that your gearing range is too high for touring with a loaded bike, so call into the next cycle shop and hope they can fix it for you while you wait.

Above all be flexible. Build some rest days and slack into your schedule so you can take a day off to do something else and perhaps sit out any bad weather. If the wind changes direction and you find yourself hopelessly battling against a headwind, either seek out an alternative route sheltered in the lea of higher ground, change plans and head off in another direction – or jump on a bus and start afresh tomorrow. It's not an endurance event; it's a holiday.

Clothing

Investing in cycling shorts with a synthetic chamois insert will provide unparalleled comfort and prevent chaffing and sores. If you don't like shorts, you can buy full-length cycling bottoms and if you don't fancy squeezing into body-hugging lycra, you can buy under-shorts that come with a chamois insert and simply wear comfortable clothing over the top. However if you do start to get problems, apply talcum powder or Cruex at the first opportunity. Likewise a good-quality cycling jersey

that wicks away perspiration and has a zipper at the neck to aid ventilation is a good investment, but launder your clothing frequently to keep it in good condition.

Eating and drinking

Cycling is strenuous and if you don't keep your energy reserves topped up all the time by eating the right types of foods frequently, you will soon feel very tired and demotivated. Try not to go overboard on a big fried breakfast as it will weigh heavy for most of the morning. It is far better to eat smaller amounts of food more frequently, so always have some favourite nibbles in your jersey pockets or handlebar bag. It is best to avoid too many sweets and confectionery which contain simple sugars that will give you a short term boost, but have limited nutritional value. Go for a balanced diet of proteins and the more complex carbohydrates such as grains, pulses, pasta and even porridge as these provide steady blood sugar levels rather than short sharp peaks.

Get into the routine of stopping frequently and taking a light snack rather than waiting until you feel hungry, as by then it is often too late and you risk 'hitting the wall'. So although places where food is available are marked with the symbol ⬛ on the maps in this guidebook, do not rely on the hotel, café or shop being open and always carry some food with you. Many cyclists carry sandwiches, fruit cake, apples and bananas, and cereal

Snack time at Sandaig on Tiree (Part 3)

bars as well as some energy gels or isotonic powders that can be added to your water bottles. That is not to say, you shouldn't enjoy a roadside café, but err on the side of caution and stick to energy-giving snacks and pastries rather than a full midday meal.

Likewise drink frequently and always carry a couple of litres of water, preferably in feed bottles rather than in a reservoir on your back as the weight will soon start to tell after a day or so. Most of the tap water in the Hebrides is collected off the hills and personally I have no apprehension about topping up bottles from clear running streams, dropping in a sterilising tablet just to be on the safe side. It is also worth carrying sachets of electrolyte replacement powder to add to water bottles in hot weather to replace vital salts and minerals.

RIDING IN A GROUP

If you are riding as part of a group you should give consideration to those around you, making them aware of obstacles such as potholes and cattle grids that they may not have seen and always alerting them to your intention to stop or turn by shouting out well before making the manoeuvre. It is only natural to ride two or three abreast on minor roads in order to chit-chat, but the 'tail-end charlie' should remain alert to traffic coming up behind and instruct the group to revert to riding in single file until the vehicle has passed.

You should also look out for each other: keep an eye on anyone who may be struggling and needs a rest. If you get into the discipline of riding as a pack (or *peloton*), as professional racing cyclists do, and take it in turns to go to the front for a few minutes at a time, others will be able to take shelter in the leader's slipstream. The benefits of doing this will vary with conditions and the number of people in the group, but it is often said that cycling in a peloton increases the overall speed by 20–30 per cent. It also gives respite to any member of the party who may be flagging, so it is well worth practising.

USING THIS GUIDE

This book caters for those who are cycle touring and those who simply want to get in a few rides while they are on holiday in the Hebrides. The longest suggested tour is over 600 miles (970km) and the shortest route (on South Uist) is a mere 12 miles (19km). There are lots in between as well and no hard and fast rules, so you can use the book to plan your own tour. And even when you are planning a tour, it is more than likely that you will want to stay put for a day and go off on one of the day rides.

Link routes

If you are touring, you can use this guide to plan your own tour through

A passing place – a refuge on the roads

Returning from Glenbrittle (Route 4.3)

the islands in the Forth of Clyde and the Hebrides. Routes are numbered by chapter with certain routes tagged as 'link routes' and these are labelled with a letter: 1A, 2A and so on. These intersect with other link routes, ferry ports and railway stations giving you complete flexibility and lots of alternatives. Cumulative distances from the start of each link route are given in miles and kilometres in brackets throughout the route descriptions like this (9/14), so you can keep an eye on your progress. These cumulative distances and the times each section of the rides should take are listed in Appendix A, which also lists where link routes intersect. In the route descriptions, places where link routes intersect are shown by this symbol: ✈.

The link routes also vary in length so that sometimes two or more can easily be ridden in a day, while the longer ones, such as Ullapool to Armadale, may stretch over two or three days. While the focus of the guide is clearly on the islands, a handful of link routes have been included to link the ferry terminals on the mainland, such as the routes from Gourock to Ardrossan and Kennacraig to Oban. Link routes tend to be the shortest and most direct route between two places, with some detours to avoid busy roads where possible. A summary of the link routes can be found in Appendix A and a summary of the ferry routes in Appendix C.

Day routes

If you simply want to do some cycling as part of a multi-activity holiday, then you should focus on the 'day routes'. These start and end in the same place and are included to give you rides to enjoy when staying in a particular location for a number of days. You can also visit neighbouring islands for the day and use your bike to get around. Appendix D shows how much time you would have on each island. There is no need to make a reservation unless you take a motor vehicle over. Many routes are circular: however, because of the relative lack of roads on some islands, some routes are out and back by the same route.

Combining the two
If you want a longer all-day ride of 30 miles (50km) or more, in certain regions, such as the Firth of Clyde or along the Sound of Mull, you can join together a series of the shorter link routes to produce a circular ride of the desired length. Similarly, even if you are touring, you may wish to stop over for a day or two and enjoy some of the day routes.

Both link and day routes can be ridden on any type of bicycle as there are no off-road sections that need a mountain bike. Quieter, second-ary roads are used as an alternative to main roads wherever possible. However the region has a limited road network so that is not always possible and although traffic is rarely heavy, you do need to be a confident cyclist.

Ferries are used to hop across to and between the islands and bus and rail services are used to get into and about the region covered by the guide, although of course you can always use your own vehicle, perhaps leaving it parked up at one of the ferry terminals where there is plenty of long-stay parking such as at Ardrossan

or Uig (see the 'Long-stay parking' box under 'Getting there' above for more details). This means that you can move around the region remarkably fast. For instance, you could arrive at Ardrossan on an early train, take a ferry to Brodick, then cycle across Arran to grab the ferry from Lochranza to Claonaig, ride across the Kintyre peninsula to Kennacraig to get a sec-ond ferry and still arrive on Islay in time for dinner. See 'Suggested Tours' below for some ideas.

Grading
Each day route, link route, and each section of the longer link routes, which are divided into sections, is graded according to the amount of physical effort involved. This reflects the amount of climbing and the steepness of the climbs rather than the length of the route. Climbs encountered on rides that use minor roads also tend to have steeper gra-dients than those on major roads and consequently rides with a simi-lar amount of climbing may have slightly different gradings. Grades are only meant as a rough guide and will be virtually meaningless in a head-wind, when even the easiest ride will become much harder. The times given for each route assume an aver-age speed of 9mph/15kph: for more on average speeds see 'Planning your trip' above.

* **Easy** – Smooth pedalling with gentle inclines

41

Approaching The Storr on the Trotternish Peninsula (Route 4.5)

- **Moderate** – Undulating with an occasional steady climb, but nothing to get you out of the saddle
- **Hard** – Involves some hard climbs with gradients up to 10%
- **Very hard** – Long steep ascents or multiple short sharp gradients that will most definitely hurt

SUGGESTED TOURS

The distances stated below only include link routes and do not include any day routes you may include in your trip. The suggested tour length is the typical elapsed time from the start of the ride to the finish, taking into account the frequency of the ferry services. In the itineraries listed below, ferries are numbered as listed in Appendix C and as on the maps, and are shown prefixed by the letter 'f', and link routes are numbered as they are throughout the text, in the table of contents and in Appendix A.

Short tours

The 5 Ferries Ride (66 miles/106km)
A pleasant loop that has been run as a charity ride in recent years – see www.5ferrychallenge.com. It takes in the main islands in the Firth of Clyde and can easily be completed in a day by seasoned riders, although most will prefer a more leisurely pace. The ride is only possible during summer months when the Lochranza – Claonaig ferry (f7) runs.

Ardrossan – (f1a) – Brodick – 1D – Lochranza – (f7) – Claonaig – 1E, 1F – Tarbert – (f6) – Portavadie – 1B – Auchenbreck – 1C – Colintraive – (f5) – Rhubodach – 1C – Rothesay – (f3) – Wemyss Bay – 1A – Ardrossan

Jumping across Kintyre to Islay (91 miles/146km)

Only possible in summer when the Lochranza – Claonaig ferry (f7) runs.

Ardrossan – (f1a) – Brodick – 1D – Lochranza – (f7) – Claonaig – 1E – Kennacraig – (f9) – Port Ellen – 2A – Port Askaig – (f9) – Kennacraig – 1F – Tarbert – (f6) – Portavadie – 1B – Dunoon – (f4) – Gourock – 1A – Ardrossan

Mull, Ardnamurchan and Morven (75 miles/120km)

Fit riders could complete this loop along the Sound of Mull in a single day – the rest of us will need longer.

Oban – (f16) – Craignure – 3A Tobermory – (f21) – Kilchoan – 3C – Salen – 3B – Lochaline – (f20) – Fishnish – 3A – Craignure – (f16) – Oban

North Uist, Berneray and Harris from Uig (48 miles/77km)

A pleasant 2/3 day tour that takes in many riders' favourite – the Golden Road in the Bays area of South Harris.

Uig – (f30) – Lochmaddy – 5C – Clachan – 5B, 5C – Berneray – (f31) – Leverburgh – 6B – Tarbert – (f32) – Uig

Medium tours

A circular tour of Colonsay, Islay and Kintyre from Oban (73 miles/117km)

This tour is only possible during the summer months when the ferry operates between Islay and Colonsay on Wednesday. So although you can ride the tour clockwise or anticlockwise, you will need to plan your schedule carefully.

Oban – (f12) – Colonsay – (f11 Wednesdays only) – Port Askaig – 2A – Port Ellen – (f9) – Kennacraig – 1F – Oban

Coll, Tiree, Barra and South Uist (27 miles/43km)

If you visit both Coll and Tiree before catching the Barra ferry that calls at both islands during its Wednesday sailings during the summer months, you can visit five Hebridean Islands at a fairly leisurely pace.

Oban – (f23) – Coll – (f23) – Tiree – (f28 on a Thursday) – Castlebay – 5A – Aird Mhor – (f29) – Eriskay – 5A – Lochboisdale – (f28) – Oban

43

Barra to the Butt of Lewis
(175 miles/280km)

This iconic route goes the entire length of the Western Isles and visits Callanish Standing Stones and other world famous antiquities. Unless you have a support vehicle or are prepared to cycle all the way back to the start, it needs careful planning. See the introduction to Section 5 for details.

> Castlebay – 5A – Aird Mhor – (f29) – Eriskay – 5A – Dalabrog – 5B – Clachan – 5C – Berneray – (f31) – Leverburgh – 6B – Tarbert – 6C – Liurbost – 6D – Barabhas – 6E – Butt of Ness

Western Isles South from Oban
(188 miles/300km)

A pleasant circuit that takes in the southern part of the Western Isles before returning across Skye and down through Morven and Mull.

> Oban – (f28) – Castlebay – 5A – (f29) – 5A – Dalabrog – 5B – Clachan – 5C – Lochmaddy – (f30) – Uig – 4B – Broadford – 4A – Armadale – (f25) – Mallaig – 3D – Salen – 3B – Lochaline – (f20) – Fishnish – 3A – Craignure – (f16) – Oban

Drying off after a dip in Calgary Bay (Route 3.5)

Skye, North Uist, Harris and Lewis (304 miles/486km)

Another fine loop that takes in Skye and the northern part of the Western Isles before returning down the west coast. The return leg from Ullapool gives you the option of testing your-self out on Bealach na Ba – 'the Pass of the Cattle' – the nearest the UK comes to a proper alpine ascent climbing over 600m (2000 feet) in about 5 miles (8km).

Kyle of Lochalsh – 4A – Broadford – 4B – Uig – (f30) – Lochmaddy – 5C – Berneray – (f31) – Leverburgh – 6B – Tarbert – 6C – Liurbost – 6D – Barabhas – 6E – Stornoway – (f33) – Ullapool – 4A – Kyle of Lochalsh

Longer tours

Butt of Lewis and back from Oban (465 miles/744km)

A complete loop of the Western Isles that starts and finishes at Oban.

Oban – (f28) – Castlebay – 5A – (f29) – 5A – Dalabrog – 5B – Clachan – 5D – 5C – Berneray – (f31) – Leverburgh – 6B – Tarbert – 6C – Liurbost – 6D – Barabhas – 6E – Butt of Ness – 6E – Stornoway – (f33) – Ullapool – 4A – Armadale – (f25) – Mallaig – 3D – Salen – 3B – Lochaline – (f20) – Fishnish – 3A – Craignure – (f16) – Oban

Butt of Lewis and back from Ardrossan (605 miles/968km)

The complete Hebridean tour that starts and finishes at Ardrossan and takes in as many islands as possible.

Ardrossan – (f1a) – Brodick – 1D – Lochranza – (f7) – Claonaig – 1E – Kennacraig – (f9) – Port Ellen – 2A – Port Askaig – (f11 on a Wednesday) – Oban – (f28) – Castlebay – 5A – Aird Mhor – (f29) – Eriskay – 5A – Dalabrog – 5B – Clachan – 5C – Berneray – (f31) – Leverburgh – 6B – Tarbert – 6C – Liurbost – 6D – Barabhas – 6E – Butt of Ness – 6E – Stornoway – (f33) – Ullapool – 4A – Armadale – (f25) – Mallaig – 3D – Salen – 3B – Lochaline – (f20) – Fishnish – 3A – Craignure – (f16) – Oban – 1F – Tarbert – (f6) – Portavadie – 1B – Dunoon – (f4) – Gourock – 1A – Ardrossan

MAPS AND ITINERARIES

This book is designed to be carried with you either in a pocket of your cycling jersey or in a map case on top of your handlebar bag. Each route is illustrated on an accompa-nying map based on OS data, and refreshment stops (🍽), cycle shops (🔧), places where cycles can be hired (🚲) and cash dispensers (💷) are all indicated. However it is advisable to carry separate maps that cover your intended route. Many seasoned cycle tourists make do with a page from a road atlas or a printout from the internet while others carry a Global Positioning System (GPS) with integrated mapping.

Ordnance Survey's 1:50,000 Landranger Series provide the right level of detail for both riding and exploring the local area, showing useful information such as hotels and public houses where there may be food and refreshments, tourist information centres and considerable detail about gradients. However if you are covering a wider area, you will need to carry a number of maps and many riders will be content with a touring map on a scale of 1:250,000 or 1:300,000 that provide an overview of the region and are useful for making changes to journey plans to avoid prevailing winds or to curtail your trip at short notice.

If you have mapping software such as Memory-Map on your computer, you can print out your intended route to any scale you wish and cut and paste a number of ribbon strips showing your route on a single side of A4 paper. If you laminate these back to back, you can often get your entire trip covering hundreds of miles on three or four totally weatherproofed sheets. You can even add text boxes containing the contact details of your accommodation. However these sheets do tend to catch the wind and it is advisable to punch a hole in the corners of each sheet and secure them to the top of your bar bag.

The same goes for your itinerary. Download any rail, ferry or bus timetables and accommodation details and contact numbers you need during your trip and cut and paste them on to an A4 sheet so they are legible but not over-large, and you can get all the information you may have to refer to on a couple of sides. This saves having endless pieces of paper that blow away or get wet at the bottom of a pannier.

Ferries are detailed in Appendix C, and the numbers used in Appendix C match the ferry numbers used on the overview maps for each section of this book and in the route tables in the appendices.

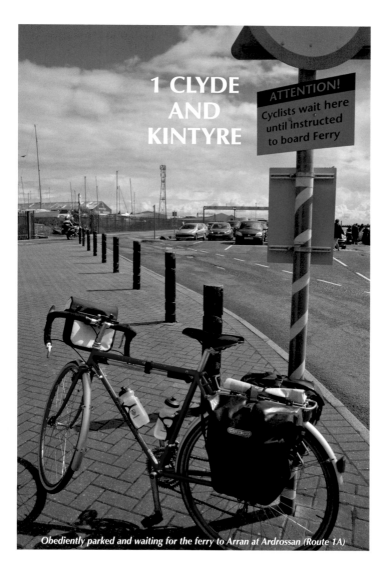

1 CLYDE AND KINTYRE

ATTENTION!
Cyclists wait here until instructed to board Ferry

Obediently parked and waiting for the ferry to Arran at Ardrossan (Route 1A)

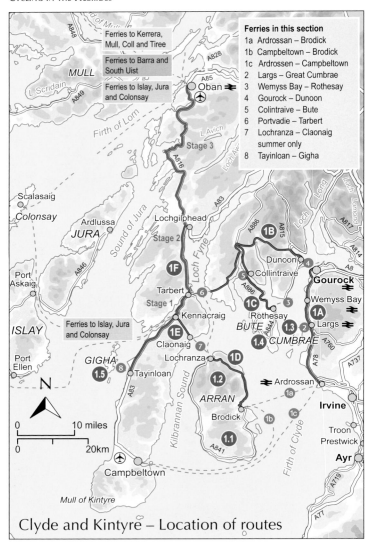

Ferries in this section
1a Ardrossan – Brodick
1b Campbeltown – Brodick
1c Ardrossen – Campbeltown
2   Largs – Great Cumbrae
3   Wemyss Bay – Rothesay
4   Gourock – Dunoon
5   Colintraive – Bute
6   Portvadie – Tarbert
7   Lochranza – Claonaig
    summer only
8   Tayinloan – Gigha

Ferries to Kerrera, Mull, Coll and Tiree

Ferries to Barra and South Uist

Ferries to Islay, Jura and Colonsay

Ferries to Islay, Jura and Colonsay

Clyde and Kintyre – Location of routes

INTRODUCTION

The Firth of Clyde was once a historically important seaway that linked the industrial and commercial powerhouse of Glasgow to the Atlantic Ocean and its overseas markets. In the late 19th century Glasgow was the fourth-largest city in Europe, after London, Paris and Berlin, producing textiles, tobacco, chemicals, engineered goods and steel, most of which were exported. It was 'the second city of the empire', building more than half of Britain's tonnage of shipping and a quarter of all railway engines in the world. This thriving manufacturing base gave rise to banking and insurance and the civic wealth that enabled many of the city's great architectural masterpieces to be built. The entire river, from the docks down to the Irish Sea, would have been busy, bringing in raw materials and exporting finished goods bound for Britain's once mighty empire.

Being sheltered from the worst of the prevailing westerly weather by the extended finger of Kintyre and the mountains of Arran, the Firth of Clyde became the weekend playground for the newly wealthy upper class. Those with a maritime bent took up sailing, while those who preferred to keep their feet on dry land either built themselves a fine holiday home somewhere within easy reach of the city or enjoyed the facilities of the growing number of hotels and 'hydropathic spas' in resorts such as Rothesay and Dunoon.

Today, Glasgow's pre-eminence in the world has waned: there is far less shipping in the Clyde and the once elegant hydros eke out a living catering for

Reaching the top of Glen Sannox with the Witch's Step visible on the skyline (Routes 1D and 1.2)

coach parties being whisked through the Highlands and Islands on a strict schedule. These faded resorts spread out along the east coasts of Arran and Bute have a genteel attraction, but as this begins to pall, you quickly leave and explore their less populated and wilder hinterland before popping out by their back doors.

Other than Great Cumbrae and Gigha, which strictly speaking belongs to the Hebrides but is included here due to its proximity to Kintyre, all of the islands and land masses in this section have front and back doors; Kintyre and Cowal could even be said to have side doors too. This gives a lot of choice in a comparatively compact and sheltered area, making Clyde and Kintyre ideal for novices, day trippers and those looking for a short break.

Kintyre is fine cycling country with two challenging circular rides that you may wish to ride as part of a longer tour. There is the excellent 63-mile (100km) loop that starts at Kennacraig and goes down to Campbeltown and back using the B842 road on the east coast and the busier A83 on the west side of the peninsula. Then, starting at Tarbert, there is a 38-mile (60km) circuit around Knapdale using the B8024 together with a short section of the A83 along the east coast. Both of these rides are best ridden to account for the prevailing wind, which would usually mean riding them clockwise.

Arran

It is claimed that Arran is Scotland in miniature, but without an equivalent to the heavily populated central belt from the Clyde to the Forth, and there is something to this claim. The Highland Boundary Fault which runs through the Great Glen splits Arran in two. To the north are shapely hills that rise to 874m/2867ft on Goat Fell. Although fairly modest in height, the traverse of the serrated ridge is

The Twelve Apostles, north Arran (Route 1.2)

continually interesting and involves negotiating the notorious Witch's Step, which gives a memorable mountain day up there with the best in Scotland. To the south are rolling moors and fertile farmland more reminiscent of the Scottish Lowlands and capable of growing similar crops. Arran's isolation from the mainland enabled Donald Mackelvie (1867–1947), a grocer from Lamlash, to breed Arran Pilot, a high-yielding variety of potato that is resistant to blight. It transformed the productivity of British agriculture between the wars and remains a stalwart of the kitchen garden. Agriculture continues to be important to the economy, supplemented today by forestry and tourism so that the island can support a buoyant population of around 5000, making it the sixth most populous Scottish island, just one place behind Bute.

Once away from tourist attractions of Brodick and the busy villages along the eastern coast, you can quickly get out into wilder country, which was until recently home to a small breeding population of ptarmigan. The road from Brodick to Blackwaterfoot – known as 'The String' – follows the line of the Highland Boundary Fault across the island and is included in both day routes. Despite being roughly the same length, and involving similar amounts of climbing, they are different in character. The northern loop has two steady climbs and a fair amount of easy pedalling, whereas the southern loop is constantly undulating, with few stretches where you can truly relax. Those wanting a more challenging ride can either do a complete 56-mile (90km) loop of the island, which, despite omitting the climb over 'The String', still entails 1800m of climbing. And if that's still not enough, then how about a 70-mile (112km) figure of eight, crossing The String in both directions and climbing over 2500m?

Off-road riding on Arran

Working with the Forestry Commission, the Arran Bike Club has developed a good selection of waymarked mountain biking trails and tracks, including some technical single track. They welcome visitors to join them on their Thursday evening and Sunday morning rides. See www.arranbikeclub.com for a downloadable map, route descriptions and a calendar of their club rides.

Arran's Milestones

Starting at Brodick Castle and running clockwise around the A841 is a series of numbered milestones that mark off the distance around the island. Being cut from soft Corrie sandstone has meant that many are so weathered as to be illegible and some are missing. Milestone number 32 actually occurs twice. The original is within the grounds of the boat house at Dougarie and a poor quality duplicate is sited outside the boundary railings to the north, presumably put there at the time the boat house was built and the old

Millport, Great Cumbrae, with the Clyde Puffer Vic 32 tied up on the quay (Route 1.3)

road re-routed with the construction of the present bridge across Iorsa Water. Locating them makes an interesting diversion on a dull day, although you might need the help of an Ordnance Survey map to spot them.

Great Cumbrae

This compact little island – just 2½ miles (1.5km) long and just over a mile wide – has a population of around 1400 people, making it the most densely populated Scottish island. However this number swells substantially during summer months and particularly at weekends due to tourists, day trippers and a high proportion of second homes. In many ways, Cumbrae is Bute in miniature and the island prides itself on being home to small things. The 'Cathedral of the Isles', which dates from 1851, is Britain's smallest cathedral, and The Wedge in the centre of Millport

is recognised as the world's narrowest house, with a frontage of 47 inches (1.19m).

Cycling is very popular with day trippers, who either bring their own bikes or hire them in Millport. However, there are few roads and it is not beyond any race-fit cyclist to arrive on one ferry, ride a complete circuit of the island and then depart on the next ferry 30 minutes later. The rest of us might want to enjoy its charms in a more leisurely manner, and the day route described here makes full use of the road network to give a longer ride with plenty of opportunities for sight seeing.

From 2000 to 2002, the BBC aired three series of *Millport*, a bittersweet radio comedy that poked gentle fun at life at the seaside resort with scripts that included scenes where free woolly socks were given away with every purchase of flip flops.

Bute

The elongated diamond of Bute is 15 miles (24km) long and 5 miles (8km) across at its widest and slots into Cowal like a piece of a jigsaw, leaving a gap that is only a couple of hundred yards across at the narrowest point of the Kyles of Bute between Colintraive and Rhubodach. In the past cattle swam across the narrows on their way to market in central Scotland. But today, the Kyles, like the rest of the Firth of Clyde, are a playground for sailors with many marinas and moorings.

Because it is sheltered from the prevailing west wind and the worst of the rain by the Arran mountains, Bute enjoys a benign climate. This and its close proximity to Glasgow mean it has always been a magnet for tourists – first the wealthy who built themselves substantial villas and frequented the once elegant hotels and then the less well-off who came 'doon the watter' to spend their holiday week at one of the many boarding houses tucked away in the back streets. When Bute was in its prime, during the 1920s, there were more than a million visitors a year arriving by a number of ferries from different mainland ports. The Winter Gardens, which date from 1923, played host to the best-known music hall entertainers of the time. Now the building is Grade A listed and the jewel in the crown of Scotland's largest urban conservation area outside Glasgow. The arrival of cheap air travel marked the end of 'Costa Clyde', although the island has sufficient attractions to maintain a viable tourist industry. Along with farming and forestry and a large retirement community, this helps sustain a population of 7000.

Mount Stuart, Bute (Route 1.4)

The gents at the ferry terminal is considered to be one of the finest examples of late Victorian lavatories left in the UK.

Like Arran, its higher and bigger neighbour, Bute is split by the Highland Boundary Fault, which runs southwest from Rothesay, following the line of Loch Fad. The land to the south is low-lying and fertile, while that to the north is more wooded and wilder, but only reaches a modest 278m at Windy Hill.

Gigha

Gigha – pronounced 'gee-ha' – vies with nearby Islay in claiming to be the southernmost island of the Inner Hebrides. It is both low-lying and influenced by the North Atlantic Drift, giving it a warmer and drier climate than that normally associated with the west coast of Scotland, and that makes for good growing conditions. Captain William Scarlett, the 3rd Lord Abinger, who owned the estate at the end of the 19th century, built Achamore House in 1884 and surrounded it with woods. By the time Sir James Horlick – brother of the inventor of the malted milk drink that found success for being able to ward off 'night-time starvation' – acquired the estate in 1944, the mature trees provided sufficient shelter from wind and sea spray to allow the planting of a 50-acre garden, now famed for its rare and unusual plants including many varieties of rhododendron, many of which were bred by Sir James and his gardeners.

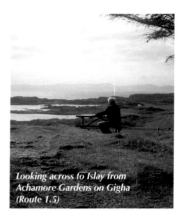

Looking across to Islay from Achamore Gardens on Gigha (Route 1.5)

This little island – a mere seven miles (11km) long and a mile wide – can perhaps justly claim to be the most beautiful in the Hebrides, with sandy bays, stunning views and breathtaking sunsets, as well as a variety of wildlife. The community purchased the island in 2002 and it is now managed by the Isle of Gigha Heritage Trust, which has initiated a number of projects that have stimulated the local economy and boosted the population, which now numbers 150. See www.gigha.org.uk.

There is a selection of self-catering cottages and short-stay accommodation available on the island as well as a well-equipped campsite, although places are limited and reservations are advised. However if you arrive on an early ferry from Tayinloan and depart in the late afternoon, you will have plenty of time to explore the delights of the island.

LINK ROUTES

ROUTE 1A
Gourock to Ardrossan

Start	Gourock
Finish	Ardrossan
Distance	28 miles (45km)
Total Ascent	1280ft (390m)
Grade	Easy
Time	3hrs
Map	OS Landranger 1:50,000 63, 70

When there are no developments, power stations or coal terminals to block out views of the sea, and the sun is shining, cycling along the busy main roads – the A770 and A78 – that link the ferry terminals along this stretch of the Clyde is just about tolerable. Only the fact that it's flat, and hence quickly over, will stop you from choosing alternative routes such as the minor road through Noddsdale and the hamlet of Garvock that could be used to link Gourock and Largs or the minor road that runs parallel to the main road between Wemyss Bay and Largs. It's best just to knuckle under and get it over with.

Looking across to Arran from the mainland

CYCLING IN THE HEBRIDES

The front at **Gourock** still has reminders of its past as a seaside resort and after decades of decay, the town is being slowly 'gentrified' as it finds favour with folk from Glasgow who would rather live on the coast. Heading south along the A770 to Cloch Point is pleasant enough, but all too soon the road turns inland to meet the A78 and the sea is obscured until you are through **Wemyss Bay** (9 miles/14km from the start).

> Pronounced 'weemz bay', **Wemyss Bay** was created in the early 19th century as a 'marine village' by Robert Wallace MP, whose lands lay behind the bay.

The road runs along the coast from **Skelmorlie** to **Largs** (15/24), another seaside resort that gained popularity when the railway arrived in 1895.

> In 1263, the Scots fought the Norwegians at the **Battle of Largs** and a small museum celebrates the town's Viking connections.

After Fairlie and the nuclear power station and coal terminal at Hunterston, the road cuts inland again, but you are soon rewarded with first a short stretch of cycle path into Seamill and then a continuous cycle path and good views of Arran all the way into **Ardrossan** (28/45). When you enter the town, stick to the coast along Eglington Road and North Crescent Road, which lead to the ferry terminal.

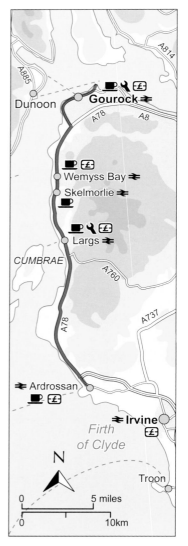

56

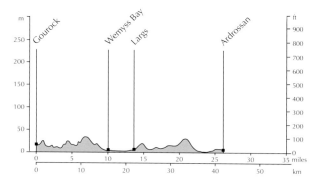

ROUTE 1B

Dunoon to Portavadie

Start	Dunoon
Finish	Portavadie
Distance	29 miles (46km)
Total Ascent	2950ft (900m)
Grade	Moderate, then Hard
Time	3hrs 10mins
Map	OS Landranger 1:50,000 62, 63

Dunoon is a mish-mash of building materials and architectural styles
ranging through white Italianate stucco to Scottish Baronial granite. But it is
pleasantly situated on the wooded slopes below the Cowal hills and spirits
will be high at the prospect of what lies before you.

If you crossed the Clyde on Argyll Ferries you will probably choose to take the
higher A885 road northwards behind the town. If you arrived at Hunter's Quay
on Western Ferries, you will inevitably take the A815 northwards along the prom-
enade. Both routes converge at **Sandbank** half way up Holy Loch, once an important submarine base for both the UK and US navies.

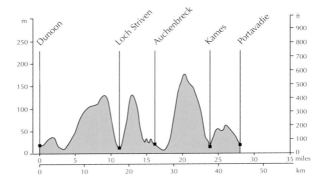

At the head of the loch, turn left on to the B836, climbing up steeply through the trees on an excellent double carriageway which turns into a single track road with passing places at Clachaig where the gradient eases off. From Loch Tarsan there is a steep descent down to the lush glen at the head of **Loch Striven** which should be ridden carefully to ensure you can stop if you meet oncoming traffic. A quick look at a map will show some short sharp inclines that reach 15% or more just above Craigendive, but a good low touring gear and steely determination will soon get you across the summit and rolling down the other side to **Auchenbreck** (15/24 ✈1C).

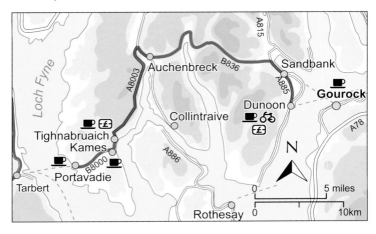

Nearing the top of a climb on the Cowal Peninsula

Turn right and enjoy the easy terrain northwards along the A886 from Auchenbreck to Waulkmill, because once you cross the River Ruel and start to turn southwards along the A8003 through Ormidale, the road climbs again although this time at a more modest 4% incline. Then, after a brief downhill section, there is another short sharp ascent to the picnic site and viewpoint, where there are good views down the Kyles of Bute. The sweeping descent back down to sea level is a joy. Turn left at the bottom of the hill if you want to visit the pretty yachting village of **Tighnabruaich** which has a gallery that specialises in Scottish artists, a gift shop and grocery store. Otherwise continue along the front into **Kames**, following the B8000 inland to Millhouse, then the minor road westwards through the conifer plantations to **Portavadie**, where the new modern marina has a restaurant and bar.

For a **longer ride**, continue south out of Kames alongside the Kyles of Bute to Ardlamont and around the loop to rejoin the route at Millhouse, adding 7 miles (11km) and 45mins.

ROUTE 1C
Auchenbreck to Rothesay

Start	Auchenbreck
Finish	Rothesay
Distance	14 miles (23km)
Total Ascent	850ft (260m)
Grade	Easy
Time	1hr 40mins
Map	OS Landranger 1:50,000 63

From Auchenbreck this route starts pleasantly enough, soon leaving the main road to meander alongside Loch Riddon, passing Colintraive's award-winning hotel – a must for a hungry traveller – and continuing via a ferry on to Bute.

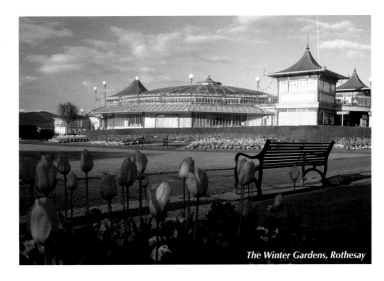

The Winter Gardens, Rothesay

Head south from **Auchenbreck** (1B), turning off the main A886 at Springfield and following the minor road alongside Loch Riddon until they come together again just before **Colintraive** (5/8).

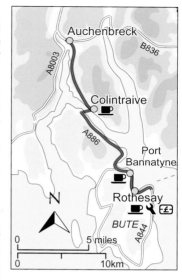

> The **name of the village** comes from the Gaelic *caol an t's-naimh* – 'the strait of the swimming place' – the narrowest point of the Kyles of Bute, where cattle reared on Bute were made to swim across to the mainland on their way to market in central Scotland.

Take the Colintraive–Rhubodach ferry (see Appendix C). The easy pedalling continues on Bute, passing herds of contented cattle with only the smallest of climbs where the road briefly turns inland between Ardmaleish Point and Undraynian Point. Bear left at the war memorial as you enter **Port Bannatyne**, and follow Shore Road through the pretty suburb of Ardbeg, rejoining the main A844 as you enter **Rothesay** (14/23).

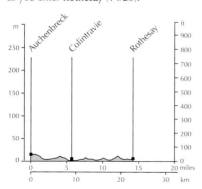

The art deco **Pavilion** dating from 1938 is a Category A listed building that was the social centre of the town during World War II when Rothesay was an important naval base and the craze was for dancing to 'big bands'. Somewhat faded since, it recently received major funding and should soon be restored to its former glory.

ROUTE 1D
Brodick to Lochranza

Start	Brodick
Finish	Lochranza
Distance	14 miles (23km)
Total Ascent	1080ft (330m)
Grade	Hard
Time	1hr 40mins
Map	OS Landranger 1:50,000 69

The traffic that comes off the ferry makes the main road through Brodick very busy, and it is best to wait for five minutes or so until it has dispersed before setting off north around Brodick Bay and below Brodick Castle. There has been a fortress on the site since the 5th century, but most of what you see today dates back to work started in 1844 when the 11th Duke of Hamilton tripled the size of the building.

Arran Distillery, Lochranza

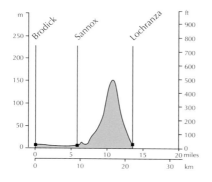

Initially, as you head north on the A841 out of **Brodick**, the road surface is not good, but this improves through the coastal villages of **Corrie** and **Sannox**. After some easy pedalling, there is a short initial climb as soon as the road turns inland followed by a steady 5% climb up to the pass at Boguillie.

On a clear day, there are **good views inland** along the serrated ridges of the Arran hills, including the obvious notch of 'The Witch's Step', which can only be crossed with some scrambling.

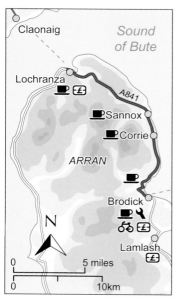

The reward for all the uphill effort is a fast run down through Glen Chalmadale into **Lochranza** (14/23), which is at its best in the early evening, when the 16th century castle and the surrounding hills glow in the setting sun. The refurbished youth hostel is delightful in itself with the added bonus that you can sometimes watch otters out on the mudflats from the lounge windows.

Independently owned **Arran Distillery** in Lochranza started producing single malts and a wide range of cask finished offerings in 1995, and opened for visitors in 1997.

63

ROUTE 1E
Claonaig to Tayinloan

Start	Claonaig
Finish	Tayinloan
Distance	19 miles (31km)
Total Ascent	1480ft (450m)
Grade	Easy, then Moderate
Time	2hrs 15mins
Map	OS Landranger 1:50,000 62

Other than a fine view back towards Arran, there is little to detain one at Claonaig. In fact the only tourist attraction in the vicinity is the castle at Skipness, which dates back to the first half of the 13th century. While not exactly on route, the café at Skipness may be the necessary incentive for the 3km detour with the promise of locally caught seafood and beers from Arran. Otherwise it's a steady climb across the peninsula, accompanied in early summer by the scratchy songs of various species of warbler hidden in the scrub alongside the road.

Head northwards on the quiet B8001 out of **Claonaig**. Once over the backbone of the peninsula, 4km of downhill leads to the busier A83 with views across West Loch Tarbert to Knapdale.

Before you set off south, you might want to drop in to the ferry terminal at **Kennacraig** (6/10 🛬 1F), which has toilets and a vending machine because, other than a garage at Clachan, there are no refreshment stops for the next 23km.

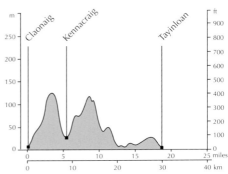

64

Low-lying Gigha from the Islay ferry

Beyond, the undulating route through **Whitehouse** and past Clachan gives frequent views across to Jura. Low-laying Gigha becomes visible once you reach Ronachan Point, which means 'the place of the seals,' so expect to find some basking on the offshore skerries. The road behind the shingle beaches is a pleasure, but it soon turns in to a three-mile straight that traffic drives at speed, so take care.

Out towards the coast at the start of this stretch are the remains of **Balure Range**, an airfield built as target practice for the fighter planes based at RAF Machrihanish further down the peninsula.

At **Tayinloan** (19/31) there is a vending machine in the general store in the village, but the tea room down at the ferry terminal has a far wider offering.

Sustrans **National Route 78** runs from Campbeltown, which now has a ferry link, to Oban and eventually Inverness, making the most of the minor roads through Claonaig, Kennacraig, Tarbert, Knapdale, Crinan and Taynuilt.

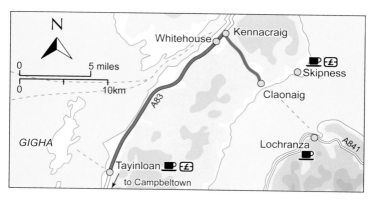

ROUTE 1F
Kennacraig to Oban

Start	Kennacraig
Finish	Oban
Distance	57 miles (92km)
Total Ascent	4630ft (1410m)
Grade	Easy to Tarbert, then Moderate to Bellanoch, then Hard
Time	6hrs 20mins
Map	OS Landranger 1:50,000 49, 55, 62

Other than a couple of climbs at Kilmartin and Glenmore, the 55 miles (90km) up the Kintyre peninsula from Kennacraig to Oban is mostly easy going and many people would comfortably ride it in a single day. But by doing so they would be missing the opportunity to explore some of the wonderful places along the way.

Tarbert is a pleasant little town with numerous cafés and galleries; Knapdale offers the opportunity of avoiding a stretch of the busy A83 for a detour through the sparsely populated villages on the west side of the peninsula and Kilmartin has such a wonderful collection of antiquities you could easily idle away half a day exploring the village.

Tarbert – a popular yachting basin on the Kintyre Peninsula

STAGE 1
Kennacraig to Tarbert

Start	Kennacraig
Finish	Tarbert
Distance	5 miles (8km)
Grade	Easy
Time	40mins
Map	OS Landranger 1:50,000 62

Easy pedalling through the mixed woodlands north of Kennacraig soon brings you to the pleasant little port of Tarbert, where there are plenty of pubs, cafés and shops. Fishing boats and visiting yachts make it a busy and colourful place to spend an hour or two.

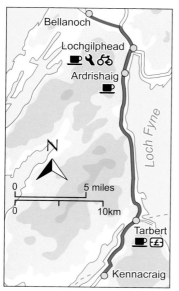

Leaving **Kennacraig** (✈1E), head north through woodland along the A83 to **Tarbert**. If you are heading to the slipway for the ferry across to Portavadie, bear right along the quay and round below the ruined 15th century tower of Tarbert Castle.

The residents of the area around Tarbert refer to themselves as '**dookers**', that being the local name for the guillemot, which formed a substantial part of their diet in the harder 19th century.

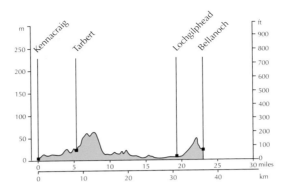

STAGE 2
Tarbert to Bellanoch

Start	Tarbert
Finish	Bellanoch
Distance	18 miles (30km)
Grade	Moderate
Time	2hrs
Map	OS Landranger 1:50,000 55, 62

Easy after the initial climb, this route gives you the option of joining the Crinan Canal Trail. Taking the towpath means bypassing Lochgilphead, a planned town dating from 1790 which gained importance after the completion of the canal in 1801. But unless you need food or supplies, it has little of interest, so it's best to take the canal all the way to Bellanoch.

North of Tarbert the A83 is generally busy, but after the short climb around Barr Hill it is easy pedalling all the way to the dour looking village of **Ardrishaig**, where you can join the Crinan Canal Trail a few hundred yards north of the village near lock 4, soon passing the village of **Lochgilphead**.

Locks on the Crinan Canal

The **Crinan Canal**, which is 9 miles (14.5km) long and has 15 locks rising to 65 feet above sea level, provides a quick link between the west coast and the Clyde Estuary, avoiding the long journey around the Kintyre Peninsula. When it was opened it was two years late, significantly over-budget and not properly finished, which led to Thomas Telford being asked to redesign parts of it in 1816.

Until the early 20th century Clyde Puffers, little coastal steamers designed to fit through canals, delivered coal to the west coast and brought back whisky and other produce. Only two of these 'Victualing Inshore Craft' remain – Vic 27, renamed 'Auld Reekie', and Vic 32, which is still based at Crinan and earns its keep carrying paying passengers, who are expected to shovel coal. (See the picture in the introduction to this chapter.) The canal no longer carries freight, although Ardrishaig is an important port for loading timber from the Kintyre forests.

Follow the canal through Cairnbaan to **Bellanoch**.

STAGE 3
Bellanoch to Oban

Start	Bellanoch
Finish	Oban
Distance	34 miles (54km)
Grade	Hard
Time	3hrs 40mins
Map	OS Landranger 1:50,000 55, 59

This route crosses the Moine Mhor, the 'Great Moss' – home to hen harriers and ten kinds of dragonfly – and passes Kilmartin, one of the richest archaeological landscapes in Scotland, before the long, twisting final stretch to Oban.

From **Bellanoch**, cross the two bridges and head north across the open expanse of Moine Mhor to join the A816 at Slockavullin. At the head of the glen is **Kilmartin**.

The **Kilmartin House Museum of Ancient Culture** has impressive audio-visual and interactive displays about the 350 ancient monuments that lie within a six-mile radius of the village.

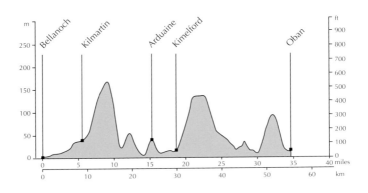

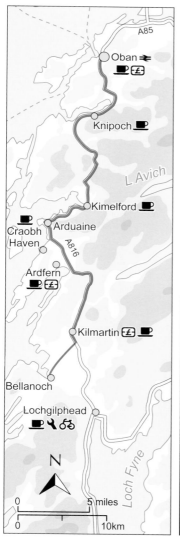

North of the village on a ridge above the A816 is **Carnasserie Castle**, built at the end of the 16th century by John Carswell who was Bishop of Argyll and the Isles during the reign of Mary Queen of Scots.

However you may wish to bypass these attractions to conserve your energy for the remainder of the ride to Oban, which has long stretches of twisting inland ascents before dropping down to cross the glens behind Loch Craignish, Loch Melfort and Loch Feochan. There are plenty of places to eat on or just off the route at **Ardfern**, and **Craobh Haven** before passing through **Arduaine**, then yet more refreshment possibilities at **Kilmelford** and **Knipoch**. But bustling **Oban** will be a welcome sight after such a long ride.

Fishing boats at Oban –
the gateway to the southern Hebrides

71

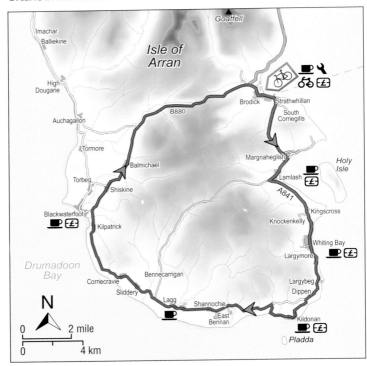

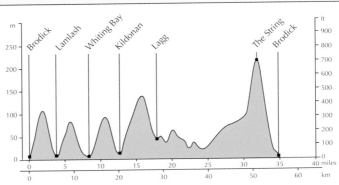

DAY ROUTES

ROUTE 1.1

Circuit of south Arran

Start/Finish	Brodick
Distance	35 miles (56km)
Total Ascent	3020ft (920m)
Grade	Hard
Time	3hrs 50mins
Map	OS Landranger 1:50,000 69
Ferries	None on the ride

It is perhaps advisable to ride around a bit to warm up before you set off on this ride, as immediately you head out of Brodick and turn inland you encounter the first of the many short hills, followed by a sweeping descent, with views of islands, the Ayrshire coast and Kintyre, that characterise this ride.

Head south out of **Brodick** and turn inland along the A841, up the first of many short hills on this ride. Thankfully it's not long, and at the summit there is a viewpoint and information board where you can stop and pick out each of the hills of north Arran. Starting off again is easy with a pleasant descent into **Lamlash.**

> **Lamlash** is the largest village on the island and an altogether prettier place than Brodick with elegant villas and broad swards of grass running along the front. Holy Isle, which provides the protection that makes Lamlash a good natural harbour, is now a Buddhist retreat but still welcomes visitors arriving on the ferry.
>
> The **Ross Road**, which runs across the south of Arran from Lamlash to Sliddery, involves an 8% climb when tackled from east to west but is much easier in the other direction and could be used to shorten this route.

The climb through the wooded slopes up and over to **Whiting Bay** gives good views north across Lamlash Bay to Holy Isle and the Ayrshire coast. In the first part of the 20th century, when Arran was a prime holiday destination, all three resorts on the east coast had their own ferry service, with Whiting Bay having the longest

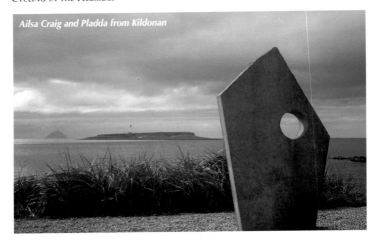
Ailsa Craig and Pladda from Kildonan

pier in Scotland. Turning the southeastern corner of Arran brings you high above the coastal village of **Kildonan**.

> Here there are views across to the islands of **Pladda** and the distant Ailsa Craig, sometimes called 'Paddy's Milestone' due to it being roughly halfway on the sea journey from Belfast to Glasgow used by many Irish labourers seeking work in the 19th century. Neither island has a permanent population.

If you keep to the main road and bypass Kildonan, you miss out on one of Arran's truly sandy beaches, but avoid a 9% climb back up again. Short climbs followed by all too brief downhill sections make it hard going through the farmlands surrounding Kilmory, **Lagg** and **Corriecravie**, but on a clear day the view across Kilbrannan Sound to the Mull of Kintrye will lift any flagging spirits. Once the sands of **Drumadoon Bay** come into view, the going gets noticeably easier and the prospect of a well-earned break in **Blackwaterfoot** will spur you on even more, so follow the main road sharply left into the village.

When you're nicely fed and watered, head back out the village the way you rode in and turn left onto the B880 along the south side of the flat expanse of Machrie Moor, through the village of **Shiskine** with its prominent red sandstone church. You are ascending all the time, gently at first but more steeply as you turn into the wooded Gleannan t-Suidhe and on to The String, which gets up to an 8% incline just before the summit. Resurfacing in 2010 almost made The

String a pleasure to ride, but a steady cadence and a low gear will soon see you to the summit and a swooping descent down Glen Shurig. Once you reach the T-junction at the bottom turn right into Brodick to get back to the start.

ROUTE 1.2
Circuit of north Arran

Start/Finish	Brodick
Distance	37 miles (60km)
Total Ascent	2490ft (760m)
Grade	Hard
Time	3hrs 40mins
Map	OS Landranger 1:50,000 69
Ferries	None on the ride

As the prevailing winds come from the southwest, it is best to do this ride in a clockwise direction, starting with the climb to the top of the infamous String road, presumably so named because its strings together the largest villages in the west coast with those on the east coast. It is an 'honest' climb with no hidden surprises, climbing at a steady 7% throughout 2 miles (3km) of ascent. The descent the other side is over all too quickly and is followed by predominantly easy and scenic cycling along the west coast to Lochranza, after which the last third of the ride soon flashes by.

Ride north out of Brodick on the A841 and then turning left on to the B880, 'the String', signposted for Blackwaterfoot. The climb to the top is rewarded by a fine view back down Glen Shurig and out over Brodick Bay.

To get a close up **view of Goatfell** and the other jagged peaks of North Arran – and a classic photograph of others in your party – you really need to clamber through the grass and heather to gain a higher viewpoint on the south side of the road.

The 6km of descent through the wooded Gleann t-Suidhe goes all too quickly, but slow down in time to turn right at the signpost for Pirnmill. This is a pleasant tree-lined road along the northern side of flat expanse of Machrie Moor. The golf

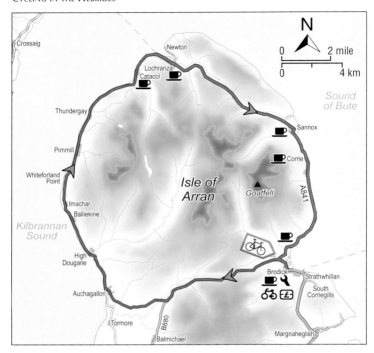

club, just to the south of the junction with the coast road, is open for refreshments during the summer months. Otherwise turn right and enjoy predominantly easy cycling for the next 20km along the raised beaches of the west coast with the sea on one side and the wooded cliffs on the other.

A thoroughly uncomfortable diversion up a poorly maintained road leads to the hamlet of Auchecar, where there is a café, but there are plenty of other more accessible cake stops further along.

> The Duke of Hamilton built **Dougarie Lodge** and its impressive boat house in 1865 as a summer retreat from his main residence of Brodick Castle.

There is an unexpected little hill just past Imachar, but otherwise it's relaxed pedalling past the shingle beach at Whitefarland and on through **Pirnmill**.

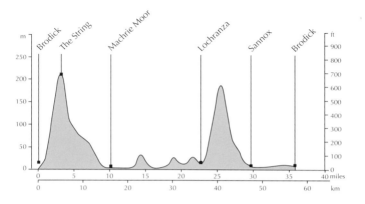

The **Twelve Apostles at Catacol** (pictured in the introduction to this chapter) are a row of uniform cottages built by the Duke of Hamilton in 1863 to house families who were cleared from their cottages in Gleann Catacol to make way for sheep. It is said that when a candle was placed in any of the differently shaped bedroom windows, returning fishermen could tell which house it was.

Parked up in the shade near Whitefarland Beach

Around the headland is **Lochranza**, a good place to take a break with a walk out to the 16th century castle or a visit to the distillery, before the steady climb up Gleann Chalmadale.

> The **summit** is 209m above sea level, only 27m less than the String, but it's an easier climb and you are soon rewarded with close up views into the Arran Hills and across the Firth of Clyde to the Ayrshire coast.

The ride back through **Sannox** and **Corrie** goes quickly, with plenty of places to eat and visit including Brodick Castle, the Isle of Arran brewery at Cladach and the Isle of Arran Heritage Museum at Rosaburn, before the return to Brodick.

ROUTE 1.3
Circuit of Great Cumbrae

Start/Finish	Downcraig Ferry
Distance	13 miles (21km)
Total Ascent	850ft (260m)
Grade	Easy
Time	1hr 30mins
Map	OS Landranger 1:50,000 63
Ferries	None on route

By including both the coastal loop and an inner loop around the inland hills, it is possible to squeeze an enjoyable 21km ride out of Great Cumbrae and, coupled with a lunch stop and a visit to the island museum housed in the beautifully restored Garrison House, this makes for an enjoyable, if short, day trip.

Once off the **ferry** at Downcraig, cycle down the east coast, passing Lion Rock and following the road around Farland Point and into the eastern end of Millport. As you swing around behind the sandy beach, turn right into Ferry Road and follow the minor road northwards through Ninian Brae. As the road starts to descend back towards the ferry, bear left and climb around Tonnel Hill to the viewpoint and picnic site at the summit of Barbary Hill.

On a clear day this is a pleasant spot with **good views** in all directions. But in the colder winters in the early half of the previous century, the high loch froze over and was used for curling, the stones coming from the now uninhabited island of Ailsa Craig which lies 20km off the southern tip of Arran.

Drop down into **Millport**, taking care as the road deteriorates on the lower part of the hill.

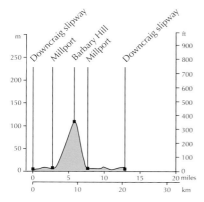

The crenellated **Garrison House** at the foot of the hill was built in 1745 to house a militia tasked with putting a stop to smuggling that was rife in the Clyde at that time. It later became a private residence, most notably for George Frederick Boyle, the 6th Earl of Glasgow, who founded The Cathedral of the Isles on ground owned by his family. After a fire in 2001, it lay derelict for a number of

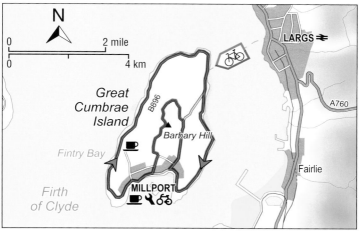

The legendary Ritz Café in Millport

years, before the community secured funding to restore it turning it into a multifunctional building that houses the island's medical centre, library and small museum as well as a bright airy café.

Continue through the town and out along the west side where there are views across to Bute and the high hills on Arran. The road passes through Fintry, where lemonade was made and bottled during the island's hey-day, before swinging round the northern tip and back to the ferry.

ROUTE 1.4

Circuit of Bute

Start/Finish	Rothesay
Distance	27 miles (43km)
Total Ascent	1840ft (560m)
Grade	Moderate
Time	3hrs 30mins
Map	OS Landranger 1:50,000 63
Ferries	None on route

This circular tour of the island goes down the sparsely populated western coast and takes in the popular gothic revival pile of Mount Stewart – the ancestral home of the Marquis of Bute, the principle landowner – before returning past the pleasant villas at the eastern end of Rothesay.

Head north out of **Rothesay** along the A844, taking a short diversion along Shore Road in **Port Bannatyne**, before rejoining the main road near the pier. Turn left by the gates of Kames Castle, originally the home of the Bannatyne family, and follow the road to **Ettrick Bay**.

Between 1902 and 1905, the **electric tramway** that ran between Rothesay and Port Bannatyne was extended to Ettrick Bay, the old route being recommissioned as the footpath that runs alongside the road.

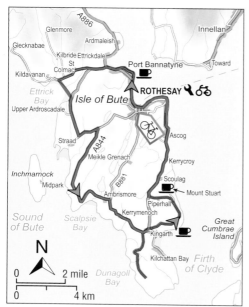

Take the track that runs behind the beach to rejoin the main road and follow it south through the quiet farmland behind St Ninian's Bay and **Scalspie Bay**.

Offshore lies the privately owned island of **Inchmarnock**, which was once used to exile alcoholics, leading to it being called 'The Drunkards' Isle'. It was later commissioned by the UK Government for training commandos in preparation for the D-Day landings in 1944.

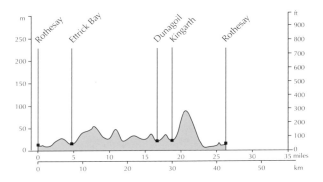

Just before Kingarth, turn right at the cemetery and take a detour to the road end at **Dunagoil**.

> Here a path leads uphill to the 12th century ruins of **St Blane's chapel** and churchyard which are hidden in a wooded valley. Extensive information boards help bring the site to life.

When you are ready to leave, return to the main road and turn right to **Kingarth**, taking the minor road that leads to Bruchag and through the quiet southeastern corner of the island before turning westwards through the woodland of the Mount

St Blane's Chapel

Stuart estate to rejoin the main A844 road. Turn right and head north back towards Rothesay, stopping off to enjoy the architectural wonders of **Mount Stuart**. Once you have paid your admission fee at the modern, minimalist visitor centre, you can ride right up to the house through the ornamental woodlands which are ablaze with rhododendrons and camellias in May and June.

Heading north, the road passes through the black and white village of **Kerrycroy**, which was built by the 2nd Marquis of Bute to make his English wife less homesick. Further on there is more for the horticulturally minded to see at Ascog Hall Fernery and Gardens on the outskirts of Rothesay, which is packed with sub-tropical ferns. Otherwise enjoy the final few miles of the ride along the sea front around Bogany Point and past the better preserved villas on the south side of Rothesay Bay.

ROUTE 1.5
Gigha

Start/Finish	Ardminish Jetty
Distance	12 miles (19km)
Total Ascent	430ft (130m)
Grade	Easy
Time	1hr 15mins
Map	OS Landranger 1:50,000 62
Ferries	None on route

The limited amount of road means that taking a vehicle across to Gigha is a pointless expense. So abandon it at the jetty at Tayinloan, where there is ample parking, and cross with your bike, or on foot if you are hiring bikes on the island. The only roadside tourist attractions are the gardens at Achamore House in the south of the island and the sandy beaches either side of the isthmus that runs out to Eilean Garbh in the north. So if the weather is fine and you fancy lounging on a beach, ride the southern end first. But if you enjoy gardens, ride the northern end first. The only places for refreshments are the community-run Gigha Hotel and the Boathouse café which are both conveniently located in the middle of the island, so you will not miss out on lunch or afternoon tea whichever way you choose.

The southern end of the island is noticeably green and pastoral, mainly due to the woods around Achamore House and Gardens, which are at their best in April and May when the camellias and rhododendron are in full bloom. There are no facilities other than a simple honesty box for admission fees and waymarked routes of varying lengths; the longest of which will take considerably less than the suggested 2hrs. At the south end of the road is the south pier with views out to the magnificently named **Gigalum Island** and **Cara Island**, which has had no permanent residents since the 1940s.

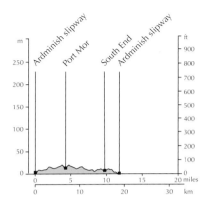

Beyond the parish church, the northern end of the island is less populated and much more rugged. The road passes below Creag Bhan, the highest point on Gigha at exactly 100m, before crossing the isthmus beyond the farmhouse at **Tarbert** and coming to an end at **Port Mor**, where there are views north to the Paps of Jura. If you want to visit the twin beaches at **Eilean Garbh**, park

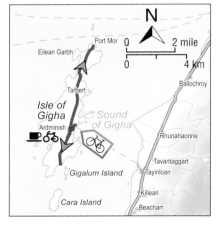

your bike below Cnoc nan Gobhar and follow the obvious track, which may be muddy and somewhat difficult to navigate in cleats. An ascent of Eilean Garbh gives good views across to Islay on a clear day.

2 COLONSAY, ISLAY AND JURA

A windless day at Port Mhor, Colonsay (Route 2.6)

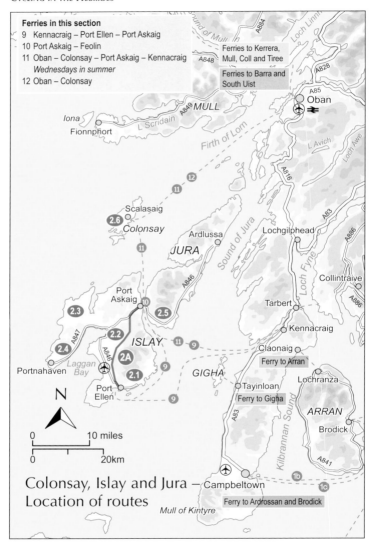

Ferries in this section
9 Kennacraig – Port Ellen – Port Askaig
10 Port Askaig – Feolin
11 Oban – Colonsay – Port Askaig – Kennacraig
   Wednesdays in summer
12 Oban – Colonsay

Ferries to Kerrera, Mull, Coll and Tiree

Ferries to Barra and South Uist

Colonsay, Islay and Jura –
Location of routes

Ferry to Arran

Ferry to Gigha

Ferry to Ardrossan and Brodick

INTRODUCTION

There are few roads on these islands, but they are an interesting and varied group particularly if you are interested in wildlife or whisky – or both. Islay and Jura can be easily visited using the frequent ferry service from Kennacraig and there are sufficient day routes and other possibilities to keep you busy for the best part of a week. Other than the link route which connects the ferry ports of Port Ellen and Port Askaig, the routes on Islay described here include mainly circular tours of the Rhinns and the central area at the head of Loch Indaal as well as an out-and-back ride along the entire south coast that visits Kildalton in the east, The Oa peninsula in the west and gives the opportunity

to stop off at any one – or all three – of the distilleries along the way. The *Velo Club d'Ardbeg* jersey is a practical souvenir of a visit to Islay. It can be bought in the café at the distillery or online at www.thecyclejersey.com.

Jura has but a single road. When the author George Orwell used the cottage at Barnhill at the northern end of Jura during the summers of 1946–1948, while writing his final, prophetic novel *1984*, he wrote that Jura was 'an extremely un-get-at-able place'. Sadly, it still is. It is effectively a dead end that requires two ferries and a journey across Islay to get to and from the mainland. A passenger ferry has recently operated between Craighouse

Abandoned tractor near Gruinart in northwest Islay (Route 2.2)

and Tayvallich on the mainland but at the time of writing this is only guaranteed to be running until the end of the 2011 season: see under 'Jura' below for more information.

Colonsay, which is served by a daily ferry from Oban, only has sufficient roads for a very leisurely day's cycling, but there are plenty of other things to explore.

You can visit all the islands in a single week-long circular tour, but this is only possible during the summer months when the ferry operates between Islay and Colonsay on Wednesdays and Saturdays. Starting from either Kennacraig or Oban, you can ride the tour clockwise or anti-clockwise, but will need to plan your schedule to make use of that critical Wednesday ferry between Islay and Colonsay. Details of long-stay car parking can be found in the 'Getting there' section in the introduction.

Islay

The southernmost of the Hebrides, Islay – pronounced 'eye-la' – is sometimes referred to as the 'Queen of the Hebrides' on account of its fertile soils and mild climate. It is world famous for malt whisky with eight working distilleries including brands such as Ardbeg, Bowmore, Bruichladdich, Bunnahabhain, Caol Ila, Lagavulin and Laphroaig. The newest distillery, Kilchoman, was the first start-up for 124 years and only released its first offering in 2009.

But there is plenty for the tourist besides whisky. Birdwatching is popular throughout the year because of the large flocks of geese which pass through every winter and the huge

Ardbeg Distillery, Islay (Route 2.1)

variety of rare birds such as the corn-crake and the chough. Islay supports around 60 pairs of resident chough, which is about a quarter of the UK population. A rare member of the crow family noted for its playful aero-batics, it has distinctive bright red legs and drooping red bill with which it extracts the grubs that are its favour-ite food from cow pats. In fact, Islay is only home to this clownish bird because of the large number of out-wintered cattle on the island.

Islay has an active cycling club, the Velo Club d'Ardbeg, which meets at Debbie's café in Bruichladdich. For the last few years, the club has organ-ised the Ride of the Falling Rain, an inclusive 100-mile event that takes place in early August and makes full use of the island's limited road network – see www.rideofthefallingrain.net.

Invading Americans

Islay has been raided by America on two occasions. During the American War of Independence (1778–1783), the colonists had no navy and relied on privateers to harass British ship-ping. One of these, The Ranger, was commanded by John Paul Jones (1747–1792), who had been born in humble circumstances in Kirkcudbright. He went to sea and rose through the ranks in his adoptive America and subse-quently became the new country's first naval hero. In the spring of 1778, The Ranger sailed into British waters and caused havoc for the British merchant shipping. He is reputed to have raided

the Islay ferry and deprived a returning Campbell of the fortune that he was bringing home from India in the all-too-portable form of gold ingots.

What is more certain is that on 4 October 1813, during the later Anglo–American War of 1812–1815, another privateer, the True Blooded Yankee, sailed into Loch Indaal and raided a number of merchant ships, setting fire to some of them and cut-ting the moorings of others. It was subsequently captured by the British navy in the Channel. However, the event did lead the island's owner to install a number of defences around Islay House and on Battery Hill above Bowmore.

Jura

The 5-minute ferry ride across the Sound of Islay takes you from popu-lous and productive Islay to barren and rocky Jura, home to a couple of hundred *Diurachs*, as the islanders are known, and five thousand red deer. The name Jura comes from *Dyr Oe*, Old Norse for 'deer island', which seems about right.

Other than a thin sliver of schist along the east coast, Jura is almost entirely made up of metamorphic quartzite. This is a poor rock that forms smooth hills and infertile soils. As a result, the small population lives along the single road that runs up the eastern side of the island, petering out into a track 17 miles (27km) north of Craighouse, leaving the rest of the island to the deer. It is the most barren

JURA PASSENGER FERRY

On the Jura passenger ferry (Route 2.5)

In recent years a passenger ferry has operated between Craighouse and Tayvallich on the mainland from the beginning of April to the end of September. It has space for 12 passengers and carries bikes free of charge so it could be used to include Jura in a tour joining Route 1F at Bellanoch on the Crinan Canal. The ride through the woodlands north of Talvallich is pleasant and as the region is on a geological fault that runs southwest to northeast, it is also very easy, although there is a brief climb from one glen over into the next.

The only reason this connection is not included as a link route is that at the time of writing the local government has only guaranteed funding until the end of the 2011 season and its future may be in doubt. So check www. jurapassengerferry.com first.

and the emptiest island in the whole of the Hebrides, today divided into a number of sporting estates.

Colonsay

Colonsay is one of the remotest communities in the UK, being 8 miles (13km) or more from its nearest neighbour. But this attractive little island has overcome its relative isolation, partly due to the careful custody of the Strathcona family, which has sympathetically developed tourism since they bought the island in 1904, and partly due to the undoubted benefit of the frequent summer ferry service from Oban, which runs five times a week. It may not be an obvious destination for a cyclist, with only 10 miles (16km) of roads, and no alternative but to backtrack to Oban, unless you make use of the Wednesday ferry that does a full rotation between Kennacraig and Oban or the Saturday ferry that goes to Colonsay and back. Using this service you can easily hop to Colonsay or Oban from Islay or Kintyre, or from Colonsay south to Islay or Kintyre. Visitors staying on Islay can also use this ferry for a day trip and enjoy six hours ashore on Colonsay.

If you do make the effort to get to Colonsay however you will be well rewarded, with two islands for the price of one! Colonsay is 8 miles (13km) long and 2 miles (3.25km) across at its widest and is known for its tranquillity, unspoilt natural beauty and a wide range of wildlife, including otters and chough. South across The Strand lies Oronsay, which is accessible for one or two hours either side of low water on an ebb tide. It is now farmed by the RSPB, with a mixed farming regime with cattle and sheep, late cut grass and arable crops grown to help conserve the corncrake and chough. Oronsay also has a 12-foot (3.5m) high medieval cross and the remains of an Augustinian priory, known to have existed prior to 1353 and now considered the second most important religious site in the Hebrides after Iona. See www.colonsay.org.uk for further information.

With very little traffic and lots of self-catering accommodation, Colonsay attracts lots of cycling families with young children.

Oronsay Priory, Colonsay (Route 2.6) (photo: Peter Edwards)

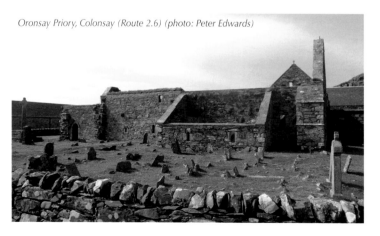

LINK ROUTES

ROUTE 2A
Port Ellen to Port Askaig

Start	Port Ellen
Finish	Port Askaig
Distance	18 miles (30km)
Total Ascent	1050ft (320m)
Grade	Moderate
Time	2hrs
Map	OS Landranger 1:50,000 60

The A846 runs across Islay, from Port Ellen to Port Askaig, and continues all the way along the east side of Jura to Craighouse and beyond. However few cyclists would want to ride the southern section past Islay airport which is relentlessly straight and featureless for 10 miles or more; the only interest coming from its wave-like undulations where sections have sunk into the peat bog that it crosses. A better and quieter alternative is to take the so-called 'High Road', the B8016, which leaves the main A846 – the 'Low Road' – at an abrupt corner just north of Port Ellen and runs parallel to it, albeit at a higher altitude.

After 5 miles (8km) on the A846 take the first right hand junction, passing the island's abattoir – one of the few features in this farming country – and bear right again at Cluanach. If it's clear, you will be rewarded with a view of the Paps of Jura to the north and over Loch Indaal to the south. If it's not, then you will be only

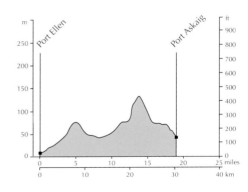

Approaching Port Ellen on Islay

too happy to drop down off the moor to rejoin civilization and the main A846 at the small village of **Ballygrant**. Turn right, passing the old chapel at **Keills**, and descend the sweeping hill down to **Port Askaig** (18/30).

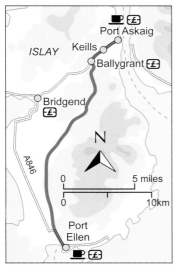

Bunnahabhain and **Caol Ila** distilleries are tucked in bays just to the north of Port Askaig.

DAY ROUTES

ROUTE 2.1
South coast of Islay

Start/Finish	Port Ellen
Distance	28 miles (45km)
Total Ascent	1870ft (570m)
Grade	Moderate
Time	3hrs 30mins
Map	OS Landranger 1:50,000 60
Ferries	None on route

Many of the main villages on Islay were founded by the Campbell family, which owned the local estate, and Port Ellen is no different, having been built in 1821 by Walter Frederick Campbell, who named it after his wife. This route heads east past three distilleries, the road sheltered by woods with occasional views out to sea, such as at Loch à Chnuic, where the grey seals that bask on the skerries can be viewed at close quarters. Further on the quality of the road varies considerably but is never too rough to ride. It then returns to through Port Ellen to The Oa peninsula to the west.

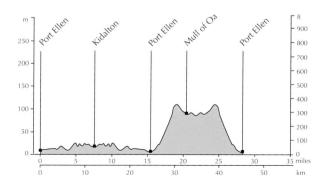

Parked up at the Laphraoig Distillery

Head east out of **Port Ellen** on the A846, stopping off to visit one or more of the three south coast distilleries of **Laphraoig**, **Lagavulin** and **Ardbeg**, all of which offer tours, sampling and cafés.

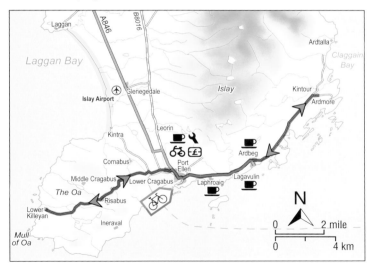

95

After the last distillery, Ardbeg, the road is no longer classified but the surface is good all the way to Kildalton.

The early Christian cross within the old parish church at **Kildalton** dates from the second half of the 8th century. It was carved from local grey-green epidiorite stone and although weathered, it is still possible to pick out the main features which include biblical scenes and celtic designs. There are a number of carved medieval grave slabs, the best of which is scattered with coins left as offerings by visitors. Outside the graveyard there is another cross which is nicknamed 'The Thief's Cross' because it stands in unconsecrated ground.

Grave slab in the old parish church at Kildalton

You can continue all the way, past Kidalton, to the road end at **Claggain Bay**, but the surface deteriorates the further you go. Most riders will be happy to retrace the route to Ardbeg back to **Port Ellen**, and then out the other side to the Mull of Oa and through **Cragabus** and **Risabus** on a quiet, twisting and occasionally steep little road.

Because the peninsula is surrounded with sheer cliffs, there are few glimpses of the sea or the hidden beaches and it can feel like riding across a moor. But it's worth persisting, even if the indifferent quality of the road surface may be leading you to question the sense of continuing to the road end at the **RSPB Oa Reserve**.

If you park your bike here, you can follow a sign posted trail walk out to the **American monument**, which commemorates the loss of life on two troop ships in 1918, taking in dramatic coastal scenery and wildlife watching as you go.

Then it's back to Port Ellen for a well-earned afternoon tea.

ROUTE 2.2

Circuit of northwest Islay from Bridgend

Start/Finish	Bridgend
Distance	26 miles (42km)
Total Ascent	1120ft (340m)
Grade	Moderate
Time	3hrs
Map	OS Landranger 1:50,000 60
Ferries	None on route

On a warm and windless day, riding west along the main road out of Bridgend can almost feel like riding alongside the Mediterranean, with Loch Indaal on your left and the lush woodlands of Islay House on your right. This loop out to the island's northwest corner takes in Islay's newest distillery and an RSBP reserve.

After 4 miles (6km) west along the A847 from **Bridgend** turn right onto the B8018, signposted for Sanaigmore, and follow this for 2 miles (3km) before forking left on the bend for **Kilchoman**.

Loch Indaal, where American privateers once burned Scottish boats

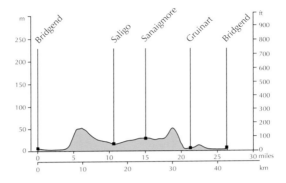

On the north side of the road lies **Loch Gorm**, the largest fresh water loch on Islay, which is renowned for its brown trout, where the overgrown ruins of Loch Gorm Castle, a stronghold of the MacDonalds are just visible on a small island.

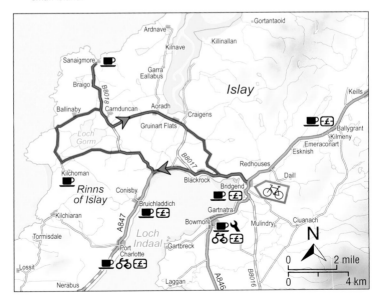

Kilchoman Distillery at Rockside Farm on the south side of the road is the smallest and most recent of the Islay distilleries, running the whole process, from growing the barley to bottling, onsite. It is open all year for tours and refreshments.

Further on, the route turns sharply northwards along the Atlantic coast with a choice of fine beaches to visit at Machrie or Saligo, both of which are favoured spots for photographing sunsets.

In the autumn, the **RSPB Reserve at Gruinart** comes alive with the honking of thousands of white-fronted and barnacle geese that arrive from Greenland.

Turning east around the northern shore of Loch Gorm, the road passes through **Ballinaby**, which is the largest village in this part of the island, to rejoin the A8018. Turn left and ride to the road end at **Sanaigmore**, where there is a welcoming gallery and café, perched above another sandy beach. Retrace the route southwards, turning left towards the RSPB Reserve at Gruinart.

The stretch of road across **Gruinart Flats** is barely above sea level, but if you leave the B8017 and keep straight on along the minor road that goes through Tighnacachla you will soon come to a challenging little climb over the shoulder of Borichill Mor, before dropping down to the main road and another easy section back into **Bridgend**.

ROUTE 2.3
Circuit of central Islay from Bowmore

Start/Finish	Bowmore
Distance	20 miles (31km)
Total Ascent	950ft (290m)
Grade	Easy
Time	2hrs 30mins
Map	OS Landranger 1:50,000 60
Ferries	None on route

Bowmore is the oldest planned village in Scotland, having been founded in 1768 by Daniel Campbell, who moved the inhabitants of the old village of Killarrow further away from the family home at Islay House. The village's original grid pattern and the small fields that were left between the rows of houses so the residents could grow food and keep a milking cow have been lost to infill development. But it's still a pretty village, dominated by the Round Church, which has a magnificent interior and is well worth a visit. Bowmore Distillery, the second oldest in Scotland, provides its surplus heat to warm the water in the local swimming pool.

Head up Main Street and turn left towards the radio mast along the minor road immediately behind the church. Turn right at the T-junction at Laggan Bridge and follow the B8016 for 1¼miles (2km) southwards, then turn sharp left onto 'High'Road and follow it through **Cluanach** to **Ballygrant**. Turn left onto the A846 and follow it on a gentle downhill slope all the way to **Bridgend** at the head of Loch Indaal.

On the north side of the road at the outskirts of Bridgend is **Islay House Square**. The buildings that sit around this one acre rectangle were once the stables, smithy and homes of estate workers from nearby Islay House, which was once the home of Campbells of Islay and subsequent lairds.

Bowmore Parish Church

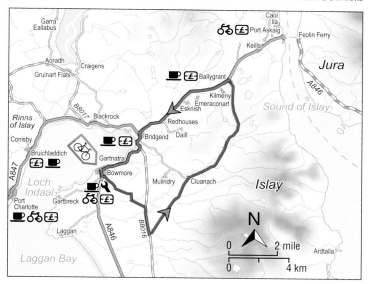

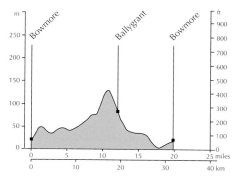

The buildings have since been converted into business units and house a variety of art and craft shops, a café and the local Islay Ales brewery.

From Bridgend it's just back along the coast on the A846 to Bowmore.

101

ROUTE 2.4

Circuit of southwest Islay (The Rhinns)

Start/Finish	Bruichladdich
Distance	21 miles (34km)
Total Ascent	1280ft (390m)
Grade	Moderate
Time	2hrs 30mins
Map	OS Landranger 1:50,000 60
Ferries	None on route

Bruichladdich has plenty of parking opposite the distillery – until recently the only one to use locally grown barley, do its own malting and mature and bottle its malts on the island. The new Kilchoman Distillery has trumped this by actually growing its own barley as well. From here this route circuits the Rhinns of Islay peninsula, passing through the picturesque villages of Port Charlotte, Port Wemyss and Portnahaven.

Head south down the western side of **Loch Indaal**, passing through the pretty village of Port Charlotte.

> Port Charlotte is another creation of **Walter Frederick Campbell**, who built it in 1828 and named it after his mother. The village was built to house workers from the Loch Indaal Distillery, which closed in 1929, its buildings now being part of the Youth Hostel and the Islay Natural History Trust.
>
> The Bruichladdich Distillery Company recently purchased the rest of the old distillery buildings and is planning to open a new distillery.

Continue south through the farming villages of **Nerabus** and **Elister** to the end of the peninsula, turning left down to **Port Wemyss**.

> Pronounced 'Port Weems', **Port Wemyss** was created in 1832 by Walter Frederick Campbell and named after his father-in-law, the 8th Earl of Wemyss. His aim was to encourage people to move off the land and take up fishing. As Northern Ireland is only 30 miles (48km) away to the south, catches were

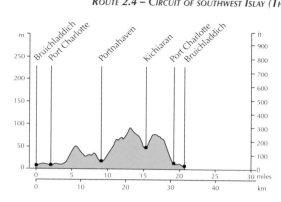

landed and processed at the Irish port of Ballycastle which had a ready market in Belfast.

Just offshore lies the island of **Orsay** and the **Rhinns of Islay lighthouse**, built in 1828 by Robert Stevenson of the famous Stevenson family of lighthouse builders. If you park your bike and take a walk along the delightful Path of the Fisherman, you should see grey seals, which haul out on a small beach across the sound, and perhaps bottlenose dolphin, which enjoy the fast tidal currents around Orsay.

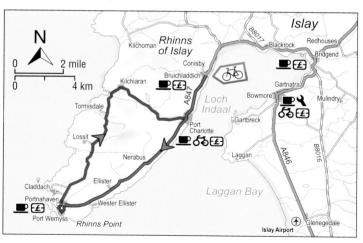

Port Charlotte lighthouse

Around the bay is **Portnahaven**, which could easily be mistaken for a Cornish fishing village, complete with a sheltered harbour and a village pub, An Tigh Seinnse, which means 'the house of singing', surely evidence of the good times still to be had there. Climb up the High Street towards the church – which is shared by Portnahaven and Port Wemyss and has separate doors for villagers from each parish – and head northwards along the quiet road that runs up the west side of the Rhins past **Lossit** and **Tormisdale** and around the top of Kilchiaran Bay to **Kilchiaran**.

From here a short climb across the wooded centre of the Rhinns, where red deer can sometimes be seen in the clearings, leads to a gentle descent to **Port Charlotte**, with good views north to the Paps of Jura. Stop off to visit the Museum of Islay Life or for a tea break – or head back northwards along the main road to **Bruichladdich**.

ROUTE 2.5

Craighouse and back from Feolin Ferry

Start/Finish	Feolin Ferry
Distance	17 miles (27km)
Total Ascent	1280ft (390m)
Grade	Moderate
Time	2hrs 10mins
Map	OS Landranger 1:50,000 61
Ferries	Port Askaig – Feolin Ferry

This route follows Jura's only road around the southern end of the island as far as Craighouse, the island's only real settlement. From here you can carry on another 17 miles (27km), if you like, before the road turns to track at Ardlussa: you can even carry on along the track all the way to Barnhill, but at some point you're going to have to turn round and head back to Craighouse and Feolin Ferry.

Set off around the south of the island along the A846, initially below low cliffs, then climbing steadily up the open hillside above the coastal flatlands of Mucraidh, where you may well see red deer.

Out to sea on the rocky island of Am Fraoch Eilean are the remains of 12th century **Claig Castle**, which helped the Lords of the Isles, the MacDonalds, to control local shipping for more than four centuries.

Further along is the green oasis of **Jura House**, which was built in 1812 as a comfortable and luxurious home by the Campbells, who occupied Jura in the 1600's.

The road undulates as it swings around to the north with a pleasant descent into **Craighouse**, where the Jura Hotel offers camping and hot showers if you are looking for an overnight stay.

You can ride much further north up the east side of Jura. The grass strip that runs up the middle of the road increases in width all the way up, suggesting the road will run out any time soon. But it only turns to track beyond Ardlussa,

17 miles (27km) north of Craighouse, although the OS map shows the road continuing as far as Glen Lealt 4 miles (6.5km) south of Barnhill. There is a sign at the road end advising of its poor condition and a chain across to stop cars going further. It is possible to ride all the way to Barnhill on a mountain bike, but road bike riders are advised

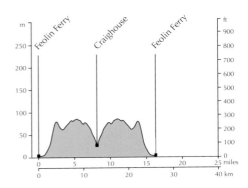

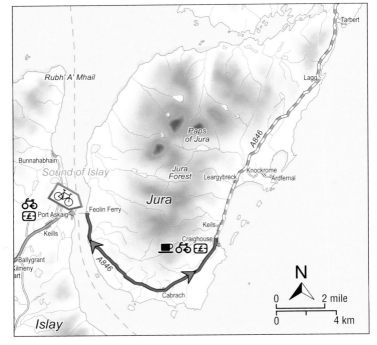

Craighouse Quay on a late summer afternoon

not to venture further than Glen Lealt and most won't want to go further than Ardlussa. But no matter how far you choose to go, you will inevitably have to head back to **Feolin Ferry**.

ROUTE 2.6

Circuit of Colonsay

Start/FInish	Scalasaig
Distance	15 miles (24km) not including Oronsay
Total Ascent	1150ft (350m)
Grade	Moderate
Time	1hr 45mins
Map	OS Landranger 1:50,000 61
Ferries	None on route

If you are planning to cross to Oronsay, first check the time of low water, which needs to be 1m or less for a leisurely visit, remembering that tide tables are always published in GMT, so you'll need to add an hour for British Summer Time. You should plan to arrive at the crossing two hours prior to low water so if low water is in the morning, ride this route anti-clockwise. Otherwise stock up with snacks at Colonsay's only shop, near the pier at Scalasaig, and head off northwards.

If riding anti-clockwise, take the B8057 northwards from **Scalasaig**. The road steadily climbs to the little coll below Beinn nan Gudairean, Colonsay's highest point at 136m, before dropping through a couple of modest hairpin

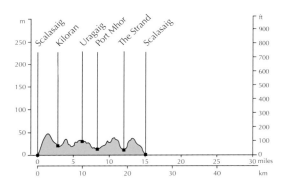

bends and crossing the chain of lochs in the central valley. Turn right on to the B8086 at the T-junction and follow the road around Colonsay House to its end at **Uragaig** above **Kiloran Bay**, considered by many to be the prettiest beach in the Hebrides. You can continue along the farm track behind the beach to the ruined chapel at **Balnahard**, perhaps catching sight of chough and Colonsay's one resident golden eagle. Parts of this undulating track are sometimes wet and muddy and you would be ill-advised to attempt it on narrow road tyres.

Return to **Kiloran** and head south through **Kilchattan** to the sandy bays of the west coast.

Standing alone above the beach at Port Mhor is **Colonsay bookshop**, which has an excellent collection of books on the highlands and islands, many of them antiquarian.

A short detour down to the airstrip leads to other beaches. Otherwise, follow the main road as it heads back inland and then turn south on the B8086 at an

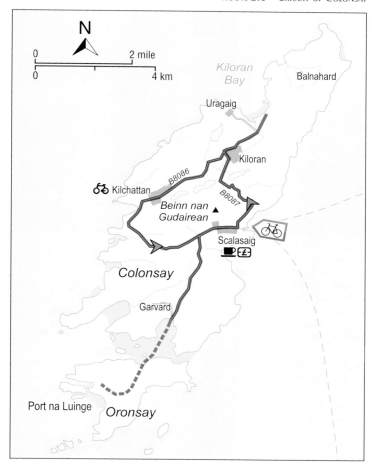

unmarked junction. Just before the road end is the ruin of a small chapel where monks used to wait to cross The Strand to **Oronsay**. As the waters recede a sand bar forms along the eastern edge of The Strand leading across to marker posts that are visible on the opposite shore. Salt water can wreak havoc with bottom bracket, gears and disk brakes and so unless the sands are completely dry, the

Sound advice at Oronsay Strand

best advice is to abandon your bike and walk across to the Priory, remembering to allow sufficient time for a safe return.

Once across, follow the track inland and around Beinn Oronsay to the Priory and the sandy beach at **Port na Luinge**. If you have time, you could also follow the 6km track that runs right around the island. When you get back to Colonsay, head back northwards along the B8086 and turn right for **Scalasaig**, passing below Dun Eibhinn on the hilltop and perhaps stopping off at the Colonsay Hotel to sample a pint of locally-brewed Colonsay beer.

Port Mhor graveyard contains the graves of several seamen whose bodies were washed up on local beaches during World War II, unidentifiable other than for their rank.

3 MULL,
COLL AND TIREE

Balevullin Bay, Tiree (Route 3.8)

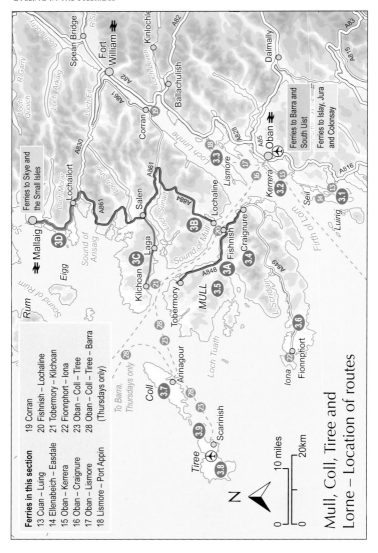

Ferries in this section
13 Cuan – Luing
14 Ellenabeich – Easdale
15 Oban – Kerrera
16 Oban – Craignure
17 Oban – Lismore
18 Lismore – Port Appin
19 Corran
20 Fishnish – Lochaline
21 Tobermory – Kilchoan
22 Fionnphort – Iona
23 Oban – Coll – Tiree
28 Oban – Coll – Tiree – Barra
(Thursdays only)

Mull, Coll, Tiree and
Lorne – Location of routes

INTRODUCTION

The 'Slate Islands' are the islands of Seil, Easdale, Luing and Belnahua, just to the south of Oban, named after the slate industry which thrived here until the early 20th century. Seil is the easiest to access, being connected to the mainland by a bridge. Kerrera, a quick hop on the ferry away from Oban, is worth visiting for its isolation and the opportunity to escape from the bustle of Oban for a couple of hours, although it's best avoided on dedicated road bikes (see under 'Kerrera' below).

Lismore, with pleasant easy riding, is worth lingering over and may be accessed by ferry from Oban to Achnacloish or the much shorter hop from Port Appin to Port Ramsay at the island's north end. The day route described here uses the first ferry to do a circular tour of the island and mainland roads back to Oban, but if you want a shorter ride and lunch at the hotel at Port Appin you could use that ferry instead.

Mull is easy to reach by ferry from Oban to Craignure, Kilchoan on the Ardnamurchan peninsula to Tobermory and from Lochaline across the Sound of Mull to Fishnish. It's a big island with very varied, often challenging cycling and makes a good base in its own right: however the easy accessibility of Mull means that it is extremely well visited. Consequently the roads are periodically busy with coaches whisking tourists around on day trips, and restaurants can be surprisingly indifferent to service and quality, while Iona, although

Tobermory (Route 3A)

Boarding the Sunday ferry across Cuan Sound (Route 3.1)

beautiful and well worth a visit, can be extremely crowded during the day in the holiday season.

Coll and Tiree, the end of the latter of which lies 60 miles (95km) off the mainland, are usually grouped in the Inner Hebrides, although Tiree extends as far west as the Isle of Harris. Both are served by the ferry out of Oban, making it easy to visit both as part of a longer trip. Alternatively, if you make use of the summer service from Oban to Barra on a Thursday, which stops at both Coll and Tiree, you could include them as part of a longer tour to the Western Isles. Tiree is roughly the same size as Coll and only two miles (3km) away across Gunna Sound, but the differences between the two islands are profound.

All the islands in this section are served by ferries from Oban, which is a convenient place to leave a vehicle.

Free long-stay car parking is available at Lochavullin Road and Longsdale Road and secure long-stay car parking and storage is provided by Hazelbank Motors – tel 01631 566476 and Timbertech – tel 01631 566660.

However, hopping between these islands is not straightforward. Mull has two 'back doors', both of them crossing the Sound of Mull northwards, either from Tobermory to Kilchoan or from Fishnish to Lochaline. These can be used to make a longer tour that starts and finishes in Oban, taking in Mull, Ardnamurchan and Morven. But visiting Coll and Tiree as part of a tour that keeps within the bounds of this section involves returning to Oban to change ferries, although on Thursdays, during summer months, it is possible to hop directly between Coll or Tiree and Barra.

Slate Islands

In the 18th and 19th centuries the slates quarried on Seil, Easdale, Luing and Belnahua roofed many of the buildings in Scottish cities and were exported across the Atlantic. The industry floundered in the early 20th century when the sea flooded the quarries and large scale extraction was no longer economic.

The days of the slate industries which give the islands of Seil, Easdale, Luing and Belnahua their names are long gone and today the main village of Ellenabeich on Seil is a busy tourist destination with a small museum, an excellent micro-brewery and is the base for exhilarating sea trips through the tidal rapids of the Grey Dog and the Corryvreckan whirlpool.

Kerrera

Kerrera, reached by a ferry trip of just half a kilometre from Oban, has history, wildlife and great scenery. But it lacks smooth tarmac roads so it's no place for a skinny-wheeled carbon road bike. Thicker road tyres would suffice in dry weather: if it's wet then you would need beefy touring tyres or a mountain bike. The tracks are generally well-drained, but need to be ridden with care due to the gravelly surface.

Lismore

The original Gaelic name for the long and low-lying isle of Lismore is *Lis Mhor*, which means 'big garden', reflecting its fertility. This is due to the underlying limestone, which was once quarried and fired in kilns to produce lime for use in local agriculture and for building, with over twenty local boats taking cargoes to Glasgow when the industry was at its peak in the second half of the 19th century. Today the only working quarry in the

Lismore Lighthouse on the way to Mull (Route 3A)

region is Glensanda on the opposite side of Loch Linnhe where a complete mountain, Meallach na Easaiche, is being removed to provide aggregate for roads all over the UK.

For its size, Lismore has a lot of history, having been the seat of the Bishops of Argyll who founded a cathedral here in the 13th century, since incorporated into the present Church of Saint Moluag. There are also the remains of an Iron Age Broch at Tirefour and a Norse castle at Coeffin. For more on the history of Lismore, visit the award-winning Heritage Museum at the centre of the island, which has the added attraction of an excellent café.

Mull

Were it not for the sea lochs and inlets that penetrate deep into its west side, Mull would be an equilateral triangle with sides of roughly 30 miles (48km). All the indentation means its coastline is a surprising 300 miles (500km) long and there are about 140 miles (224km) of road on the island which give a couple of excellent circular rides as well as a long out-and-back to the iconic island of Iona. There is fine cycling to be had amid stunning scenery and a couple of magnificent day routes that are arguably the best that the Hebrides has to offer.

Iona

Tiny Iona, just 3½ miles (5.5km) long and a mile (1.5km) wide, is the place where Colm Cille, an Irish priest and prince who was to become revered as Saint Columba, established an outpost for Celtic Christianity in the 6th century. Missionaries and craftsmen spread out across northern Europe, resulting in Iona becoming a place for

Summer in the gardens of Iona Abbey (Route 3.6)

pilgrimage and the burial of important people thought to include 48 Scottish, eight Norwegian and four Irish kings. The monastery flourished until the Reformation, when most of the buildings, and all but three of the 360 crosses that had been set up, were systematically destroyed. In 1899 the 8th Duke of Argyll granted Iona to the Church of Scotland, but limited restoration work was carried out until 1938, when the Reverend George MacLeod and a group of followers started to rebuild the abbey, eventually founding the Iona Community.

Today the island has two hotels, a number of guest houses and self-catering cottages and a hostel for the use of the large number of visitors who stay on the island. But the crowds of day trippers that pack the abbey and craft shops mean that anyone looking for peace and tranquility needs to get well away from the main village of Baile Mor.

Erraid

Just to the south of Fionnphort, past the campsite at Fidden, is the island of Erraid. David and Thomas Stevenson used it as a base in the years between 1867 and 1872 when they were building the Dubh Artach lighthouse, which is 9 miles (14km) offshore and marks the Torran Rocks. The building of the lighthouse was prompted by a violent storm at the end of 1865 which resulted in 24 ships being lost in the area, and if you look at a map you will see the hazard. The writer

and sailor Hamish Haswell-Smith describes the rocks as 'being scattered over a wide area like dragon's teeth. They lurk menacingly just beneath the surface, occasionally showing themselves in a froth of white spittle'.

During the years the lighthouse was being built, Thomas's son, the author Robert Louis Stevenson, visited the island and was so taken with its beauty that he used it as the setting for the shipwreck in his novel *Kidnapped* (1886). The lighthouse was automated in 1971 and the keepers and their families left the island. Today Erraid is in the custody of a small group of members of the Findhorn Foundation who enjoy a simple life based on work, play, celebration and meditation. You can visit for a day or stay for a week. See www.erraid.com.

Coll

Superficially, Coll and Tiree appear to have a lot in common. They are treeless and low-lying, enjoy a mild climate and the highest levels of sunshine recorded anywhere in the British Isles, typically averaging over 220 hours during May. But this comes at a price. The average wind speed is between 18 and 24mph – a fresh breeze – which attracts sand-yachters and all types of surfer to the wide sandy bays, and helps drive away rain and midges. However cyclists should expect some strenuous pedalling.

Coll is 13 miles (21km) long and 4 miles (6.5km) across at its widest point, giving it roughly the same area as its neighbour Tiree. The north of the island is rocky and barren and overall only a tenth of the land is cultivated, the majority being left for cattle and sheep to graze. Because of this the island has never been heavily populated, the current number of residents being approximately 200. The situation is not helped by a large population of wild rabbits, estimated to number 100,000 or more and said to consume as much grass as 10,000 head of sheep.

Tiree

Tiree means 'the land of corn' in Gaelic and has been called the granary of the Hebrides. It is certainly the most fertile, with crops benefiting from the long sunny days and good rich soils. The island has an outer ring of *machair* that is wider on the west side where the prevalent southwesterlies have blown the shell sand further inland, a middle area of well-drained, arable land and a central area of wetter, peaty ground called *sliabh* (pronounced 'slieve'). When the crofts were set out over a century ago, the land was apportioned to give each crofter a fair share of each type of land; the middle area for growing corn or grass for hay and silage; sliabh for summer grazing and machair for winter grazing.

Today farming remains the island's main source of income, supplemented by fishing and a growing tourist industry, particularly for the windsurfers and kite surfers who come to Tiree because the wind is reliable and there are beaches on every side of the island. This buoyant economy enables the island to sustain a population of around 800, together with a good selection of accommodation and a couple of well-stocked shops. In fact the only thing Tiree happily does without is the rabbit, which was systematically eradicated at the beginning of the 19th century. See the community website at www.isleoftiree.com for visitor information.

The commonest geese on Tiree are the native Greylag, the monochrome Barnacle and the Greenland White-Fronted goose – although others do occur.

Tigh gael, Sandaig, Tiree (Route 3.8)

LINK ROUTES

ROUTE 3A
Craignure to Tobermory

Start	Craignure
Finish	Tobermory
Distance	17 miles (27km)
Total Ascent	1380ft (420m)
Grade	Easy to Salen, then Moderate
Time	2hrs 30mins
Map	OS Landranger 1:50,000 49, 47

There are frequent ferries on the 45 minute sailing between Oban and Craignure even during the winter months so the journey across to Mull is more like a bus ride than an adventure. But the views up and down Loch Linnhe are spectacular and in really rough weather the transit over the overfalls south of Lismore Lighthouse is unforgettable. Pity the same cannot be said of Craignure, which is an entirely functional ferry terminal.

The road north has few views out across the Sound of Mull, but the surface is good and if you're rushing to catch a ferry at **Fishnish** (6/10), you might want to test your time-trialling abilities. The confining forestry finishes at Fishnish Bay and the views open up all the way to **Salen** (12/20), where there is an excellent coffee shop and an entrepreneurial Post Office that also has a take-away food counter and a launderette.

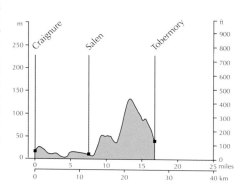

Rotting boats at Salen, Mull

After the 13th century Aros Castle, once a stronghold of the MacDougalls, Lords of Lorn, the road climbs steadily up to Gualan Dhubh – 'the black shoulder' – from where it's mostly downhill all the way to **Tobermory** (23/37).

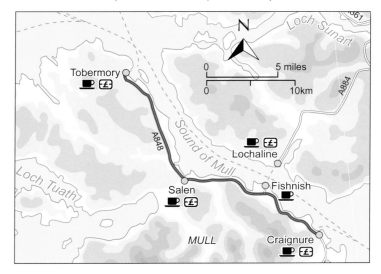

This busy, picture-postcard fishing village at the foot of steeply wooded hills was chosen by the BBC as the setting for the popular children's television series **Balamory**. You could easily idle away a day here visiting the distillery, taking a boat trip and finishing with a good dinner of local seafood.

ROUTE 3B
Lochaline to Salen

Start	Lochaline
Finish	Salen
Distance	30 miles (48km)
Total Ascent	1280ft (390m)
Grade	Hard
Time	3hrs 30mins
Map	OS Landranger 1:50,000 40, 47, 49

As soon as you leave Lochaline, you are into the empty roads of Morven with some climbing before a fast descent down to Loch Sunart and a chance for refreshments at Strontian. From then on, the route undulates along the north side of the loch to Salen.

Happy to be going downhill towards Loch Sunart

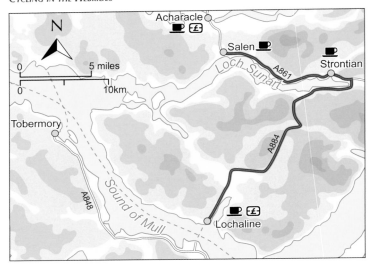

In the summer months, there is a welcoming café near the pier, where you might want to take a break before starting out, but otherwise climb up out of **Lochaline** on the A884 as it runs along the shore of Loch Aline to the north of the village.

At the head of the loch, the pink harled walls (harling is the covering of rough stonework with a slurry of small pebbles or fine chips of stone) of the 15th

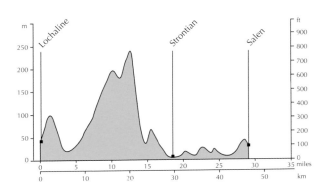

century **Kinlochaline Castle** stand proud above the trees. It was once the home of Clan MacInnes but is now a comfortable private residence.

The road meanders beside the River Aline, before climbing alongside Abhainn a' Ghlinne Ghil and then finally dropping down to Loch Sunart at a steady 8% incline that provides effortless exhilaration for 4km. After that cycling on the flat road alongside the loch may seem like hard work. When you reach the junction, turn left onto the A861 for the short ride into **Strontian**.

> The village grew up as a centre for **lead mining** but found fame in 1790 when French prisoners of war who were working the mines to provide shot to the Napoleonic Wars discovered the ore from which the new element strontium was eventually isolated. Mining ceased in 1930 and today the village is a centre for tourism.

Continuing west along the A861, which was built under the guidance of Thomas Telford, the road rises and falls all the way to **Salen** (30/48 ✗ 3C, 3D).

ROUTE 3C

Salen to Kilchoan

Start	Salen
Finish	Kilchoan
Distance	20 miles (32km)
Total Ascent	2330ft (710m)
Grade	Moderate to Laga, then Hard
Time	2hrs 20mins
Map	OS Landranger 1:50,000 40, 49

The road drops sharply at the beginning of this route, before getting into the familiar rhythm of short ascents and descents that are typical of lochside roads.

Leave **Salen** (✗ 3B, 3D) on the B8007. Once the road cuts inland it climbs around the southern slopes of Ben Laga before dropping down into the small village of Laga (6/9).

Further along, set high above the road and concealed by shrubbery, is **Glenborrowdale Castle**. It was built in 1900 for a South African diamond magnate and subsequently owned by Lord Trent who was the son of Jesse Boot, founder of 'Boots the Chemist'. Today it is privately owned and available for private hire.

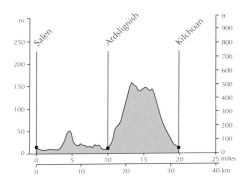

At the head of Glenmore Bay is **Glenmore Natural History Centre**, which during summer months, puts on interactive exhibitions about the natural environment of Ardnamurchan and has a very welcome tea room – the only 'cake stop' along the route. If it's open, it is worth dropping in, because things are about to change!

After **Ardslignish**, the road turns inland traversing high above the sandy beach at Camas Na Geall before climbing up between Ben Hiant and Beinn Bhuidhe to Loch Mudle with views northwards to the Small Isles and beyond to Skye. Towards dusk, when the sun is sinking into the west and you are exhausted after

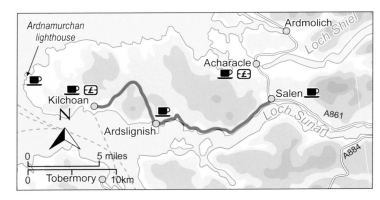

Looking back to Mull at sunset

a long day in the saddle, this is a magnificent place to rest. But there is still good riding to come.

After turning left at the junction, there is 3 miles (5km) of glorious descent to **Kilchoan** (20/32), a perfect way to end a day.

Ardnamurchan Lighthouse, the most westerly in mainland Britain, is 5 miles (8km) from Kilchoan and open to visitors from April to October.

ROUTE 3D
Salen to Mallaig

Start	Salen
Finish	Mallaig
Distance	38 miles (60km)
Total Ascent	4070ft (1240m)
Grade	Hard
Time	4hrs 25mins
Map	OS Landranger 1:50,000 40

Trains run from Lochailort, halfway along the route, to Mallaig, stopping at Beasdale, Arisaig and Morar and giving the weary and those who don't enjoy riding main roads the opportunity to grab a lift to the destination of their choice. Be aware that trains only stop at Beasdale on request of the driver. However trains are infrequent and the addition of a cycle route that runs most of the way from Loch Nan Uamh to Mallaig along either a dedicated cycle lane or quiet backroads means you only have to ride 5 miles (8km) directly on the main A830, making riding the whole way more tempting.

A few minutes ride northwards up the A861 from **Salen** (✗ 3B, 3C) is **Acharacle**, the largest village in Moidart. Telford's road weaves its way through this low-lying, and consequently midge-ridden, area, crossing the outflow of Loch Shiel by a new triple-arched bridge built in the 1970s to replace Telford's original bridge, which still stands 500m downstream.

> Just after the bridge, a 3km (2 mile) diversion northwards through a steeply wooded valley leads to Loch Moidart, where you can walk across a sandspit to the impressive ruins of **Castle Tioram** – pronounced 'chee-rum' and meaning 'dry island'. Parts of the castle date from the 13th century, but the impressive tower and other internal buildings were built between 15th and 17th centuries. It was the seat of the Clan MacDonald of Clan Ranald, but was seized by Government forces around 1692 and held by them until the Jacobite Uprising of 1715, when Allan of Clan Ranald recaptured and torched it to keep it out of the hands of the Hanoverian forces. It has remained unoccupied ever since.

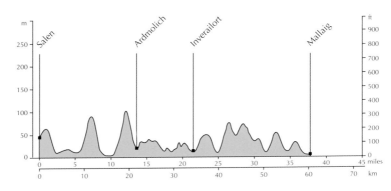

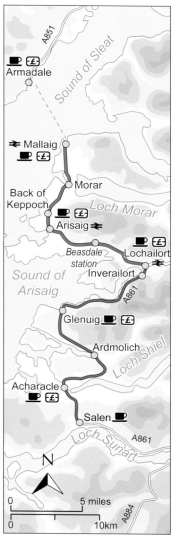

Back on the A861, the road goes eastwards through Mingarry, Dalnabreck and Langal before a steep climb up past Captain Robertson's Cairn and down through the woods to **Ardmolich**, where another newer bridge stands side by side with an older one.

The cairn commemorates **Captain WJ Robertson**, a member of an eminent local family, who was buried at St Finan's Chapel, Kinlochmoidart in 1869.

Just outside the village, in the meadows between the road and Loch Moidart, are '**The Seven Men of Moidart**', a row of seven beech trees planted more than 200 years ago in memory of the seven men who accompanied Bonnie Prince Charlie in the 1745 Jacobite uprising. Today there are four mature trees and three replacement saplings that will hopefully grow to restore the row to somewhere near its former glory in time for the tri-centenary of the dismal event!

Castle Tioram

Eigg and Rum from Inverailort on the way to Mallaig

The road climbs steadily below the steep wooded hillside before turning inland up the appropriately named Bealach Carach – 'the rocky pass' – at a steady 10% gradient for almost half a mile (1km). Over the summit, the hard work is immediately rewarded with a descent to **Glenuig**, with views north across the Sound of Arisaig. As you head eastwards along the south side of Loch Ailort, en route to **Inverailort**, stop and enjoy the view behind you to the Small Isles.

> Down below the road is the **Roshven House**, which is still owned by the family of Glasgow mathematician, Professor Hugh Blackburn and his wife Jemima who purchased it in 1854. Jemima, 1823–1909, was an eminent bird artist, who was admired by Sir Edwin Landseer and later Beatrix Potter, and was such a good ornithologist that Darwin referred to her observations in *The Origin of Species*. She entertained some of the most celebrated Victorians here, including John Ruskin, Sir John Everett Millais, Lord Kelvin, Anthony Trollope and Benjamin Disraeli.

At **Lochailort** (21/34), from where trains may be taken to Mallaig via Beasdale, Arisaig and Morar or back towards Fort William, turn left, signposted for Mallaig, and climb across the neck of the Ardnish peninsula, with the railway and remnants of the old road beside you.

A cairn at the head of **Loch Nan Uamh** – 'loch of the cave' – commemorates both Bonnie Prince Charlie first landing here on 25 July 1745 on his way to eventual defeat at Culloden and then his subsequent departure aboard a French ship on 20 September 1746. The cave, one of many attributed as his hiding places and shown on OS maps, is further around the shore and best approached on foot on a track behind Arisaig House Hotel.

In 2001, scans of the Loch nan Uamh **railway viaduct** confirmed the tale that a horse and cart had fallen into the cavity of the large central pier during its construction in 1900.

The road climbs inland past **Beasdale Station** and pleasantly onwards beneath massive oaks and beeches to **Arisaig**. Here the cycle route turns left down through the village and out the other side on the B8008 to **Back of Keppoch**. This stretch of coast has some fine sandy beaches and an excellent panorama of the Small Isles and the Skye Cuillin on a clear day, making it popular with holiday makers. Although this means there are plenty of well-equipped campsites, it is something of a relief to reach the quieter beaches at Camusdarach and the outflow of Loch Morar, made famous in the film *Local Hero*. The cycle route crosses the main A830 and goes under the railway and alongside the often dramatic River Morar before turning into the village of **Morar**. Once back to the main road, a cycle path takes you right into **Mallaig** (38/60).

Prior to the arrival of the railway in 1901, **Mallaig** was just a collection of isolated cottages. But it quickly outgrew nearby Arisaig, where the Road to the Isles used to end, to become the major fishing port and transportation hub on the west coast. It's utilitarian, rather than picturesque, with good facilities for weary travellers who need to refresh before moving on elsewhere.

DAY ROUTES

ROUTE 3.1
Slate Islands

Start/Finish	Kilninver
Distance	33 miles (53km)
Total Ascent	3020ft (920m)
Grade	Moderate
Time	3hrs 40mins
Map	OS Landranger 1:50,000 55
Ferries	Easdale – Easdale Island; Cuan Ferry – Luing

This ride starts and finishes at Kilninver just off the main A816 Oban to Campbeltown road and visits the three accessible islands. However you could easily shorten or lengthen the ride to suit.

An exhilarating ride across Cuan Sound

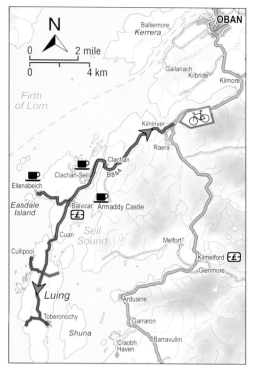

Park considerably at **Kilninver** and follow the road south to Seil where the steeply-arched Clachan Bridge, which was designed by the prolific road builder and architect Thomas Telford, has effectively spanned the Atlantic Ocean since it was completed in 1793. Continue southwards alongside Seil Sound, turning right at **Balvicar** to **Ellenabeich** and Easdale.

At the highest point of this undulating stretch of road there is a bench on the left-hand side of the road which gives extensive views out to sea and down on Easdale showing the prominent cliff left after the quarrying.

If you decide to visit **Easdale Island**, it is best to leave your bike on the quayside at Ellenabeich as the island has no roads.

When you are ready to leave Ellenabeich – the micro brewery is a gem but the tourist crowds deter staying longer – head back to the main road and turn south for **Cuan** and the ferry to the island of **Luing** – pronounced 'ling'. Normally this is a small roll-on–roll-off ferry, but on Sundays it is replaced with the smallest ferry boat you are likely to encounter in the Hebrides, carrying a maximum of twelve passengers: see Appendix C for details. At mid-tide, when the sea is rushing through Cuan Sound, it is an exciting crossing.

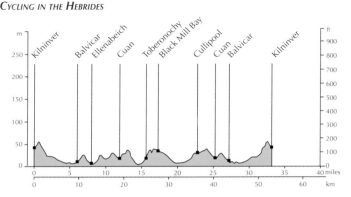

Ride south past the island's school and church to reach the graveyard and remains of 13th century **Kilchattan Chapel**. Inland Luing is farming country, famous for having its own breed of cattle.

Down the road end to the east is **Toberonochy**.

This **unspoilt village** has a pretty collection of miner's cottages and the remains of a once busy quay that shipped slate from the quarry behind the village.

On the west is **Black Mill Bay**, with the ruins of another pier. Besides shipping slate, the village was an important stop-off for passenger steamers going between Glasgow, Oban and Fort William, at one time being the main sorting office for mail in and out of the Slate Islands.

Head back to the northern end of the island. The long village of **Cullipool**, home to the island's only shop, lies to the west.

At the far end of the village are water-filled quarries and out to sea lies **Belnahua**. Quarrying here was brief and effectively ended in 1914 when all the able-bodied men went off to fight in World War I and the remaining population abandoned the island.

On the east side is the small settlement of Ardinamir. Retrace your route northwards across Cuan Ferry and back to **Kilninver**.

ROUTE 3.2
Kerrera

Start/Finish	Oban
Distance	13 miles (21km)
Total Ascent	2030ft (620m)
Grade	Moderate
Time	2–3hrs
Map	OS Landranger 1:50,000 49
Ferries	Kerrera ferry from Gallanach Road

If you are staying in Oban, ride south through the town, past the vehicle entrance to the ferry terminal and along the Gallanach road to the Kerrera ferry, which you may have to hail by following the instructions and rotating the sign board.

Leave the ferry and head south, following the sign for Gylen Castle: you'll feel as if you're stepping back in time to a quieter way of life before even the bicycle was invented.

Waiting for the Kerrera ferry

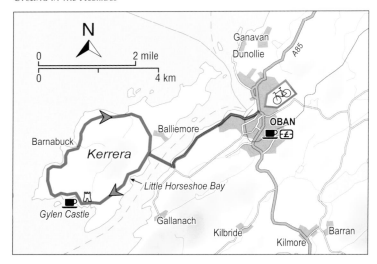

The next generation of egg producers in Kerrera Tea Gardens

A field above Horsehoe Bay bears the name the '**King's Field**', after Alexander II of Scotland who died here in 1249 while preparing to reclaim the Hebrides from Norse rule. His campaign was abandoned but the Norse were finally routed at the Battle of Largs in 1263 and the fleeing Norse are said to have reassembled here before sailing home for good.

Next you come to **Little Horseshoe Bay**, with its pretty whitewashed row of cottages, originally built to house slate workers and their families.

You may become aware of some of the exotic noises of the jungle. Your ears are not deceiving you: the owner of the first cottage in the row runs a **parrot sanctuary,** where you can view the aviaries in return for a donation.

For fifty years, the bay was an important centre for the **lobster industry**, with consignments being sent south to London and beyond by rail, which arrived in Oban in 1880. Business was so good that the Oban postmaster eventually decided to run a telephone cable to Kerrera rather than employ yet more telegram boys, making this the first Hebridean island to be linked into the national network. You can buy an excellent visitor guide on the ferry that tells lots about the island's history.

The track continues uphill past the farm at Upper Gylen and then downhill through a gate to the tea rooms and bunkhouse at Lower Gylen, where you can enjoy their cottage garden complete with a magnificent cockerel and his harem of hens. A grassy path just before the tea rooms leads over to **Gylen Castle.**

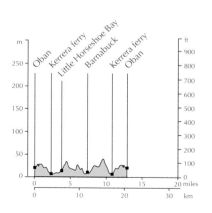

The castle was completed by the MacDougalls in 1582 and occupied for only 65 years until it was attacked and burnt by Government troops during the **English Civil War**. When **JMW Turner** visited Kerrra in 1831 he was so taken with its dramatic position that he did 25 sketches of it.

After passing through the gate alongside the tea room the track deteriorates, although it is generally well-drained and can be ridden most of the way. As it passes below low cliffs, there are views out to the islands of Seil, Insh, Scraba and the Garvellachs and around to Mull. You may need to dismount and push your bike up past the cottage at Ardmore, but are rewarded at the top with an easy grassy path and a view along the narrow island of Lismore set against a panorama of the higher peaks of Mull and Morven.

The track descends to the whitewashed farm at **Barnabuck**.

Although it is now very peaceful here, up until 1860 **Barnabuck** was the main port for ferries to Mull, Coll and Tiree and would have been thronged with travellers and cattle. The farm was an inn and down on the shore, you can still see the remains of the quay and other outbuildings.

Barnabuck's decline was due to David Hutcheson who established a regular steamer service that by-passed Kerrera. Ironically, he is commemorated by an obelisk at the north end of the island whose demise he brought about. When he retired in the 1870s, his partner David MacBrayne took over the business and renamed it. His name lives on in today's state-owned Caledonian MacBrayne.

Initially the ascent out of Barnabuck is steep and twisting, but the surface is sound and you are soon at the top. Pass through one final gate and then follow the track down past the old schoolhouse and back to the ferry. While waiting for the ferryman to return you're likely to find yourself reflecting on how much you've enjoyed your visit despite the island's lack of proper roads.

ROUTE 3.3

Circuit across Lismore from Oban

Start/Finish	Oban
Distance	42 miles (67km) (including 7-mile ferry crossing)
Total Ascent	2560ft (780m)
Grade	Moderate
Time	4–5hrs
Map	OS Landranger 1:50,000 49
Ferries	17 and 18

Lismore is an excellent island for gentle family riding and many people will be happy to spend the entire day on the island. The prospect of a good lunch at the hotel at Port Appin may encourage you to go across and back from there on the ferry. But those riding all of this route should take the ferry from Oban to Achnacroish, half way up the island's east coast. Details of the ferry can be found in Appendix C.

Once you've disembarked at **Achnacroish**, head up the hill to the T-junction and turn left towards the southern end of the island. Ignore the turning to the right, which leads to the southwest corner of the island, and continue on the B8045 past **Baligrundle** on what feels like a country lane in a leafy shire rather than an island road in the West of Scotland.

> Kilcheran Loch lies on the right of the road, but it is the **view back to the mountains on the mainland** that attracts most interest. Close inshore are the Kilcheran Islands where a prominent rock stack on Eilean na Cloiche could be easily mistaken for an ancient keep, except by a native Gaelic speaker who would know that the island's name means 'island of the rock'.

Contented cattle on Lismore with the distinctive rock plug of Eilean na Cloiche in the distance

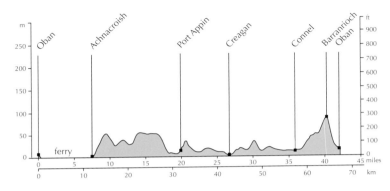

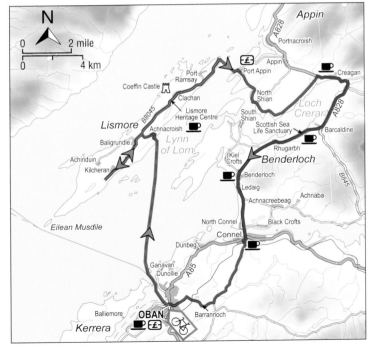

Go through the gate near the wooded farmstead at **Kilcheran** and continue south to another gate by a farm building. If you have a mountain bike and wish to idle away some time, you can continue past Loch Fiart to the southern tip at Dalnarrow and the lighthouse on **Eilean Musdile**. Otherwise retrace the route to the centre of the island and head north, past the Post Office at Balliveolan and the **Lismore Heritage Centre** at Killandrist. Further on, just before the island's church, a track leads westwards to the ruins of 13th century Coeffin Castle, which was once a stronghold of the MacDougalls. It is worth leaving the bike and going to explore. **Port Ramsay**, a pretty village made up of terraced cottages that were once homes to kiln workers is also worth a brief detour before heading down to the ferry across to **Port Appin**.

Once back on the mainland head up around the hotel and take the quiet, wooded backroad, signposted for **North Shian** which runs along the north side of Loch Creran to join the A828 just north of **Creagan**. After the meander through the woods, there is a certain excitement of joining a fast and well-surfaced road. However care needs to be taken as it is the main road that links Oban with Fort William and is busy with traffic travelling at high speed. There is a cycle path down to the **Scottish Sea Life Sanctuary** that makes use of forest trails and a disused railway track. But from there on there is no alternative than to join the road, where the long straights will soon find you stepping up your pace. **Benderloch** has a pleasant cake stop-cum-bookstore and from there on it is easy going to the bridge at **Connel**, where you can often see kayakers riding the overfalls on the Falls of Lora as the tide floods and ebbs through the narrows of Loch Etive.

Lismore Heritage Centre

Connel bridge, completed in 1903, was originally built to carry a branch line
of the Oban to Callander railway northwards to Ballahulish. Like many other
minor lines it was closed, this one in 1966.

Rather than ride the main road back to Oban, turn left just as you come off the
bridge and follow the quiet, undulating road through open country to **Barranrioch**.
Here a road on the right leads sharply uphill into the woods, before a final exhilarating descent past the town reservoir and under the main railway line back into
Oban.

McCaig's Tower was built as a family monument at the end of the 19th century by a banker wanting to provide work for unemployed stonemasons and
labourers.

ROUTE 3.4
Circuit of central Mull

Start/Finish	Craignure
Distance	48 miles (78km)
Total Ascent	2950ft (900m)
Grade	Hard
Time	5hrs 20mins
Map	OS Landranger 1:50,000 47, 48, 49
Ferries	None on route

This varied and very scenic ride takes in the coasts of the Sound of Mull, the
wilder sea lochs of Mull's west coast and the quieter lochs Spelve and Don,
via three increasingly long passes over inland glens that range from gentle
and wooded to a bare U-shaped glacial valley. The ferry schedule means
that it is possible to do the ride as a day trip from Oban even during the
winter months, when you would still get 8hrs ashore.

After disembarking at **Craignure**, ride north on the A849 past **Fishnish** to Salen,
following the first part of Link Route 3A. At **Salen** turn left on the B8035 and climb

Below the cliffs of Creag Mhor, Mull

gently across the wooded isthmus to the head of **Loch Na Keal** and through the hamlets of **Gruline** and **Knock**.

Alongside the road is the deer larder of the **Benmore Estate** that provides stalking for the impressively large Mull stags from mid-August to mid-October when the rut begins.

Just off the road at Gruline is the mausoleum of Ulva-born **Lachlan Macquarie** who was Governor of New South Wales from 1810 to 1821 and is widely recognised as 'The Father of Australia'.

Less than 2½ miles (4km) away inland is the summit of **Ben More** – the only island Munro (Scottish summits above 3000 feet) outside Skye – but down on the undulating shoreside road it's easy pedalling past the uninhabited island of Eorsa out in the centre of the loch.

If you need an excuse to stop for some sightseeing, **Staffa**, the island famous for its basalt columns and Fingal's Cave, lies 7½ miles (12km) to the west.

The strange four-storey house on **Inch Kenneth** has a bizarre history. Built around a former building by Sir Harold Boulton, writer of the lyrics to the *Skye*

Boat Song, in the early 1930s, it was occupied by the Mitford sisters – Nancy, Unity, Diana, Decca, Pam and Deborah – between 1938 and the 1960s. Diana married the British fascist Oswald Mosley: Unity was a close friend of Adolf Hitler, and became so distraught on the day World War II was declared that she shot herself in the head. She survived and her family arranged for her to move to Inch Kenneth, out of the public eye, where in 1948 she died of meningitis, a direct result of the bullet that was still embedded in her brain.

The gradient starts to increase below the impressively high cliffs of Creag Mhor and continues as the road turns south and twists its way up below the cascading waterfalls of the Gribun, to reach the summit of **Gleann Seilisdeir**. The descent through the conifer woods down to **Kilfinichen Bay** on Loch Scridain goes quickly, but needs care as the surface is occasionally poor.

Just above the road is a bird hide that gives good views out over the loch. **White-tailed sea eagles** were reintroduced on Mull in 1975 and the first chicks were successfully reared at Loch Frisa in 1998. Since then they have spread right across the Hebrides. However Mull remains their stronghold and they can be regularly seen around Loch na Keal, Glen More and Loch Scridain. Just look for that distinctive white band across the tail feathers.

At the high point of Glen More, Mull

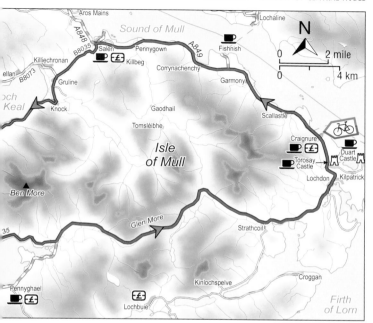

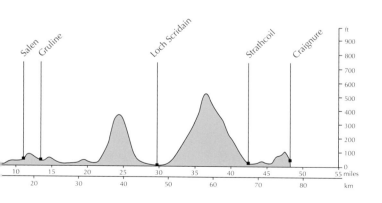

The road around the head of Loch Na Keal to the junction with main A849 is pleasant but all too brief, as once you turn left back towards Craignure there is 5 miles (8km) of steady ascent up to the summit of **Glen More**, a typical bare and empty U-shaped glacial valley.

The 5 mile (8km) descent down Glen Lussa to **Strathcoil** and the head of Loch Spelve soon restores flagging spirits and by this time many would welcome a 'cake stop'. In the summer season, you can make a short detour to visit 13th century **Duart Castle**, home of the Clan Maclean, or **Torosay Castle**, which was built in the Scottish baronial style in the 1850s and is famed for its extensive gardens. From either it's just a short ride back to **Craignure**.

ROUTE 3.5

Circuit of northern Mull

Start/Finish	Tobermory
Distance	43 miles (70km)
Total Ascent	4230ft (1290m)
Grade	Very hard
Time	4hrs 45mins
Map	OS Landranger 1:50,000 47, 48, 49
Ferries	None on route

One of the unwritten laws of cycling in the Hebrides is that as soon as the road leaves the coastline, there is always going to be an ascent. It happens repeatedly throughout this ride, the climb out of Tobermory setting the tone. After pleasant pedalling down the Sound of Mull the route turns right to cross a narrow wooded isthmus to the head of Loch Na Keal, turns right again along the shores of Loch Na Keal and Loch Tuath to Ulva Ferry, Calgary and Dervaig. With no more road junctions, from here it's just a matter of following your nose back to Tobermory.

Climb steeply out of **Tobermory** southbound on the A848. The ascent continues until the aptly named Gualan Dhubh ('the black shoulder'), with views down the Sound of Mull, then it's easier pedalling past the ruins of Aros Castle into **Salen**. Turn right and follow the B8035 across the wooded isthmus to the head of Loch

Looking down on Tobermory

Na Keal, then turn right again on to the B8073 following signs for Ulva Ferry, Calgary and Dervaig.

As you get level with the island of **Eorsa** out in the loch the road heads inland and so, inevitably, climbs, in this case up the southern slopes of Cnoc na Di-Chuimhne – 'the forgotten hill' – before descending to Ulva Ferry.

In the Napoleonic Wars the supply of potash, used in the manufacture of soap, glass and chemicals, was cut off. As a substitute, on Ulva and across the Hebrides a **kelp burning industry** developed. Despite it taking 20 tons of seaweed and lots of back-breaking, dirty work to produce a single ton of potash, the owner of Ulva is reputed to have 'trebled his income and doubled his population by careful attention to his kelp shores'.

Once the Napoleonic Wars ended in 1815 supplies of foreign potash were restored and the kelp burning industry collapsed. The population of around 600, complete with shoemakers, boat builders, tailors, weavers, blacksmiths, masons and merchants, living in sixteen villages whose ruins can still be seen today, were brutally cleared by a new owner, Francis Clark. When his tombstone was being ferried across to Ulva to be placed in his mausoleum, it was said to be too heavy to lift because of the 'weight of evil that was in it'. Today the island has a population of 16, which makes it the most de-populated Hebridean island, apart from those that are now uninhabited.

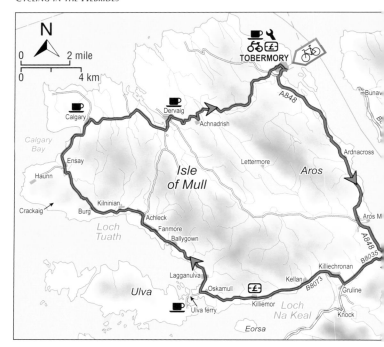

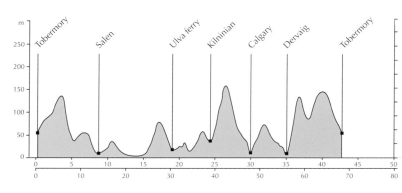

If you're feeling hungry, the licensed tea room on **Ulva** offers a range of snacks and local foods including its own recommendation of oysters and Guinness. Otherwise, continue around the head of Loch Tuath – 'North Loch' – where the final cascade of Eas Fors drops straight into the sea. The road continues through the hamlets of **Ballygown**, **Fanmore** and **Achleck**, where a minor road over the 'Pass of the Mirror' to Dervaig gives an opportunity to shorten the ride.

> It is pleasant riding through this wooded corner of Mull, with the **Treshnish Isles** strung out in the middle distance and low-laying **Tiree** and **Coll** occasionally visible on the horizon.
> From Cracaig House just past Kilninian, a track leads 1¼ miles (2km) across the moor to the cleared village of **Crackaig** where there are a number of ruined blackhouses.

The easy riding changes at **Kilninian**, where a collection of medieval graveslabs in the small church gives an excuse for a rest before a short climb up to the watershed and a glorious descent down the hillside and below the crags into **Calgary**.

> With its wide sandy beach and turquoise seas, this is perhaps the **prettiest place on Mull** and always attracts the crowds.

After a short climb out of the village, it is easy going above Loch a Chumhainn and down into **Dervaig**.

Fast approaching Calgary Bay after a long descent

This is another pretty village with a street of white cottages and the interesting early 20th century **Kilmore church,** which has a pencil steeple that was directly inspired by Irish round towers and a highly decorated interior that defies its simple exterior.

There is only 7½ miles (12km) to go but there is no respite with a snaking climb out of Dervaig and another alongside Loch Carnain an Amais – a loch that changes its name along its length. The final 5km is a fast, twisting, descent entering **Tobermory** by the back streets high above the harbour – a perfect end to a magnificent ride.

ROUTE 3.6

Out to Iona

Start/Finish	Craignure
Distance	70 miles (112km) plus ferry to Iona
Total Ascent	4400ft (1340m)
Grade	Hard
Time	7hrs 40mins
Map	OS Landranger 1:50,000 48, 49
Ferries	None on route: ferry to Iona at end

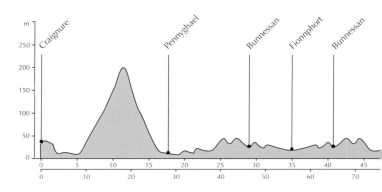

Approaching Iona on the Fionnphort ferry

Even in winter, when the ferry timetable gives you 8–9hrs on Mull, you could ride out to Iona and back as a day trip from Oban – a round trip of 72 miles. However most people will prefer more time for sight-seeing and relaxing and will want to make it a two-day trip. But given the number of visitors, it is best to reserve your accommodation and book dinner well in advance.

Initially the route reverses the final leg of Route 3.4, south out of **Craignure** on the A849 and up through **Glen More**, with close views of Ben More, which at 3169 feet is the only Hebridean Munro outside of Skye. At the summit of the climb, you are rewarded with views to the south along the line of lochs beneath Beinn Fhada and Ben Buie and then a wonderful descent to the head of Loch Scridain.

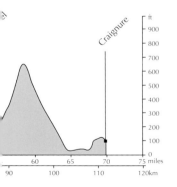

The date of 1897 on the remaining ten **cast iron mileposts** alongside the A849 from Craignure to Iona suggests they were erected to celebrate Queen Victoria's Diamond Jubilee. They were made to a standard design cast at the Tyneside foundry of Smith, Patterson & Co Ltd which ran from 1870 to 1954. Other examples can still be found near Drimnin and Salen on the Morven peninsula and many that remain are now listed as being of special architectural or historic interest.

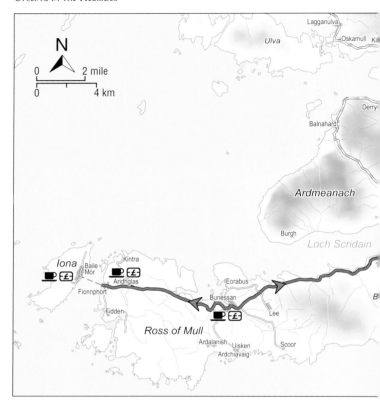

There are a couple of small hotels near **Pennygael**, but they are only open to non-residents at limited times and you may need to grab a coffee and a snack from the shop. In Gaelic, *ros* means 'long peninsula', and the constantly undulating Ross of Mull can seem to go on for ever with few reasons to stop until you get to **Bunessan**.

Pretty in pink – one of the few surviving Victorian mileposts along The Ross of Mull

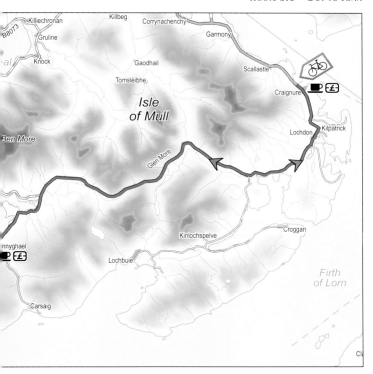

Thankfully there is plenty of interest across the **other side of Loch Scridain** with an unfolding view of the vertical cliffs of the Burg and eventually the sight of Staffa and the unmistakable island of the Dutchman's Cap out to sea.

There are wonderful **sandy beaches** to visit on the south side of the Ross at Uisken and Fidden and on the north side at Kintra.

Nearly a quarter of a million people visit Iona each year, periodically swamping **Fionnphort**, which is a pleasant, white-painted village with a large car park that probably contains most of the vehicles that have been speeding past you for the last few hours. But if you have been riding most of the day, you will most likely be arriving when the crowds are beginning to disperse: perfect for taking a late ferry over to **Iona** and enjoying the island in splendid isolation.

ROUTE 3.7
Coll

Start/Finish	Arinagour Quay
Distance	27 miles (43km)
Total Ascent	1480ft (450m)
Grade	Moderate
Time	3hrs
Map	OS Landranger 1:50,000 46
Ferries	None on route

About half the population of Coll lives in the main village of Arinagour. The ride starts and finishes here and makes full use of the island's limited roads. The unofficial website www.visitcoll.co.uk is a good source of information. A day trip from Oban on a Thursday during the summer months gives ample time to ride the entire island and still have plenty of time to enjoy an excellent dinner of local seafood while waiting for the evening ferry to return. Although the OS 1:50,000 Landranger 46 is listed in the box above, Explorer 372 covers all of Tiree and Coll at twice the scale for an additional £1.

Leave the quay and ride up towards **Arinagour**, passing a row of traditional *tigh gael* (cottages), then turn left at the signpost for the airfield and head along the south side of the island. For a while the Caledonian MacBrayne ferry will accompany you as it makes it way to Tiree, but you will soon find yourself stopping to take in the views of Mull and Iona to the south and the ferry will inevitably take the lead. Turn left at the airfield. Then once around the corner, turn left again and ride down the track to the castles at the head of Loch Breachacha.

> Both of the **castles** are privately owned and a sign asks that you respect their privacy. The older castle dates from the 15th century and was once a stronghold of the MacLean clan. The newer Georgian castle dates from around 1750 and was visited by Dr Johnson and James Boswell during their tour of the Hebrides in 1773. They considered it to be 'a mere trademan's box'.

The two castles at Breachacha

Park your bike near the farm buildings on the right and slip through the gate and out on to the beach, from where you get the best view of both of them without being intrusive.

Head back to the road and turn left. The road eventually turns into a sandy track, but if you have wider tyres you should be able to ride this quite safely.

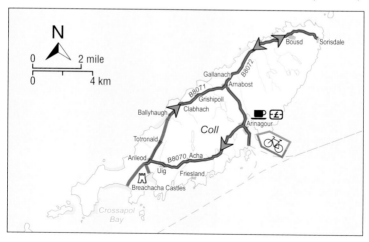

153

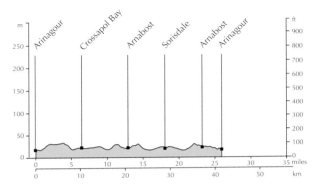

Otherwise get off your bike and either abandon it or push it down to the wonderful beach at **Crossapol Bay**. It's well worth the effort and makes an excellent place for a break. When you can pull yourself away, head back through the dunes and retrace the route back to the airfield. Take the minor road on the west side of the airfield and ride past the croft houses to the gate at the road end at **Totronald**. Go through the gate and follow the sandy track through the RSPB reserve to **Ballyhaugh**. Again you may find it safer to walk if you have skinny tyres. To get back to the road that runs along the north side of the island, you need to go through the grounds of the The Hebridean Centre, which is the home of the Project Trust, an educational trust which sends young people abroad to work alongside local communities.

> The star of the show at RSPB Totronald is the elusive **corncrake**. Encouraging crofters to mow outwards from the centre of their fields have helped this once common bird re-establish itself.

Although there are beaches on the north coast of Coll, they are not visible from the road and you will need to park up and walk down to them. The road passes the isolated farms at **Clabhach** and **Grishipoll** and the Coll Golf Club to the unmarked T-junction at **Arnabost**. If you want a shorter ride, turn right here and head back across the island to Arinagour. Otherwise continue north through similar terrain to the road end at **Sorisdale**, where there is a collection of houses above a sandy beach. Inevitably the only way back is to retrace the route back to the junction at Arnabost and turn left to Arinagour, although you can break your journey with a visit to the sandy beach at Bagh an Traillech, which is marked by a sign alongside the road.

ROUTE 3.8
Circuit of west Tiree

Start/Finish	Scarinish
Distance	23 miles (37km)
Total Ascent	520ft (160m)
Grade	Easy
Time	2hrs 30mins
Map	OS Landranger 1:50,000 46
Ferries	None on route

Because it is so fertile, Tiree has many farms and crofts that are scattered all over the island and linked by pleasant and relatively flat roads. On calmer days, this makes it an idyllic island for cycling and you can gently roll along the roads that run behind the many sandy bays and take in the distant views of other islands in every direction. On windy days, give it a miss as with so little shelter you will quickly find yourself struggling into a headwind. With so many roads to choose from, with the aid of a map you can easily tailor a ride to suit yourself. The ride described here is simply the longest loop possible.

Start at **Scarinish**, where there is a shop selling snacks and drinks, and head west along the B8065 across the unfenced grazing of The Reef, where the small commercial airport is located.

> The numerous **concrete bunkers** date from World War II, when Tiree was an important RAF base for patrolling the Atlantic and protecting commercial shipping.

Pass through **Crossapol**, where there is the only other shop on the island, then turn left at the T-junction and follow the B8066 south through **Balemartine** and down to the end at the Skerryvore Museum at **Hynish** (see box).

On leaving Hynish, retrace the route north through Balemartine and turn left to **Balinoe**, following the road around the north side of Loch a Phuill, which is an important reserve for overwintering duck and geese. When you reach the parish church at the crossroads, turn left to rejoin the B8065 signposted for **Barrapol** and Sandaig.

155

If you are **ready for a break** or need a break from the wind, ride down the open grazing to Traigh Ghriehel and shelter among the rocks above the beach. On a clear day you can see the Skerryvore lighthouse to the south.

HYNISH – THE VILLAGE BUILT TO ERECT THE SKERRYVORE LIGHTHOUSE

If you look out to sea as you cycle in the southwest of Tiree on a clear day you can see the Skerryvore lighthouse which marks a low reef just over 10 miles (16km) away. In the 18th and early 19th centuries, when trade with America was booming, many ships going in and out of the growing port of Glasgow were wrecked on the reef. This

Hynish Village built as a base for the construction of the Skerryvore Lighthouse

led the Northern Lighthouse Board to appoint Alan Stevenson, of the famous Lighthouse Stevenson family, to build a lighthouse there in 1837. To minimise the amount of work that needed to be done on the reef, Stevenson decided to work each stone to the exact size needed on land and built a shore station at Hynish on Tiree to house the masons and eventually the lighthouse keepers. Over the last 20 years this purpose-built village has been restored to provide low-rent housing, holiday accommodation and a small museum that tells the amazing story of Stevenson's not-so-flat-pack lighthouse.

Stevenson and his workers landed on the reef in 1838 and set about building a wooden barracks that would enable a 17-hour working day during the summer months. He had to rebuild it the following year after it was destroyed in an autumn storm. This meant that construction did not commence until 1840, but using Stevenson's approach progress was rapid and the lamp was ready to be manned in April 1844, the final stages of completion of the tower being left to younger brother Thomas following Stevenson's promotion to the post of Engineer to the Lighthouse Commissioners.

The tower is 48m (156ft) high and tapers from 13m (42ft) at the base to 5m (16ft) at the top and many claim it is the world's most graceful lighthouse. Hynish, where the granite quarried on Mull was brought to be worked by the masons, is hardly less wonderful and it is well worth taking a short diversion off the island's main loop of roads to pay a visit.

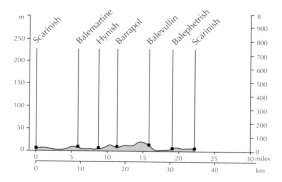

The road continues northwards below Beinn Hough, passing the remains of a medieval chapel at Kilkenneth to reach **Balevullin**, where the houses are arranged either side of the road and you could almost believe you had entered a picture-book English village. Here the route turns eastwards to follow the B8068, although there is no signpost to let you know.

> From the junction it's well worth riding the extra few hundred yards down to Sraid Ruadh and the road end above Traigh Boll a Mhurain. The **beach** gives good views across the Minch to the Western Isles and there is the unexpected delight of two of the best-preserved cottages on the island, both with traditional marram thatching.

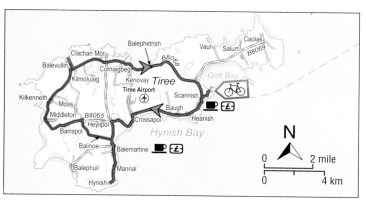

Tarred roof and thatched roofs at Balevullin

The road along the north side of the island first passes Loch Bhassapol, which is the retreat of windsurfers in stormy weather, and then the remains of an old water-mill at Cornaigmore, a reminder of a time when barley was extensively grown on Tiree, much of it finding its way into whisky production. The road then skirts around Balephetrish Bay and passes through **Balephetrish** before turning south across the island to **Gott Bay**, with good views of Ben More, the only Munro on Mull, on a clear day. Then all too soon, you're back in **Scarinish**.

ROUTE 3.9

Fishbone ride in east Tiree

Start/Finish	Scarinish
Distance	20 miles (32km)
Total Ascent	590ft (180m)
Grade	Easy
Map	OS Landranger 1:50,000 46
Time	2hrs 30mins
Ferries	None on route

If you like wildlife watching then the eastern end of Tiree deserves a visit, but there are no road loops and the only way to visit the area is to go up and down the eight road ends that lie either side of the B8068. Collectively they make the shape of a fishbone – hence the title of the ride. On a clear day, the rocks and beaches at these road ends give good views all around the Inner Hebrides and across to the southern tip of the Western Isles.

The ride gives plenty of opportunity for watching wildlife so it's worth carrying binoculars and taking a break at every road end to see what's about. Because wildlife watching is the big attraction of this ride, it is best to visit the road ends on the north side of the island earlier in the day and leave those on the south side until later, that way the light will be behind you and there is less chance you'll be watching silhouettes! The rocky foreshore and numerous small skerries around this end of the island are particularly good for spotting otter.

Starting at Scarinish ride east along the B8068, taking the turn for **Caolas** at the western end of **Gott Bay**. The first road end goes to Gott, but unless you want to park up your bikes and follow the footpath 3km over to the north side of the island to visit the Ringing Stone – a glacial erratic that rings when hit with a rock - you can give this one a miss. The second, alongside the hotel at **Kirkapol**, leads to two medieval chapels.

The chapel nearest the road is the old **parish church** and is now the roost and nesting site of a raucous pair of ravens. The smaller 13th century **chapel**

Medieval chapels at Kirkapol

is thought to have been an oratory for the clergy to use and is dedicated to St Columba.

The next road end, on the left, is at **Vaul**, where there is a fine sandy bay.

> If you look left at the penultimate house you will see a post in the crags. This marks the remains of **Dun Mor Bhalla** – a first century broch built as an emergency refuge. It is a short walk down the grassy track and across a stile.

The fourth road end (again on the left) leads to **Salum** and another sandy bay, with views across the Minch to the Western Isles. The last road end on the north side leads to **Miodar**, with the Isle of Coll less than two miles away across Gunna Sound. Follow the grassy track on the left of the last house and cycle across the grazing to reach the headland at **Urvaig**, remembering to keep low as you approach so as not to alert any wildlife on the shore and the nearby skerries.

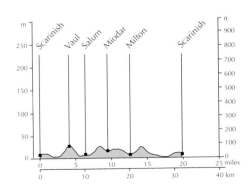

160

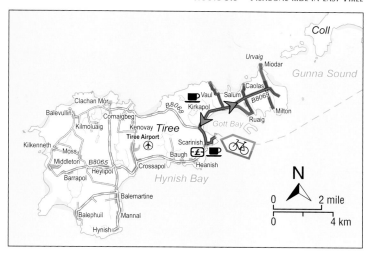

Now, heading back west towards Scarinish, the first road end on the south side is unmarked, but as soon as the tarmac ends you are presented with a choice of heading left over the grazing to the beach near Eilean Liath, or right to the cliffs at Port Ban, where there is a solitary cottage above a narrow sandy beach hemmed in by the crags. Heading westwards, the next road end leads to **Milton**.

Watching an otter at Urbhaig on the eastern end of Tiree

161

Heading home through the tarred roofs of the cottages at Brock

This is home to Tiree's small **fishing fleet**, which sells most of its catch of crab and lobster to Europe.

The final road end southwards is signposted for **Ruaig,** and leads down to the eastern end of Tràigh Mhor, the 4km stretch of beach around Gott Bay.

As you head back to the main road, turn left along a track to visit **Brock**, where there is a fine collection of *tigh gael* – traditional white cottages – with tarred roofs.

From here, cycle across the grazing, rejoin the road and head back to **Scarinish**.

In spring, one of the fields down this road end is amass with **daffodils** – remnants of the 1950s, when crofters on Tiree were encouraged to propagate bulbs.

4 SKYE AND RAASAY

Isleornsay (Route 4A)

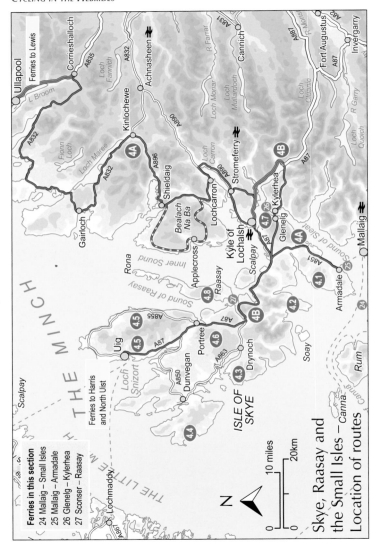

Skye, Raasay and
the Small Isles –
Location of routes

Ferries in this section
24 Mallaig – Small Isles
25 Mallaig – Armadale
26 Glenelg – Kylerhea
27 Sconser – Raasay

Ferries to Lewis

Ferries to Harris
and North Uist

INTRODUCTION

The Black Cuillin from the Old Sligachan Bridge (Route 4.6)

It may be the most visited of the Hebridean islands, rich in history and legend, but Skye lost some of its romance for many people when the bridge that now joins the island to the mainland at Kyle of Lochalsh was opened in 1995. Gone are the days of waiting for the ferry and the building anticipation of going over the sea to

Skye. It no longer feels like an island. Hamish Haswell-Smith, renowned sailor and author of the definitive *The Scottish Islands*, clearly agrees. He defined an island as any piece of land that is over 40 hectares (100 acres) at high tide and completely surrounded by sea water at low tide, so that you can only get to it by getting your feet wet or by boat. Once the bridge was opened he dropped Skye from his list and over the years other islands that are now linked by bridges and causeways such as Scalpay and Berneray have suffered the same fate.

The lighthouse at Neist Point on the Diurinish Peninsula (Route 4.4)

Skye is the largest and most northerly of the Inner Hebrides, but it is also worthy of being labelled the 'High Hebrides', with its dramatic mountains and vertical sea cliffs. All of this makes for harder riding and you are advised to choose a route that keeps you in your personal comfort zone. Skye's popularity and growing population also means that the main roads that link the main ferry ports and centres of population are busy and this does not make for relaxed cycling.

There is growing recognition of the need to provide a traffic-free alternative to many of the busiest sections, but don't hold your breath as it could be years before plans come to fruition. But despite all these reservations, it is a magnificent island for cycling, especially the day routes out around the peninsulas of Trotternish, Duirinish

and Sleat, out along the less populated south coast and deep into the mountains.

Skye

The name 'Skye' comes from the Norse word *skuy*, meaning 'cloud'. It is an appropriate name for an island where the jagged Cuillin is frequently wreathed in mist and where sea haze drifts into the sea lochs that cut so deeply inland that the island is sometimes called 'The Winged Island'. Because the steep streams rapidly drain water from the mountains and nowhere is far from the sea, Skye has few inland lochs.

Raasay

Raasay – 'the isle of the roe deer' – has a checkered history. It was ruled by the MacLeods from the 16th to the

19th centuries, then owned by a series of private landlords, who systematically cleared the land for sheep and then deer before it was bought by a mining company which extracted iron ore from a mine in the south of the island until it was exhausted in 1921. Subsequently the government purchased Raasay and used part of it as a camp for prisoners of war before transferring it into public ownership. Raasay House, which was visited by James Boswell and Samuel Johnson during their famous tour in 1773 and substantially added to during the 19th century, is now an outdoor centre.

Calum's Road

Malcolm (Calum) MacLeod (1911–1988) was a crofter, part-time postman and Assistant Keeper of Rona Lighthouse who famously built Calum's Road, which runs from Brochel to Arnish. After the inhabitants of the northern end of Raasay had unsuccessfully campaigned for a proper road that would alleviate some of the hardship of living there, Calum decided to take matters into his own hands and build the road himself.

He bought a second-hand copy of Thomas Aitken's manual *Road Making and Maintenance: A Practical Treatise for Engineers, Surveyors and Others* for half a crown (25p) and started work on upgrading the existing narrow footpath. It took him ten years to complete the 1¾ miles (2.5km) of road using little more than a shovel, a pick and a wheelbarrow, supported by the Department of Agriculture's Engineering Department, who funded and carried out essential blasting and drilling. Several years ·after it

The start of Calum's Road on Raasay (Route 4.8)

NAUTICUS – AN EARLY 'WHEELMAN' ON SKYE

There was a golden age of cycling from the 1870s through to the 1900s, when the first motorcars arrived on our roads. New technologies, such as ball bearings and pneumatic tyres, made riding more comfortable, which drove demand. During the first half of the 1880s tricycles were more popular than bicycles, primarily because they were seen as being more genteel by the upper-class men and women who could afford them.

There was probably no one more adventurous in using a tricycle to explore the UK than Commander Charles Edward Reade of the Royal Navy, who wrote up a number of his journeys under the pen name 'Nauticus'. These were first published as articles in the *Boy's Own Paper* and later as books, which are still available as reprints from on-demand publishers.

None was more ambitious than the 69-day tour north of the border that he recorded in *Nauticus in Scotland – A Tricycle Tour of 2,462 Miles, Including Skye and the West Coast*, which was first published in 1882. He rode a Coventry Machinists Cheylesmore Tricycle, as supplied to HRH The Prince of Wales, the King of Siam, the Emperor of Russia and other worthies. The company's name betrays its origins making sewing machines, and the Cheylesmore was an ingenious piece of engineering, with the rider sitting between two penny-farthing sized wheels with a smaller wheel at the rear for stability. There was a constant need for running repairs, such as gluing the tyres back on the rims with compound, relining the brakes or getting a local blacksmith to forge replacement washers and bolts.

During the potato famines of the 1850s and 60s, the authorities had funded road construction and repair as part of the relief programme, so surfaces were perhaps better than we might assume. But Reade still encountered some horrendous roads and, despite the discomfort of solid tyres, he managed to cover 36 miles (58km) on an average day and on his 56th day managed 80 miles (130km) between Forres and Peterhead at an average speed of 9mph. It certainly kept him trim; the engravings that accompany the text show a dapper man with the distinctive physique of a performance cyclist.

A born adventurer, he had fought in the New Zealand Wars against the Maori chiefs and travelled in the Pacific, using his experiences as the basis for lecture tours to North America and Australia. But he never married and spent a long solitary retirement living in lodgings in London before dying at the age of 80 in 1922, showing that cycling promotes health and longevity!

Reade started his tour in Newcastle, rode through the Scottish Lowlands to Glasgow, then north through Oban, Fort William and Shiel Bridge, where he and his contraption were ferried over to Skye, a particularly heroic part of the trip. Of the ascent of Bealach Ratagan he wrote 'I was aware that any slight inattention on my part, or any derangement in the machine, might launch me a distance of five hundred feet or more'. He carried on noting that once over the summit, 'I ran for nearly, if not quite, six miles without putting foot to pedal'.

Nauticus on the Trotternish Peninsula

Once across the Glenelg ferry, he continued to Broadford and the next day to Portree. From there he rode to Uig and then across the Trotternish peninsula to Staffin, stopping off to view the Quiraing and climb onto the Table, before returning to Uig Inn for the night. Next day he left Uig at noon and rode to Dunvegan, and then on to the Sligachan Inn, arriving at 11pm after cycling part of the way in the dark. He wrote, 'As it was almost dark, I had to take every possible precaution. Fortunately, the road was perfect, and as I ran slowly down, the baying of a dog in the depth below was the only sound that broke upon the still night air'. He ended his visit to Skye with a walk out to Loch Coruisk before heading back to the mainland.

Returning to the mainland he rode all the way up and along the north coast through Durness, Thurso and John O'Groats before returning south, finally crossing back into England at Gretna Green and finishing his adventure at Penrith.

Tokavaig beach on the west of the Sleat Peninsula (Route 4.1)

was completed, in 1974, the local council finally adopted and surfaced the road and Calum was awarded a British Empire Medal 'for maintaining the Rona light', the real reason being something of a sore point with the authorities. Ride it – it is one stretch of road that you will never forget!

The Small Isles

Muck, Eigg, Rum and Canna that make up the Small Isles have less than 6 miles (10km) of road between them but if you choose your day, you can land and spend a few hours on Muck, Eigg or Rum: see Appendix D for details.

Muck has less than 2 miles (3.25km) of tarmac road; the community-owned Eigg just over 3 miles (5km) and Canna and Rum no more than a few hundred yards each, although Rum once had more. Sir George Bullough, who inherited Rum in 1891 and spared no expense in

building Kinloch Castle as a hideaway for the glitterati of Edwardian society, had 14 full-time road menders on his staff to maintain 10 miles (16km) of track to such a high standard that he could race his two Albion sports cars across the island. Years of neglect mean that the surface has deteriorated but they are still passable on a mountain bike. A visit on Saturdays or Sundays during the summer months gives ten hours ashore, which is plenty of time to visit all parts of the island and take a tour of the castle. Alternatively, there is accommodation or camping available – see www.isle-ofrum.com for details.

For those who need time out of the saddle, the ferry from Mallaig provides a relaxing day out and gives plenty of opportunity to see the islands and wildlife at close quarters with the possibility of spotting a basking shark or even an orca.

LINK ROUTES

ROUTE 4A
Ullapool to Armadale

Start	Ullapool
Finish	Armadale
Distance	151 miles (242km)/179 miles (286km)
Total Ascent	13,160ft (4010m) (main route)
Grade	Moderate–hard/very hard–moderate
Time	16hrs 50mins/19hrs 40mins
Map	OS Landranger 1:50,000 19, 24, 25, 32, 33

Most people will want to spend two or more days over this link route – the natural way to get back down south after a traverse of the Western Isles (usually done north-to-south with the prevailing wind). The route is varied and the landscape is stunning, with white sandy beaches and high mountains. It is also challenging, especially if the additional 28-mile (44km) loop around Applecross (Alternative stage 4) is included, with the demanding ascent of the Bealach na Ba. This is a must for any enthusiastic road cyclist wanting to retain their self-respect, as the first question they will get asked on arrival back from holiday is 'What was the pass like?'.

Heading towards Liathach

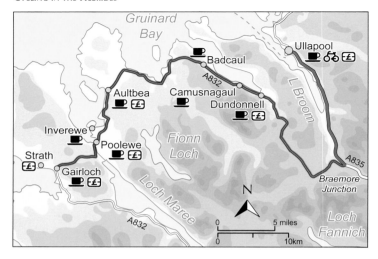

STAGE 1

Ullapool to Breamore Junction

Start	Ullapool
Finish	Breamore Junction
Distance	12.5 miles (20km)
Grade	Moderate
Time	1hr 20mins
Map	OS Landranger 1:50,000 19

Ullapool was created as a herring port in 1788 and laid out by Thomas Telford. Today it is a busy ferry terminal with a reputation for arts, music and culture with numerous events throughout the year.

Head south on the A835 following signs for Inverness, with easy pedalling alongside Loch Broom until a steady gradient leads up to **Braemore Junction**.

Test your head for heights at the **Corrieshalloch Gorge** where the Victorian bridge gives views of the Falls of Measach 60m below.

STAGE 2
Breamore Junction to Gairloch

Start	Breamore Junction
Finish	Gairloch
Distance	43 miles (69km)
Grade	Moderate
Time	4hrs 40mins
Map	OS Landranger 1:50,000 19

This route heads anti-clockwise around the mountain of An Teallach (1062m) which means 'The Forge' in Gaelic on account of appearance of the red Torridonian sandstone in the evening sun, descending to the coast at Gruinard. In 1942, British military scientists tested the anthrax virus on Gruinard Island as part of the war effort and following decontamination it was only officially declared safe in 1990. Then its a couple of steep climbs before the stage ends in a descent into Gairloch.

From **Braemore Junction**, turn right onto the A832 following signs for Gairloch. The road climbs steadily alongside the Abhainn Cuileig before turning northwards to reveal fine views of An Teallach. There is a well-earned descent down to **Dundonnell**, before more steady climbing through **Camusnagaul** and past **Badcaul**, until the road turns to the west and drops to Gruinard. With its sandy beach and wooded shoreline, **Gruinard Bay** is idyllic. But everything changes around the corner at Little Gruinard, where the road ascends 100m in 500m (20%). You may decide it is technically a ramp being uniformly straight and steep throughout its length.

Thankfully, it's soon over and it's back to gentler inclines up and over to **Aultbea** and around the shores of Loch Ewe, which was an important base for shipping convoys and accompanying submarines setting out into the Atlantic Ocean during World War II.

Passing Inverewe Gardens at Poolewe

Further round the bay at **Inverewe** local man Sir Osgood Mackenzie created his famous gardens during the last quarter of the 19th century. He packed them with subtropical plants that thrive due to the warmer water bought up from the Caribbean by the Gulf Stream and the strategic planting of trees to provide a windbreak.

Nearby **Poolewe**, once an important centre for smelting iron ore, has a choice of places to eat including a café where the owner betrays his enthusiasm for cycling with a wrought iron planter in the shape of a bike. You are unlikely to feel guilty about stopping for cake as there is a steep climb out of the village up to Loch Tollaidh before descending into **Gairloch**.

STAGE 3
Gairloch to Shieldaig

Start	Gairloch
Finish	Shieldaig
Distance	37 miles (59km)
Grade	Hard
Time	4hrs 40mins
Map	OS Landranger 1:50,000 19, 24, 25

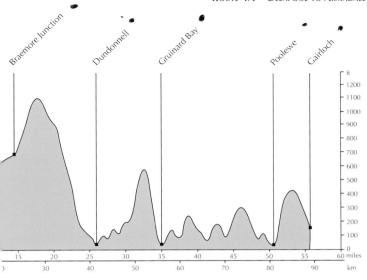

Being a major tourist destination, there is plenty of accommodation in Gairloch, although both hostels are a few miles off-route on the north side of the bay. Their spectacular locations and the prospect of a sunset over The Minch amply compensate for such a minor inconvenience.

Although the next 50 miles passes through some of Scotland's most spectacular mountain scenery, it is easier going than the preceding 50 miles along the coast.

Initially the road climbs up alongside the River Kerry before cutting over to the shore of Loch Maree with its myriad of islands that have the oldest and least disturbed woodland in Britain. As you pass through Talladale and below the sugarloaf of the Slioch (981m) at the head of the loch, one expects a climb around every bend in the road. But it never comes and you are soon in **Kinlochewe**.

Leave the village heading west on the A832 following signs for Torridon.

175

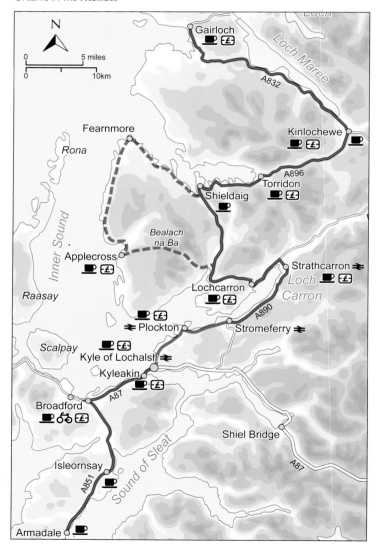

On a fine day, this is glorious cycling with such **magnificent scenery** that you are oblivious to the gradual ascent up to Loch Clair. The road passes directly below Beinn Eighe (993m) and Liathach (995m), with the horned Beinn Alligin (986m) high above Torridon: each one a distinct mountain with steeply tiered sides.

Once through Annat you may wish to take a break at the hotel in preparation for the climb up and over to **Shieldaig**.

STAGE 4
Shieldaig to Stromeferry

Start	Shieldaig
Finish	Stromeferry
Distance	26 miles (42km)
Grade	Hard
Time	2hrs 50mins
Map	OS Landranger 1:50,000 24, 25

Shieldaig is a pretty village founded in 1800 as a base to prepare seamen for war against Napoleon, but it soon became a herring port and today is a holiday destination.

If you are going around the coast road to Applecross, you need to turn right just outside the village. Otherwise continue south on the A896 which has a gradual climb up Glen Shieldaig and over to Tornapress. There is a good view up Coire Na Ba as you approach Sanachan, so you can see why it has such an awesome reputation. There is another steady climb over to Lochcarron, a loch-side village which is home to the world's largest manufacturer of authentic tartans. Imagine the freedom that comes from cycling in a kilt and make a purchase. You will never regret it – at least not until the wind gets up!

19th century **Courthill House** in the woods near Sanachan was abandoned in the 1930s and had its roof removed in 1946, but the late Victorian chapel is intact and open to visitors.

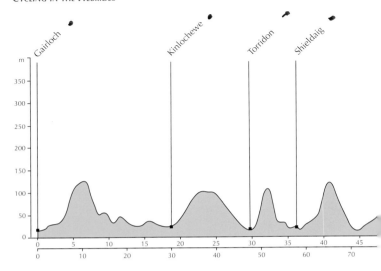

After all those hills, it's virtually flat all the way around the head of Loch Carron and along the first stretch of the A890 through **Strathcarron**. But it all changes again along the southern shore of the loch with a sharp little climb just before Attadale and another longer climb up through the woods to the viewpoint above **Stromeferry**.

In poor weather or if you need a break from riding, you could always jump on to one of the infrequent trains at any of the stations alongside this stretch of the route.

Traveller and ex-Monty Python member **Michael Palin** included the line in his top rail journeys in the world due to the superb views and its closeness to the shore, made possible by the extensive use of bridges, causeways and cuttings.

178

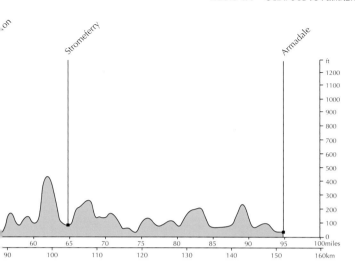

ALTERNATIVE STAGE 4

Shieldaig to Stromeferry via Applecross and Bealach na Ba

Start	Shieldaig
Finish	Stromeferry
Distance	54 miles (87km)
Grade	Very hard
Time	5hrs 40mins
Map	OS Landranger 1:50,000 24, 25

If you want a challenging diversion that adds an additional 28 miles (44km) to this route and climbs from sea-level to 626m (2053ft) in roughly 10km (6 miles), reaching gradients approaching 20%, then this is the route for you: a classic Scottish cycling challenge. If not, go the easier route described above.

From Shieldaig turn west around the head of Loch Shieldaig. Initially the going is quite hard, with a succession of short sharp climbs, but once past **Fearnmore** the west side of the peninsula is far easier, with fine views out to Raasay, Rona and beyond to the Trotternish peninsula on Skye. **Applecross** is a good place to overnight and stock up on food ready to take on the infamous Bealach na Ba. In Gaelic, the name means 'the Pass of the Cattle', reflecting its past as the route drovers took cattle reared on the fertile coastal plain to markets in Central Scotland.

Until 1975, when the road linking Applecross with Shieldaig was completed, the only supply routes into Applecross were the weekly steamer or the **Bealach na Ba**, which would have been impassable for weeks on end during the winter months (it is still regularly closed due to snow). The ascent from the Applecross side is long and steady, but once over the summit, there are tight hairpin bends and steep gradients that make it feel like the Alps. Even on a sunny day, it can be decidedly chilly at the summit and you will need a windproof jacket to keep you warm both while you enjoy the view and when you hurtle down the exhilarating descent on the other side.

For the last few years, there have been two separate **cycling events that climb the pass**, the 90 mile Bealach Mor in September and the 43-mile Bealach Beag in May. Both attract a large number of riders of all standards, so early entry is advised: see www.handsonevents.co.uk for details. Riding over the pass makes a challenging day – it is rated 11/10 in Simon Warren's *100 Greatest Cycling Climbs; A Road Cyclist's Guide to Britain's Hills*.

Testing the brakes on the descent from the Bealach na Ba

Between storms at Loch Carron

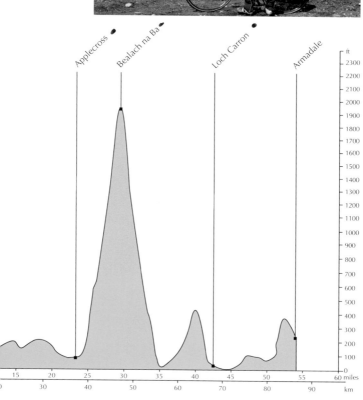

STAGE 5
Stromeferry to Armadale

Start	Stromeferry
Finish	Armadale
Distance	32.5 miles (52km)
Grade	Moderate
Time	4hrs
Map	OS Landranger 1:50,000 25, 32, 33

Ferries stopped sailing from Stromeferry in 1970 when the railway was converted to single track to make room for a road alongside Loch Carron. Today it's a quiet village at the bottom of a steep dead end. The next village on the route, Plockton, is another classic Scottish fishing village and might look familiar because it has featured in numerous television series and films, including *Hamish Macbeth* and *The Wicker Man*. It was established as a fishing community in an attempt to stem emigration, but today is a haven for sailors, artists and tourists with a good selection of places to eat. Despite being a shopping centre for the region, since the Skye Bridge opened in 1995, replacing a ferry that had run for four centuries, both Kyle of Lochalsh and Kyleakin on the opposite shore seem to have lost their reason to exist.

Pretty Duirinish village on the way to Kyle of Lochalsh

Caisteal Maol at Kyleakin

Ignore the road sign that says 'Stromeferry – No Ferry' and turn right at the next junction signposted for Achmore along a green shady road that meanders below high crags all the way to **Plockton**.

Following the road signs for Kyle of Lochalsh takes you down minor roads through the picturesque villages of Duirinish, Drumbuie, Erbusaig and Badicaul which all pass in quick succession before **Kyle of Lochalsh** is reached.

Kyle-born **Alexander MacRae** (1888–1938) emigrated to Australia in 1910 and founded the swimwear giant Speedo – an idea that would perhaps not have occurred to him had he stayed home.

A cycle track starts at the traffic lights on the edge of the village and goes right across the bridge, but it may be wise to get off and walk in wind.

Eilean Ban, the island used for the foundations of the two spans that make up the bridge, is now a museum celebrating the life of **Gavin Maxwell**, the naturalist and writer best known for his books about otters. After his main house at Sandaig burnt down, he spent his final years at the keeper's cottage. The lighthouse was built by David and Thomas of the famous 'Lighthouse Stevensons' family and opened in 1857. Today it is dwarfed by the bridge.

The Ring of Bright Water Centre on the quay in **Kyleakin** also has exhibits and displays about the history, heritage and wildlife of Eilean Ban and Maxwell.

Kyleakin, once the 'gateway to Skye', is now a dead end and is slightly off route for anyone not staying in the village overnight. But it is well worth a visit with good views of the bridge, a number of places to eat and a little working harbour tucked in below the ruins of 15th century Caisteal Maol, which was once a stronghold of the Mackinnon clan.

Other than views of the islands in the Inner Sound and the distant Cuillin, there is little of interest along the A87 – yet another road built by Thomas Telford - until the crofts at Breakish mark the beginnings of **Broadford** (✗ 4B), the main town of southern Skye.

For Armadale turn left on to the A851 at Skulamus a mile or so before the town. Stretches of the old single road run parallel to the new road, which was constructed with funding from the European Union and comes complete with idiosyncratic bridges clearly influenced by a visit to Disneyland. But the surface is excellent and the long open ascent up and over to Duisdalemore goes by quickly. The natural harbour at **Isleornsay** (*Eilean Iarmain* in Gaelic) was once home to a fleet of boats that fished for herring and a popular stop-off for steamers coming up the west coast from Glasgow via the Crinan Canal. Today a collection of pretty white houses cluster around the hotel and gallery making it one of the most attractive villages on Skye.

> **Isleornsay lighthouse** was built by the same Stevensons who built the Kyleakin lighthouse first lit on the same day – 10 November 1857. Gavin Maxwell owned the keepers' cottages here too.

Further on the road cuts inland with an inevitable ascent before dropping back to the coast at Teangue. From here, it is easy pedalling with wooded slopes on the right and views across the Sound of Sleat to the Knoydart peninsula on the left. There is an interesting collection of shops and galleries at **Armadale** (157/251) and a hotel with a popular bar just down the road in Ardvasar.

ROUTE 4B
Stromeferry to Uig

Start	Stromeferry
Finish	Uig
Distance	81 miles (130km)
Total Ascent	8070ft (2460m)
Grade	Very hard–hard–moderate
Time	8hrs 35mins
Map	OS Landranger 1:50,000 25, 32, 33

This route, the mainland section of which is very tough, is only possible when the Glenelg to Kylerhea ferry, the last manually operated turntable ferry in Scotland, is running. Operated by the Isle of Skye Ferry Community Interest Company, it runs every 20mins or so between 1000hrs to 1800hrs Easter to October, so this route cannot be done in winter.

STAGE 1
Stromeferry to Kylerhea

Start	Stromeferry
Finish	Glenelg Ferry
Distance	27.5 miles (44km)
Grade	Very hard
Time	2hrs 50mins
Map	OS Landranger 1:50,000 25, 33

The route is dominated by two ascents, the first over the Kyle isthmus to Dornie, where tourists congregate at the ubiquitous and much-restored 13th century Eilean Donan Castle, which is an essential attraction for whistle-stop coach tours of the Highlands and Islands. Then easy cycling round Loch Duich leads to the big, steep ascent of Bealach Ratagan. Then it's downhill all the way to the Skye ferry.

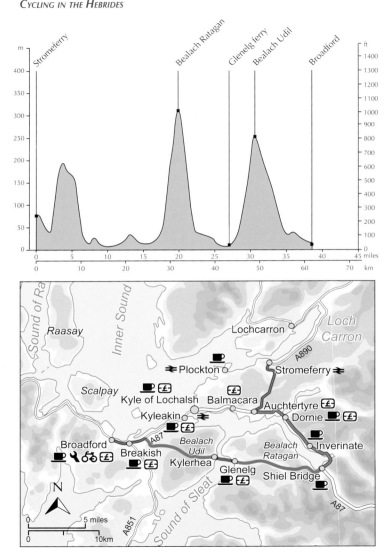

Eilean Donan Castle

After the briefest stretch of downhill, the A890 climbs steadily up through the woods, before breasting the summit to reveal Loch Alsh and the mountains of Kintail, Glen Shiel and the Cullin away to the west. After a sweeping descent to **Auchtertyre** turn left on to the A87 following signs for Inverness. The village of **Dornie** was once an important ferry crossing, but is now by-passed by the causeway that spans Loch Long.

The easy pedalling continues through **Inverinate** and around to **Shiel Bridge.**

> Here a flock of **wild goats** frequently scares revellers walking back to the campsite after an evening at the hotel bar.

Soon after the road turns inland, turn right onto an old military road signed for Glenelg. Those soldiers must have been fit because the road over **Bealach Ratagan** starts steep and just gets steeper. The gradients approach 20% around the switchback hairpin bends just below the viewpoint.

> Stop and enjoy the **view** – you deserve it. Kintail is a Munro bagger's paradise with three among the The Five Sisters on the east of the valley and seven on the Glensheil ridge opposite.

If you can stop yourself from looking across to the next major climb across on Skye, the swooping descent down through the conifers and out above the green

Classic cars leavng the ferry at Glenelg

pastures of Glen More is a delight. **Glenelg** is a pleasant village of regimented cottages built to house the officers responsible for the garrison housed in Bernera Barracks near the shore. They were completed in the early 1720s and a century later found use as the local poor house before being abandoned.

A short ride leads round to the community operated ferry – the last turntable ferry in Scotland – that crosses the 550m of Kyle Rhea, running every 20mins between 1000hrs and 1800hrs, Easter–October, across to **Kylerhea**.

Until the railway came to Kyle of Lochalsh this was the **main crossing place for Skye**, much used by passengers and drovers who swam their cattle across at slack water on their way to market.

STAGE 2
Kylerhea to Broadford

Start	Kylerhea
Finish	Broadford
Distance	11.5 miles (18km)
Grade	Hard
Time	2hrs 50mins
Map	OS Landranger 1:50,000 32, 33

Just north of Kylerhea is an otter hide that gives good views down on to the shore and the prospect of a sighting, a good place to rest before the steep climb that starts this short but steep stage. But Bealach Udil is never quite as fierce as the previous ascent over Bealach Ratagan.

You can't put off the inevitable climb up to **Bealach Udil** forever. Once over the summit the the descent through Glen Arroch to the sounds of cuckoos, pipits and babbling streams will soon raise flagging spirits. Once you reach the main A87 at **Breakish** turn left into **Broadford** (✗4A), which is a good place to top up on supplies, grab a bite to eat or simply idle away some time browsing the galleries and shops. You might need a break as there are more big climbs ahead.

After the Jacobite uprising of 1715, George I sent **General George Wade** to Scotland with orders to get the rebellious clans under control. He recommended building barracks and roads, and between 1725 and 1737 oversaw the construction of 250 miles (400km) of road, and more than 40 bridges, to link garrisons at Ruthven, Fort George, Fort Augustus, and Fort William.

However he was not responsible for the military road through Glen Shiel, connecting Fort Augustus to the Bernera barracks in Glenelg. This was built by his successor **William Caulfeild** and although he is not as well known as Wade, he was responsible for the construction of 900 miles of roads and over 600 bridges.

STAGE 3

Broadford to Portree

Start	Broadford
Finish	Portree
Time	2hrs 45mins
Distance	25 miles (40km)
Grade	Hard
Time	2hrs 45mins
Map	OS Landranger 1:50,000 32

This stage has two main climbs, the first of which, from the head of Loch Ainort, can be avoided by taking the minor road that runs down the north side of Loch Ainort to Moll and around the headland to rejoin the main road just south of Sconser. It adds an extra 3km but avoids most of the climbing. There is no easy alternative to the next climb up through Glen Varrigall Forest.

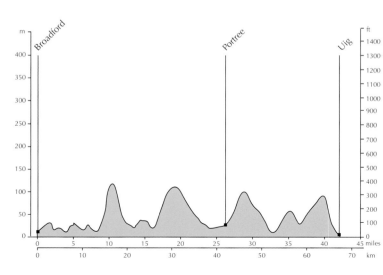

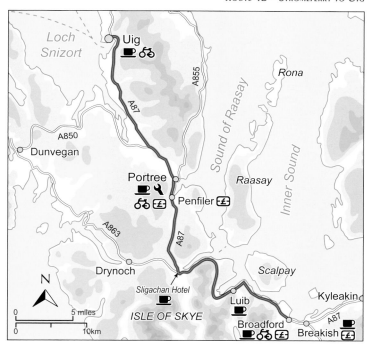

Initially the road climbs up through the conifer plantation, but it soon reaches the coast, to give easy riding through Strollamus and Dunan and close up views to Scalpay across the straights. As soon as the road turns inland through **Luib** you can see the climbing to be done at the head of Loch Ainort, and this is where you need to make a decision either to ride the main road, with 4km of steady ascent past the dramatic waterfalls that run off the Red Cuillin, the only downside being the traffic that congregates at this busy viewpoint, or to turn right along the north shore of Loch Ainort.

The road turns inland again, undulating all the way to the **Sligachan Hotel**, a long-established centre for climbers and mountaineers and a good place for a rest before the climb up through Glen Varrigall Forest, which is never too steep and you can always entertain yourself looking for sea eagles, which are frequently seen in the area. Once over the top, there is a welcome descent to **Portree**, with a backdrop of The Storr on a clear day.

191

STAGE 4
Portree to Uig

Start	Portree
Finish	Uig
Distance	17 miles (27km)
Grade	Hard
Time	1hr 45mins
Map	OS Landranger 1:50,000 23, 32

Portree has everything you might need and more besides, with eateries offering menus that run from fast food to fine dining, a cycle shop, a bookshop and even a traditional music shop.

The main supermarket, which is just north of the town alongside the A87, is the last place to stock up before a long and slightly featureless ride to **Uig**, with only the final descent around Uig Bay being at all memorable.

Local landlord Major William Fraser built **Uig Tower** around 1860 and used it as a place to collect rents.

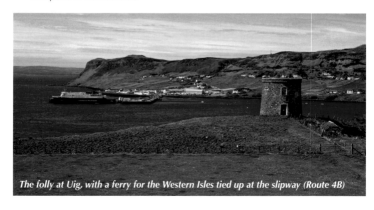

The folly at Uig, with a ferry for the Western Isles tied up at the slipway (Route 4B)

DAY ROUTES

ROUTE 4.1
Across the Sleat Peninsula from Armadale

Start/Finish	Armadale
Distance	21 miles (34km)
Total Ascent	3670ft (1120m)
Grade	Hard
Time	2hrs 15mins
Map	OS Landranger 1:50,000 32
Ferries	None on route: Mallaig – Armadale at start

Being close to the Armadale, this is an ideal ride for those holidaying on the mainland near Mallaig and especially those whose family or friends are set on visiting Armadale Castle, home of the Clan MacDonald. Although it is only a short ride, it is challenging with plenty of little climbs and takes you to both coasts of the Sleat peninsula with excellent views of the Cuillin to the west and the Knoydart peninsula to the east.

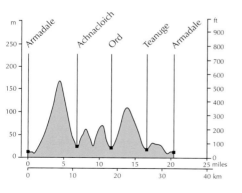

If you have a vehicle with you there is plenty of parking near **Armadale** pier or in one of the many lay-bys along the A861 towards Armadale Castle.

Only parts of the original **Armadale Castle** and later 19th century additions remain, supplemented by the more recent Museum of the Isles.

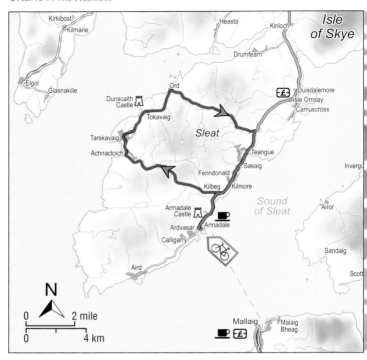

Head northwards on the A851 following signs for Broadford and Portree until the village of **Kilbeg.**

> Kilbeg is home to **Sabal Mhor Ostaig**, part of the University of the Highlands and Islands that specialises in Gaelic language, history and culture.

Turn sharp left, following signs for Tarskavaig, Tokavaig and Ord, steadily climbing up past Ostaig fank (sheep sorting pens), and over the southern flank of Sgurr na h-Iolaire ('the Hill of the Eagle'). Your efforts are rewarded with a fast descent past Loch Dhoghaill and down through the birch woods to the crofts and houses at **Achacloich**. Riding along the coast inevitably means inclines and you are immediately hit with a short steep ascent as the road climbs up behind the scattered village of **Tarskavaig**, which can be visited by adding a short loop. Most people will be happy to continue along above the village, especially on a clear day when you can see the whole of the Cuillin, 12 miles (19km) to the west beyond the Strathaird peninsula. Past Loch Gauscavaig, the road descends to the wooded Ob Gauscavaig, where the remains of **Dunscaith Castle** sit on a prominent rock at the northern end of the bay.

> **Dunscaith Castle**, which was built by the MacAskills in the 14th century, is thought to be the oldest standing castle on Skye; although very little still stands today.

More steady climbing leads up through the birch woods to the scattered village of **Tokavaig** and a short 20% descent into **Ord**, where a stoney beach and views of the Cuillin make a welcoming place for rest. Then it's back across the peninsula, with further climbing up alongside the Ord River and over and down through the conifer plantation to rejoin the main road. Turn right, heading south on the A851 through the coastal villages of **Teangue**, **Saasaig**, **Ferindonald** and **Kilbeg**, to return to **Armadale**, making use of what appears to be a good, yet unsigned, cycle lane.

> On a clear day there is an **excellent view eastwards** across the Sound of Sleat to the mighty Ladhar Bheinn (1010m), the most westerly mainland Munro and the main summit on the landlocked Knoydart peninsula.

Tarskavaig on the west side of the Sleat peninsula with the Cuillin behind

CYCLING IN THE HEBRIDES

ROUTE 4.2

Elgol and back from Broadford

Start/Finish	Broadford
Distance	30 miles (48km)
Total Ascent	2690ft (820m)
Grade	Hard
Time	3hrs 15mins
Map	OS Landranger 1:50,000 32
Ferries	None on route

With close views of the Cuillin and the opportunity to take a sea trip to Rum or to view basking sharks and even whales, Elgol and the single track B8083 can get busy. Riders need to be attentive to vehicles approaching from the rear, always checking whether there's more than one before pulling back out into the road, as well as to the possibility of meeting traffic at blind summits and sharp bends.

Novice riders may also find the amount and severity of some of the ascents on the Strathaird peninsula between Torrin and Elgol too challenging to be enjoyable. Despite these qualifications, this ride has to be one of the very best dead-end rides in the UK.

There are plenty of places to park at the start of the B8083 in Broadford opposite the hotel. Initially it is fast and easy riding along Strath Suardal all the way to **Torrin**. This gives you plenty of time to warm up and will again be a welcome respite on the ride back.

> For three hundred years through to the last century, this quiet valley was a **hive of industry** with industrial buildings, workers cottages and even a railway to carry the Skye marble that was quarried on the south side of the glen down to the sea at Broadford. The community would have worshipped at 16th century **Cill Chriosd**, built on a site with Christian connections going back to the 7th century and used until it was abandoned in the 1840s. Small quantities of Skye **marble** are still quarried in the area. The jagged Black Cuillin was formed out of hard, rough gabbro, which gives climbers an excellent grip, while the lower, smoother Red Cuillins are of softer granite.

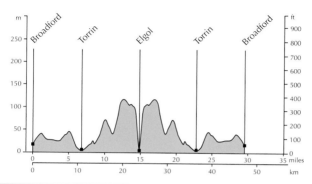

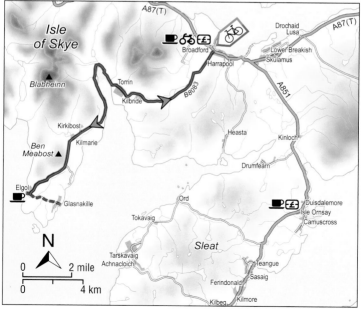

Looking up Loch Scavaig to the Black Cuillin from Elgol

The easy pedalling continues all the way around the head of Loch Slapin too, but you will want to stop frequently to take in the jagged panorama of **Blabheinn** and Garbh-bheinn, the highest summits of the Red Cullins, towering above the opposite shore. But soon the road turns inland through **Kirkibost** and **Kilmarie** and the climbing begins in earnest and continues all the way up around the flanks of Ben Meabost until a steep and fast descent leads down to **Elgol**.

> The **views** are spectacular. To the north across Loch Scavaig is the Black Cullin, which many consider provide the ultimate mountaineering experience available in the UK with a traverse of the ridge requiring ropes and confidence in climbing short rock pitches.
>
> Directly west is the low-laying island of **Soay**, where Gavin Maxwell, the author of *Ring of Bright Water*, tried to establish a commercial whaling station in the 1940s. Further around to the south lies **Rum**, which the Nature Conservancy Council has managed as a nature reserve since it acquired the island in 1951.

That steep and fast descent into Elgol becomes a challenging 20% climb back out on the return. But all the really hard work is over by the time the road drops down to the shore of Loch Slapin and it's easy pedalling all the way back to **Broadford**.

You can add another 4 miles (6.5km) to this ride by going over to **Glasnakille** on the east coast of the peninsula and back.

ROUTE 4.3

A three-legged ride from Carbost

Start/Finish	Carbost
Distance	38 miles (57km)
Total Ascent	7710ft (2350m)
Grade	Hard
Time	4hrs 15mins
Map	OS Landranger 1:50,000 32
Ferries	None on route

There may be some whisky-loving cyclists whose idea of heaven is to visit every Hebridean distillery in a single tour. Such a tour would involve visiting Carbost, a pleasant village on Loch Harport, home of the Talisker Distillery and the central village on the Minginish peninsula, an ideal place to start a three-legged ride to three road ends.

Looking down towards Glendale from Carbost

The first 'leg', a round trip of 28km with 600m of ascent, goes out of the village to **Merkadale**, then takes the minor road to **Glenbrittle**, passing through Glenbrittle Forest and out into green pastures of Glen Brittle to the campsite at the road end. For a ride which is such easy pedalling, it's hard to believe that the 3000-feet plus summits of the Cuillin are less than 1¾ miles (3km) from the road. Allow 2hrs.

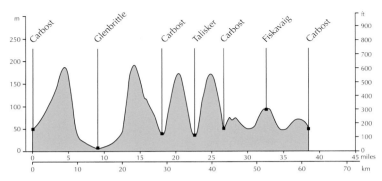

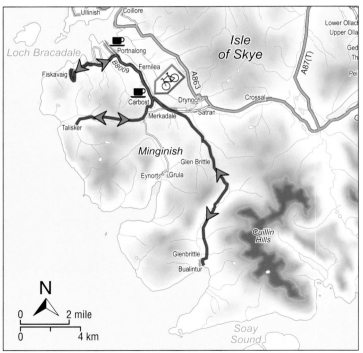

Tight in beneath the Cuillin on the way back from Glenbrittle

For the second leg, a round trip of 14km and 400m of ascent, from **Carbost** take the road signposted for Talisker. It leaves the village near the distillery, then climbs steadily up through rounded hills before dropping gently into Gleann Oraid to reach the road end in the woods at **Talisker** House.

> When **Dr Johnson and Boswell** stayed at Talisker House during their tour of the Hebrides in 1733, Boswell scrambled up nearby Preshal More by a route that still carries his name.

Repeatedly riding past a distillery and a pub may test one's resolve on a hot day, so quickly on with the third and final leg – a round trip of 16km, with 470m of ascent. Leave the village following signs for Portnalong and Fiskavaig. The road climbs steadily up above the shore of Loch Harport revealing increasing fine views of the Cuillin on a clear day. Just before the hotel in **Portnalong**, bear left following signs for Fiskavaig. Initially the road drops down above the Fiskavaig Bay before climbing up through **Fiskavaig**, to reveal views of the island of Wiay out in Loch Bracadale and the instantly recognisable MacLeod's Tables. Now back to **Carbost** for that well-earned treat.

ROUTE 4.4
Around the Duirinish Peninsula

Start/Finish	Dunvegan
Distance	25 miles (41km)
Total Ascent	4630ft (1410m)
Grade	Moderate
Time	3hrs 15mins
Map	OS Landranger 1:50,000 23
Ferries	None on route

Another route that cunningly starts from a major tourist attraction that will detain friends and family for the couple of hours needed to ride around the Duirinish peninsula in the far northwest of Skye.

Head south out of **Dunvegan** towards Sligachan on the A863 and turn right onto a narrow road marked for Glendale. This is a shortcut around the head of the bay and soon joins the B884 at a T-junction. Turn right again, still following signs for

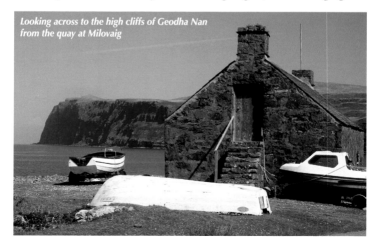

Looking across to the high cliffs of Geodha Nan from the quay at Milovaig

Glendale, with **Loch Dunvegan** to your right and the flat summits of the instantly recognisable Macleod's Tables on your left. Ride through the loch-side villages of **Skinidin** and **Colbost**, where there is a folk museum, and up and over into **Glendale**.

> This is countryside characterised by **linear villages** set out so that each croft has an equal share of good pasture in front of the croft house and less fertile hillside behind. Not that many houses remain as working crofts: the majority are smartly maintained holiday homes or retirement retreats.

After climbing out of Glendale, turn right along the western shore of Loch Pooltiel following the road through Lower Milovaig and back around to **Upper Milovaig** – a loop that is worth adding just to get a closer view of the 300m-high cliffs of Biod an Athair across the loch. Turn right and ride down through the green sheep pastures of Waterstein to **Neist Point**, which is a popular viewpoint with dramatic

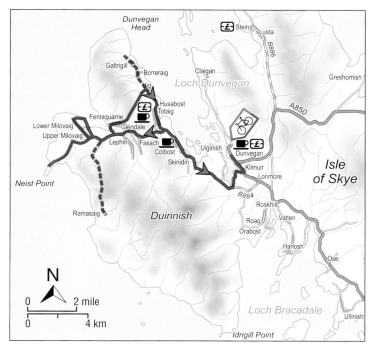

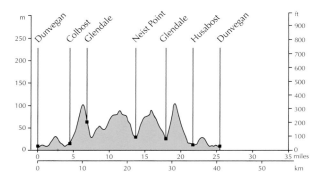

cliffs in every direction and a reputation for being the best place to see whales, dolphins, porpoises and basking shark.

> You can add another 16km to this ride by visiting the road ends at **Ramasaig** and **Galtrigill**, where a museum commemorates the MacCrimmons, who were pipers to the Clan MacLeod for generations.

On the return, follow the road back to **Glendale** and turn left to **Feriniquarrie** just before the bridge over the Hamara River. The road climbs steadily around the flanks of Ben Ettow, with its prominent radio mast, before an enjoyable serpentine descent to **Uig**. Turn right and follow the road through **Husabost** and **Totaig** before turning left onto the B884 and following it back to **Dunvegan**.

ROUTE 4.5
Circuit of the Trotternish Peninsula

Start/Finish	Portree
Distance	49 miles (78km)
Total Ascent	3580ft (1090m)
Grade	Hard
Time	5hrs 15mins
Map	OS Landranger 1:50,000 23
Ferries	None on route

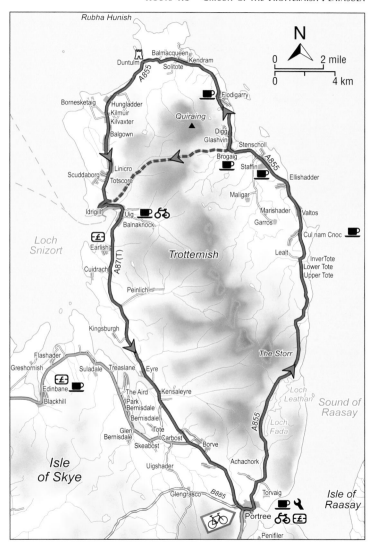

A wonderful reconditioned road below The Storr

With consistently good roads and stunning scenery, this loop around the Trotternish peninsula will appeal to committed road cyclists looking for a fast ride as well as those who simply want a wonderful day out. If you need to leave a vehicle, there is free long-stay parking as you enter Portree.

Ride or walk to Bank Street above the harbour and turn left up Bosville Terrace, following the A855 and signs for Staffin. The road climbs gently out of the town past **Achachork**, gradually levelling off to reveal **The Storr** and a fast smooth road past **Loch Fada** and **Loch Leathan**.

A 100m walk at **Inver Tote** gives good views of the waterfall and down on to the industrial remains of a former diatomite mine.

On a clear day there are **extensive views** across to Rona and Raasay and further to the high mountains of Applecross and Torridon in Wester Ross.

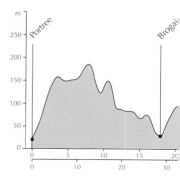

The easy riding continues making for rapid progress through Tote, **Cul nam**

Cnoc, **Valtos** and **Eilishadder**, past pretty white croft houses scattered in the pastures that run up to the continuous line of crags. The viewpoint at Kilt Rock looks down onto the basalt sea cliffs that line this stretch of the coast, then a fast descent leads down into the large village of **Staffin** and around the bay above the long strips of croft land to **Brogaig**. Taking the minor road between Brogaig and Uig shortens this route by 10km while adding 200m of ascent through hairpin bends to the top of the escarpment – a location once much loved by car advertisers.

There is a steady ascent up through **Digg** and around the eastern flanks of the cylindrical **Quairang** to **Flodigarry**, before the road turns westwards through the exposed villages of **Kendram** and Kilmaluag at the extreme north of the peninsula.

> This is **Golden Eagle** country, so keep an eye out for something the size of a ironing board hovering along the cliffs.
>
> The stepped or 'trap' **geology** of the Trotternish peninsula was formed when basalt lavas flowed over softer sedimentary rocks from the Jurassic period to give characteristic flat-topped hills. The weight of the heavier lavas, glaciation and years of steady erosion resulted in huge landslides that have left steep crags and numerous isolated blocks and pinnacles that today have evocative names such as the Old Man of Storr, the Table, the Needle and the Quirang.

The road continues to **Duntulm.**

The remains of a **castle** that dates back to the 14th century sit on a basalt plug above the bay, with views across The Minch to the distant Harris Hills. During the 17th century it was the base of the MacDonalds of Sleat, but was abandoned in 1732 when Sir Alexander Macdonald built Monkstadt House, a more comfortable mansion a few miles to the south.

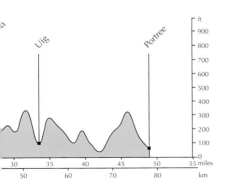

The road climbs away from the shore and out onto the pasture lands on the west coast.

The **Skye Museum** at Hungladder is located in a group of restored black-houses and in the cemetery beyond is the grave of Uist-born Flora MacDonald (1722–1790), who enjoys a permanent place in history after a mere 36 hours spent helping Bonnie Prince Charlie evade the government forces following the defeat of the Jacobites at Culloden in 1745. After a spell in America, where her army officer husband fought for the Hanoverians during the American War of Independence, she returned to farm at Kingsburgh in the southwestern corner of the Totternish peninsula.

She had two daughters and five sons, who mostly joined the British army or navy, so clearly her big adventure had no lasting impact on her family. Either that or they never mentioned their mother's maiden name on the application form.

As long as there is no headwind, it is easy pedalling through **Kilmuir**, **Kilvaxter** and **Linicro**.

Out between the road and the sea is an area of **meadow** that is lower than the land nearer the coast. Before it was finally drained by the Macdonalds of nearby Monkstadt House in 1821, this used to be Loch Chaluim Chille and is now effectively a piece of fenland in the Hebrides.

A fast descent leads down to the ferry port of **Uig**, which is home of the Skye Brewery, an undoubted magnet for beer lovers. The main A87 road back to

Skye Folk Museum at Hungladder

Portree can be busy especially if a ferry has just come in: perhaps, one day, the stretches of the old road that run alongside it will be repurposed as a cycle track.

The **Skye Sportive Mor** annual road race combines Routes 4.5 and 4.6, to make a route of 96 miles with 1800m of ascent – with the shorter option being just Route 4.5.

ROUTE 4.6
Circuit of Central Skye

Start/Finish	Sligachan Hotel
Distance	53 miles (85km)
Total Ascent	4070ft (1240m)
Grade	Hard
Time	5hrs 45mins
Map	OS Landranger 1:50,000 23, 32
Ferries	None on route

Being a circular route, you could start this ride anywhere along the way, but I've chosen the Sligachan Hotel, because the prospect of a cool beverage may provide some necessary motivation towards the end.

Join Route 4B, Stage 4, heading north on the A87 through **Portree** to **Borve**, then turn left on to the A850, following signs for Dunvegan.

Crossing the peninsula between Loch Snizort Beag and Loch Greshnishorn involves some up and downs, but once through **Edinbane** there is 5km of steady climbing up and over the Waternish peninsula before a welcome descent into **Dunvegan**.

The **castle**, which has been the stronghold of the Chiefs of MacLeod for nearly 800 years, is tucked away behind a screen of trees. The 1861 guidebook *Black's Picturesque Tourist in Scotland* described it as 'less picturesque than might be expected', and the village too is something of a disappointment, saved only by a good cake stop. By cutting the corner on the way in, it can be avoided altogether.

Common seals regularly haul out on the islands in Loch Dunvegan and can be viewed from the road to the north of the castle.

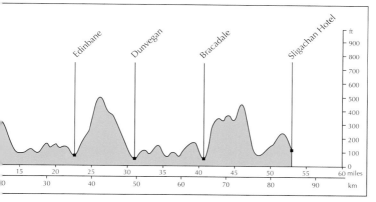

When UK roads were categorised and numbered in the early 1920s, someone deemed that Clan MacLeod still deserved the respect of having the dead end that runs up to the castle door classified as part of the A850. So as you leave the village, you are now following the A863, which is altogether a much better road with hills that are positively enjoyable and excellent views all the way back to the Sligachan Hotel. There are rolling hills through the villages of **Roskhill**, **Caroy** and **Ose**, but with the stunning scenery of MacLeod's Tables on your right hand side and Loch Bracadale out in front, the miles pass by easily.

After **Struan** the road drops down through **Bracadale** and around the head of Loch Beag, before a sharp climb back up the other side.

A **viewpoint half way up** has good views of the cliffs either side of Loch Bracadale and down to Gesto Farm, a well-preserved Victorian steading complete with a circular hen house heated by a central chimney.

Now you are riding with the magnificent panorama of the Black Cuillin directly ahead and it gets even better, with a fast and twisting descent down to the head of Loch Harport. The excellent views of the Cuillin stay with you through Glen Drynoch and all the way to the **Sligachan Hotel**.

ROUTE 4.7

Skye Bridge/Glenelg circuit from Kyle of Lochalsh

Start/Finish	Kyle of Lochalsh
Distance	39 miles (62km)
Total Ascent	4760ft (1450m)
Grade	Very hard
Time	4hrs 10mins
Map	OS Landranger 1:50,000 33
Ferries	Glenelg ferry (see Appendix C)

Although it can only be ridden during the summer months when the Kylehera Ferry operates (runs every 20mins 1000hrs to 1800hrs maybe later in summer, Easter–October), this is just too much of a good ride to leave out.

The ride starts easily along the shores of Loch Alsh and Loch Duich, but then come two punishing climbs over Bealach Ratagan and Bealach Udil before a flat run-in culminates with a crossing of the Skye Bridge. But be warned; while it is a wonderful ride for a fit rider, it would be a truly memorable ride for an unfit one.

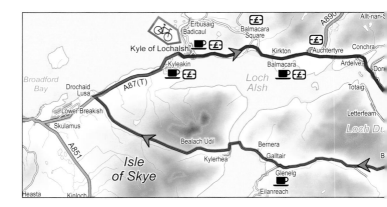

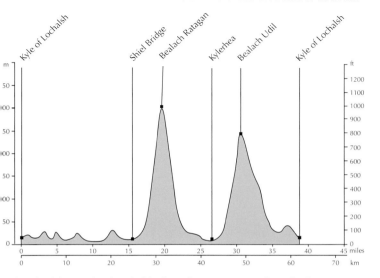

Ride inland from Kyle of Lochalsh along the A87, passing through **Blamacara** to join Route 4B, Stage 1 at **Auchtertyre.**

Follow Route 4B through **Dornie** and **Shiel Bridge** to **Glenelg.** Once across the ferry, following Route 4B, Stage 2 up over **Bealach Udil** before turning right onto the A87 just before **Breakish** and **Broadford** and then Route 4A, Stage 5 in reverse along the A87 and over the Skye Bridge to **Kyle of Lochalsh**.

213

ROUTE 4.8

Raasay

Start/Finish	Sconser on Skye
Distance	23 miles (37km)
Total Ascent	2920ft (890m)
Grade	Hard
Time	2hrs 15mins
Map	OS Landranger 1:50,000 24
Ferries	Sconser to Raasay

There is a frequent ferry service from Sconser to Raasay every day but Sunday, when there is a single outward sailing in the morning and a return sailing in the afternoon. It can get busy, but there is no risk of being left on the island if the last ferry is full as they always run an additional sailing to clear any remaining vehicles.

This is another excellent ride with fine views in each direction and some short sharp climbs at the northern end that hit you one after another with little time to recover. The OS Landranger map shows 11 chevrons to indicate gradients of 14% to 20% and more in a mere 2½ miles (4km). But as the road surfaces are never that good, Raasay is not an island to bring your best carbon-framed road bike or your ultra-skinny tyres.

Once off the ferry, head up towards the village and immediately left up through the woodland behind Raasay House, following signs for the cemetery and **Oskaig**. There are good views northwards across the Sound of Raasay to the Trotternish peninsula. After **Holoman**, the road leaves the coast and swings back on itself, past a side road to **Balachuirn** and up the hill to a T-junction. Turn left and head northwards past the crofts and grazing cattle at Brae and onwards across the open moor. After a right-hand bend the road drops sharply down to **Brochel**.

> Here the ruins of a late 15th century **castle**, said to have been built by Calum, Raasay's first Macleod chief, sit dramatically on a volcanic plug. With good views of any shipping sailing through the Inner Sound between Raasay and the mainland, it served as a base for the marauding Macleods until it was abandoned some time around 1671.

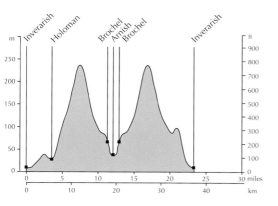

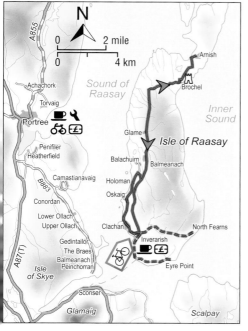

Nearby a sign and suitably battered wheelbarrow (pictured below) mark the start of Calum's Road and a series of punishing little climbs up over to Loch Arnish, where the road is wedged in above the cliffs. Finally, and perhaps not soon enough for many, you reach the road end at **Arnish**, where you may be greeted by the crofter's friendly pigs.

The reward for riding back up those hills is that once they are over with and the road heads south across the open moor, it is easy pedalling with a magnificent panorama of the Cullins

215

The start of Calum's Road on Raasay

to lift flagging spirits. Ignore all junctions and continue past the hostel and down through the shade of Raasay Forest, turning right at the road junction in **Inverarish** to return to the pier.

Visits to the road ends at **Eyre Point** and **North Fearns** at the south of the island extend this ride by 16km.

5 BARRA AND THE UISTS

Tied up on the Eriskay ferry (Route 5A)

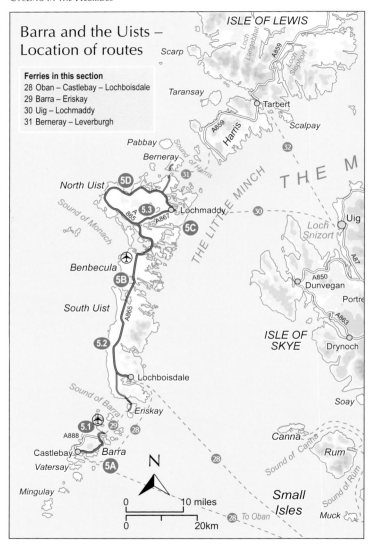

Barra and the Uists – Location of routes

ISLE OF LEWIS

Ferries in this section
28 Oban – Castlebay – Lochboisdale
29 Barra – Eriskay
30 Uig – Lochmaddy
31 Berneray – Leverburgh

Scarp

Loch Langabhat

Loch Siophort

A859

Taransay

Tarbert

Pabbay

Harris

Scalpay

Berneray

Sound of Harris

THE M

North Uist

5D

A865

5.3

A867

Lochmaddy

31

32

THE LITTLE MINCH

30

Uig

Loch Snizort

5C

Sound of Monach

Benbecula

5B

A850

Dunvegan

Portre

South Uist

A865

A87

5.2

A863

ISLE OF SKYE

Drynoch

Lochboisdale

Sound of Barra

Eriskay

Soay

5.1

29

28

Canna

Sound of Canna

A888

Castlebay

Barra

Vatersay

5A

Rum

Mingulay

N

Sound of Rum

0   10 miles

0   20km

28

Small Isles

28 To Oban

Muck

INTRODUCTION

Crossing from Eriskay to South Uist (Route 5A)

TRAVERSING THE WESTERN ISLES

The sparsely populated string of islands that make up the Outer Hebrides or Western Isles are a magnet for cyclists who relish isolation, haunting beauty and the obvious challenge of riding their entire length from Castlebay to the Butt of Lewis. Although it is a relatively modest ride of just less than 150 miles (240km), this is undoubtedly one of the great cycling journeys in the world, packed with antiquities and taking you past dazzling white beaches, alongside turquoise seas and through dramatic hills.

However, unless you do some detailed planning or have a back-up vehicle to accompany you, the logistics can become a nightmare or even ruin a holiday. I have met numerous cyclists in the hotel bars of Tarbert who set out to ride the length of the Western Isles but curtailed their journey to return southwards. Typically they end up going back down to Lochboisdale to catch the ferry to Oban and are somewhat disheartened by their perceived failure to achieve their original aim of cycling the length of the Western Isles. Chatting to them often reveals they have either overestimated their fitness or, more typically, have not done sufficient planning.

Getting back to Oban

If you do what many people do, which is leave a vehicle at Oban and take the ferry to Castlebay, when you finish the ride at the Butt of Lewis you are faced with the challenge of getting back to Oban. If you can spare the time, one of these options may suffice.

- You could ride south back to Tarbert (61 miles/98km), take the ferry to Skye, then cycle across Skye (66 miles/106km) to take the ferry from Armadale to Mallaig, finally riding down to Oban through Fort William (86 miles/138km).
- Or ride back to Stornoway (26 miles/42km), take a ferry to Ullapool and then ride down the west coast to Oban (167 miles/267km), following Routes 4A, 3D, 3B and 3A.
- Or once at Ullapool you could catch the Inverness–Durness–Inverness Service 804 operated by D&E Coaches from mid May until the end of September (see www.decoaches.co.uk) that has room for 16 bikes on a trailer. However it doesn't arrive back in Inverness until after the last train back to Oban so you'd need to stay the night.
- Alternatively you could ride from Ullapool to Garve (32 miles/51.5km) to catch the lunchtime train via Inverness and Glasgow that will get you back to Oban 8–9hrs later.
- If you've been blessed with fair weather and seduced by the charms of the Outer Hebrides, you might be more than happy to ride back to Lochboisdale

(133 miles/214km) and catch a ferry back to Oban. You can vary your route through South Harris and around North Uist, but most of the way you would be retracing the route.

- All of the coaches that serve the major routes through the Western Isles have space for a couple of bikes in their cargo hold if these are not already taken. See www.cne-siar.gov.uk/travel for timetables. Using this service, which involves making a couple of connections, you could get back to Castlebay in just less than 12hrs. Be aware there are no bus services on Sundays and on other days there is only one service that enables you to complete the journey in a single day, and that departs from Lionel near the Butt of Lewis at 0755hrs. Therefore unless you organise overnight accommodation in the Ness area you will find it easier to split the journey over two days. It is also advisable to pre-book with the individual coach operator during the peak summer months.

Getting back to Uig

Those with time constraints may consider leaving their vehicle near the ferry terminal at Uig, where there is ample long-stay parking, and taking an early ferry to Lochmaddy (1hr 45mins). From there you can catch a bus to Eriskay (2hrs 30mins) and a second ferry to Barra (40 mins). With some short waits for connections the entire journey will take up the best part of a day, but you can enjoy the sights and will get to meet fellow passengers. And after spending so much time sitting on a bus, you might be grateful of the opportunity to cycle the final few miles around to Castlebay – riding the road on the opposite side of the island to the way you intend to cycle on your journey northward. When you have completed the tour, it's a short ride from the Butt of Lewis to Lionel where you can catch a bus which, with a change at Stornoway, will take you to Tarbert (2hrs 45 mins) to catch a ferry back to Uig (1hr 40mins). On some days of the week, as long as you arrive at Lionel to catch the lunchtime bus, it is possible to get back to Tarbert in time for the afternoon ferry to Uig.

On other days you would need to be at Lionel for the first bus at 0755hrs, which probably entails staying overnight locally.

Another option is to hire. Rothan Cycles – www.rothan.com – based at Howmore in South Uist hire bikes out and will deliver them to Eriskay or Lochboisdale and collect them from Stornoway. All you then need to do is get yourself home.

Barra

Barra has everything that a lover of Hebridean islands could wish for – hills, white sandy beaches, flower-strewn machair, deeply incut sea lochs and a castle – all contained within 27 square miles. Kisimul Castle, out in Bagh a' Chaisteil, dates back to the 15th century and was once a stronghold of Clan MacNeil. A descendant rescued it from dereliction

Head around the north of Barra (Route 5.1)

in the 1930s and leased it to Historic Scotland for the annual rent of £1 and a bottle of whisky. It can be visited during the summer months.

The Uists

Until they were linked by causeways, Eriskay, South Uist, Benbecula, North Uist and Berneray were distinct islands. Some were separated by fords that could only be safely crossed on foot at low water while others needed ferries. Today, it is a continuous 60-mile (95.5km) stretch of fast road that it is all too easy to speed along without stopping to enjoy some of the hidden charms that lie at the dead ends either side of the main road. On the west coast there is an almost continuous stretch of sand backed by flat, fertile machair which is ablaze with flowers in early summer. To the east, small fishing villages are tucked in around the sea lochs that cut deeply into the higher hills. Take the time to visit one or two and let the gentle charm of these islands sink in.

MARGARET FAY SHAW – CYCLE TOURIST

In 1924, before the American-born folksong collector Margaret Fay Shaw met her ideal partner in John Lorne Campbell and went on to become the chatelaine of Canna, she undertook an extended cycling tour of Britain with some friends. They went up through the Cotswolds, over to the Lake District and across Scotland to Skye, using buses and trains between the less picturesque bits.

Two years later she returned with an American female friend for another tour, cycling the length of the Western Isles from Barra to the Butt of Lewis. In her autobiography *From the Alleghenies to the Hebrides* she records that 'a cart took us across the half-mile ford from Uist to Benbecula, and with the rising tide, the two-wheeled cart filled with water. The horse had to swim a few strokes, and myself sitting at the rear tried to keep our bikes upright with our luggage tied on. I was soaked.'

Soon after this trip she returned to South Uist, where she spent five years living in a blackhouse with two sisters learning Gaelic, collecting songs and taking photographs with a heavy plate camera. In 1934 she met John Lorne Campbell when he walked into Lochboisedale Hotel, where she was playing piano to accompany some youths learning the pipes. He was doing similar things across on Barra and it was a perfect match. They spent the best part of 60 years together, most of it on Canna, which they gave to the National Trust for Scotland in 1981. John died in 1996 and Margaret died in 2004 at the ripe old age of 101. She is buried in the churchyard at Hallan in South Uist.

LINK ROUTES

ROUTE 5A

Castlebay to Lochboisdale

Start	Castlebay
Finish	Lochboisdale
Distance	26 miles (42km)
Total Ascent	1570ft (480m)
Grade	Moderate to Aird Mhor, then Easy
Time	3hrs 5mins
Map	OS Landranger 1:50,000 31

Strictly speaking, if you want to lay claim to having ridden the length of the Outer Hebrides you should start not in Castlebay itself but at the road end near the burial ground in Vatersay, which is visited here on the circular Route 5.1 below. So if you are a perfectionist, make an excursion out there. Residents started to campaign for the causeway that now links Vatersay and Barra in 1986 after a prize bull called Bernie drowned while swimming across the 250m channel.

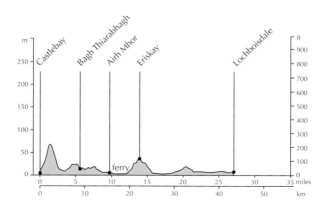

Otherwise head east out of **Castlebay** on the A888, which immediately climbs up around the shoulder of Sheabhal, where a statue of the Virgin and the Child on the hillside above looks out to sea. The rest of the route is easy, quickly reaching **Bagh Thiarabhagh** ('Northbay'), a thriving fishing community with a hotel. Turn right and follow the signs for ferry terminal at **Aird Mhor** (15/24), where there are toilets, a shower and a small tea shop.

In fine weather, the 40 minute ferry ride across the Sound of Barra to **Eriskay** (see Appendix C for details). gives good views of the offshore islands, including Eilean Leathan immediately to the south of Eriskay, where the ruin of Caisteal an Reubadair (Weaver's Castle) is clearly visible.

This was the home of a **notorious pirate** called MacNeil who raided ships and looted wrecks – evidently a common activity on Eriskay!

The terminal building on Eriskay has a shower and a café, but you will soon want to set off and explore this magical little island. The road climbs above Coilleag a' Phrionnsa ('Prince's Beach'), where Bonnie Prince Charlie landed on his way to his disastrous defeat at Culloden in the 1745 Rebellion, before dropping to the main settlement of **Am Baile**, ('the town').

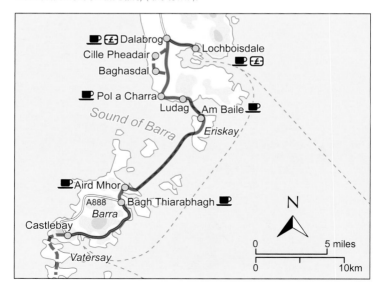

Crossing Eriskay on the way to South Uist

There is a good community shop at the road junction and down to the left is **Am Politician**, a pub named after the SS Politician which went aground off Eriskay on 5 February 1941 with over a quarter of a million bottles of whisky – and apparently some bicycle parts – in its holds. The pub contains memorabilia from the wreck, including a couple of the original bottles of whisky, but alas no bicycle parts.

The causeway that has linked Eriskay with South Uist since 2000 is a good place to pause and look for otters, particularly if you are passing during a rising tide at dawn or dusk when they are most likely to be seen. Enjoy riding above the shore from **Ludag** to **Pol a Charra**, where there is a hotel that marks the old crossing point to Barra.

> Once you turn north towards Dalabrog you enter a terrain of moorland and lochs with only the hills to the east to break the empty horizon. Rising out of this flat landscape at Gearraidh na Monadh is **Our Lady of Sorrows**, a modernist church from the 1960's that looks like a wedge of cheese topped with a neon cross. Its starkness fits well with the surrounding landscape.

From here on, it's gentle riding into **Dalabrog** (5B), but if you've had enough of the main road, a detour through the townships of **Baghasdal** and **Cille Pheadair** takes you to the dunes and eventually a back road into Dalabrog (25/40), while only adding 2 miles (3km) to the route.

Dalabrog is the undoubted centre of South Uist, with a well-stocked supermarket and a busy hotel. In contrast, Lochboisdale (28/45) is a sleepy ferry terminal.

Looking out to Rum from Lochboisdale

However it does have some saving graces. Lochboisedale is a **natural harbour**, set at the head of the deeply indented Loch Baghasdail and sheltered by Beinn Ruigh Choinnich to the north and Beinn Beag to the south. This means there is only a narrow view out across The Minch. But on a clear summer evening, there is no better place to be than sitting outside the **Lochboisdale Hotel** at the end of a long ride with a cool drink in your hand and a distant view of the mountains of Rum perfectly framed in the gap. Even if you are not departing on the ferry, it's worth the detour.

Lochboisdale looks set to change with plans to **develop the harbour** and construct a seaweed processing plant to manufacture commercially valuable alginates.

ROUTE 5B
Dalabrog to Clachan

Start	Dalabrog
Finish	Clachan
Distance	31 miles (50km)
Total Ascent	820ft (250m)
Grade	Easy
Time	3hrs 20mins
Map	OS Landranger 1:50,000 31

Unless you are cycling into a head wind, the miles pass by remarkably fast along this link route, leaving few memories other than isolated croft houses, the causeways across South and North Fords, lots of water – and big, big skies.

The first stop on the A865 north of Dalabrog (✗5B) is **Mingearraidh**, just north of which, off the main road, is the supposed birthplace of Flora MacDonald – the woman who famously helped Bonnie Prince Charlie evade the government forces and escape to Skye dressed as her Irish maid, Betty Burke.

There is not much to see, but the South Uist Historical Society has a museum a little further north at Cill Donnain, housing a collection of **local archaeological and historical artefacts** – and a **café**.

Further on, near the Gatliff hostel at **Tobha Mor**, are the ruins of two medieval churches and two surviving chapels as well as a picturesque group of thatched cottages.

The only other significant landmark along the main road is **Our Lady of the Isles**, another statue of the Madonna and Child from the 1950s on the western flank of Ruabhal. However it is entirely spoilt by the communication station behind it.

If you want to see anything of South Uist and Benbecula other than the main road, you have to leave the main road. On the fertile west coast is the machair: any road

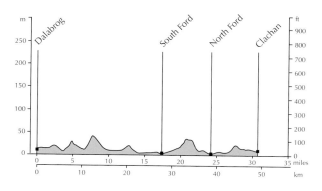

227

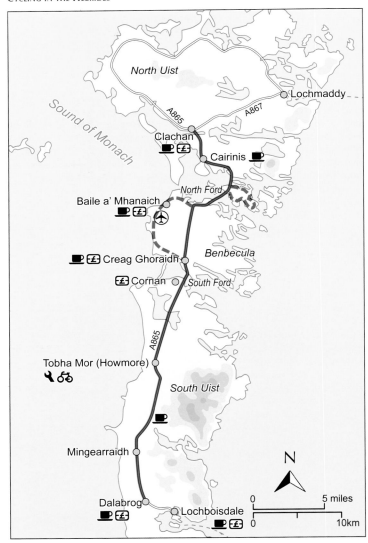

will get you there, but perhaps the most convenient is a detour around the west side of Benbecula, which adds 3¾ miles (6km) to the route.

The **machair** – the 'shell meadow' – is carpeted with wild flowers early summer. Most of the plants are commonplace – ragwort, buttercup, clover, daisy, various vetches and trefoils and, in later months, rarer orchids – but collectively the effect is unforgettable.

Immediately after the causeway across **South Ford**, at **Creag Ghoraidh** on Benbecula there is a supermarket and hotel – and soon after the turn for Baile a' Mhanaich, a small museum, before you reach the machair and some fine beaches that are close to the road. The deeply incut beach at Culla provides good shelter from the wind and is well hidden from nearby **Baile a' Mhanaich**.

This is the **main centre of population** on Benbecula, but with its utilitarian airport buildings and barracks, it is best forgotten.

If you want to visit the rocky east coast with its deeply incised sea lochs, turn right after the first section of the causeway across the North Ford and ride the 9km circuit around **Grimsay**.

There is a busy little harbour at **Ceallan**, at the eastern end of the island, which is an important base for fishing for shellfish. The Boatshed, a marine repair facility, promotes traditional boat-building skills and has a small museum.

Crossing the second section of the causeway across **North Ford** brings you to **North Uist**. At **Cairinis** there is a hotel, a pub and the ruins of Teampall na Trianaid, an important pre-Reformation church and site of learning that was still in use in 1728. From then on it's a straight run into **Clachan** (✗ 5C, 5D), which has a well-stocked grocery store.

ROUTE 5C

Clachan to Berneray

Start	Clachan
Finish	Berneray
Distance	19 miles (30km)
Total Ascent	690ft (210m)
Descent	340m
Grade	Easy
Time	1hr 55mins
Map	OS Landranger 1:50,000 14, 18

The eastern side of North Uist is a maze of fresh water lochs and deeply incut sea lochs, while the north and west coasts are gouged by vast sandy bays with low-laying islands that are only accessible at low tide with the endless Atlantic Ocean as a backdrop. So, unless you are bound for a ferry at Lochmaddy, you are faced with a choice. Both have their attractions.

Route 5C starts by crossing the open moor land dominated by the twin hills of Li a Tuath and Li a Deas – 'North' and 'South Lee' – and Eaval, the highest point on North Uist. It is an undulating route, constantly rising and dipping along its length, but even its highest point is a modest 30m.

Head northeast out of **Clachan** (✈5B, 5D) for 1¼ miles (2km) on the A867 to **Barpa Langass** on the north side of Beinn Langais.

This is a **megalithic tumulus** dating from 3000BC consisting of a large mound of stones with an entrance on its east side that leads to a burial chamber of some unknown warrior. It is perhaps not for those who suffer from claustrophobia. Within easy walking distance across on the south side of Beinn Langais is Pobull Fhinn – 'Finn's People' – the most complete prehistoric stone circle in the Uists.

Follow the gently undulating main road to **Lochmaddy**, a scattered, utilitarian village that is said to take its name from the Madadh ('the dogs'), the distinctive black pyramidal rocks that guard the southern entrance to Loch nam Madadh.

James Hogg, the artisan poet known as the Ettrick Shepherd, wrote that 'it is not easy to conceive a more dreary and dismal looking scene than the environs of this harbour' when he passed through **Lochmaddy** in 1803. On a dull day, it is difficult to disagree with him, but it does have its attractions. There

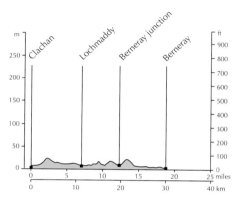

are some good examples of colloquial 19th century architecture, two hotels, a supermarket and a bank. Tourist attractions are limited to Taigh Chearsabhagh, an excellent arts centre with changing exhibitions, shop and café.

The next section is a short ride along the A865 on the western shore of Loch nam Madadh. The stage

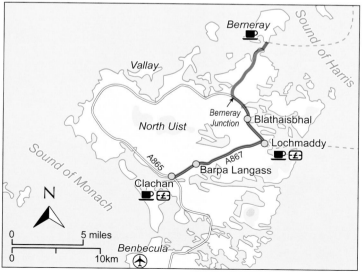

starts with a pleasant meander above the many skerries out in the loch and finishes with a couple of short climbs around the shoulders of **Blathaisbhal** and Crogearraidh Beag to reach the **junction** with the B893 that leads to Berneray. It is a short route but it conceals a hidden gem.

> If you turn off the main A865 just before the second bridge out of Lochmaddy (at OS grid reference NF902701) and ride 1¼ miles (2km) down to the pier you will come to **Both nam Faileas** – 'Hut of the Shadows' – a grass-roofed stone tumulus built by land artist Chris Drury in 1997. It is located on the end of a spit of land and surrounded by sea, skerries and sky. A curved passageway leads to a small chamber which, by means of a lens and three mirrors built into a wall, acts as a camera obscura, projecting an image of the landscape outside on to the opposite wall. You can also get to it directly from Lochmaddy by going over a footbridge near the Outdoor Activity Centre.

The third section of Route 5C is a short run to **Berneray**, which is the only permanently inhabited island in the Sound of Harris with a small but thriving population tucked in around the harbour and bays on the east coast. If you have had a long day already, the short, sharp, incline around the flank of Beinn Mhor will test your stamina. But the anticipation of visiting another island and the prospect of food at the tea rooms make it all worthwhile.

> The **causeway** that joins the island to North Uist was opened in 1998, although Berneray remains part of the parish of Harris, where many of its past residents are buried in the churchyard of St. Clements at Roghadal. Perhaps the most infamous was Donald Ruadh Macleod (1693–1781), who was married three times and fathered 29 children in all, seven following his last marriage, when he was 75 years of age. Another famous son of Berneray is Angus Mor MacAskill, who was born in 1825. Known as Giant MacAskill, he was 7 feet 9 inches tall and weighed 425 pounds. A memorial to him stands near the new graveyard. Clearly there is something in the fine Hebridean air!
>
> Berneray is an excellent place to take a rest day and enjoy some **walking**. Either follow the waymarked walk around the north of the island or wander along the 5km beach on the west side. But even if you only have an hour to kill while waiting for a ferry, ride through the village and enjoy the scenery. There is a small museum of local history, a rock near the post office where seals haul themselves out of the water, and at Baile the delightful Gatliff hostel set immediately above a white shell beach. But most of all, just enjoy the community atmosphere. There may not be many people here, but they know

how to make tourists welcome. There is even a coin-operated shower down in the fishing harbour that is available for public use.

If you are holidaying on North Uist or Berneray, using the early ferry to Leverburgh you can get 10 hours on Harris – plenty of time to enjoy Route 6.1

ROUTE 5D
Clachan to Berneray Junction

Start	Clachan
Finish	Berneray Junction
Distance	20 miles (32km)
Total Ascent	690ft (210m)
Grade	Moderate
Time	2hrs 10mins
Map	OS Landranger 1:50,000 31

On a fine day, this route around the west side of North Uist is far more rewarding than Route 5C, with views of the open sea and the prospect of a glimpse of St Kilda. Immediately you set out, there are good views of the Monach Islands, 5 miles (8km) out to sea beyond Kirkibost Island and Baleshare. It is said that they were connected to North Uist by a sand bar until it was swept away by a tidal wave in the 17th century. Despite its fertility, the last inhabitants left in the 1940s, although the islands are still used for grazing.

Heading west out of **Clachan** (✗ 5B, 5C) on the A865 there are few opportunities for refreshments, and there'll be nothing on the north coast, so grab a bite while you can. The Westford Inn at **Claddach Kirkibost** does not open until 5pm, but the Claddach Kirkibost Centre, just north of Clachan, is open during the summer months. It has a small exhibition area, an internet café and sells a range of locally-produced preserves. Further on, there are some gentle climbs and good views to the south and west. But the townships all lie at ends of side roads and the beaches and bays are hidden below the flat coastal grasslands, so it's worth making a few detours.

The loop around **Ceann a' Bhaigh** and **Paibeil** takes you past a grocery store and an animal sanctuary with a small café. The loop at **Balranald** leads to the RSPB reserve.

Balranald Reserve RSPB (NF 706 707) has sandy beaches, rocky foreshore, marshes and sand dunes and is renowned for its pioneering work in helping the corncrake re-establish itself in the Hebrides. The reserve is open daily from April to August, but the best months to visit to stand any chance of seeing a corncrake are May and June.

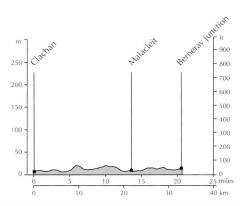

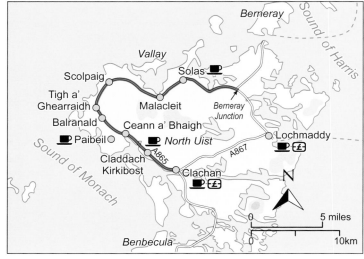

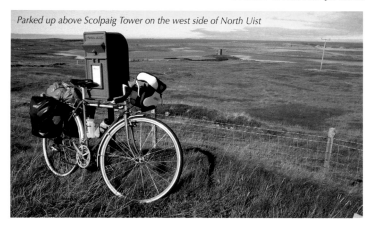
Parked up above Scolpaig Tower on the west side of North Uist

Although related to moorhens and coots, **corncrakes** live on dry land and are very secretive; spending most of their time hidden in tall vegetation. This proved to be their downfall as the introduction of mechanised mowers for haymaking drove them to seek refuge in the remaining standing grass where they were slaughtered in their thousands. Since then, mowing from the inside–out and paying crofters subsidies for growing late-cut varieties of grass that provide cover for longer has helped the breeding population recover – not that they were ever rare in continental Europe.

You can return to the main road by going through **Tigh a' Ghearraidh**, before the road starts to turn eastwards along the north coast at **Scolpaig**.

Here **Scolpaig Tower**, a folly, sits out in the loch on the site of an older dun. It was built in the 1830s by local surgeon, engineer and land improver Sir Alexander Macleod, who is better remembered today for meddling with antiquities.

On a clear day, there are views of more uninhabited islands. **Haskeir Island** is 8 miles (13km) to the northwest and another 33 miles (53km) beyond it is the **St Kilda** group. They are almost in a straight line, so if you cannot see two distinct groups, then you definitely cannot see St Kilda. Come back another day when visibility is better.

Passing a traditional tigh gael at Malacleit, North Uist

The north coast of North Uist has a surprising large conifer plantation and more sand bars and offshore islands. Vallay is accessible for two hours either side of low tide, but don't attempt it without consulting tide tables or local knowledge as the waters of the Sound of Harris are treacherous.

> The island has a number of **important ruins** – two duns and three chapels – as well as the ruins of Vallay House, an imposing Edwardian mansion built in 1902 by linen magnate, author and archaeologist Erskine Beveridge, who owned the island. His son George inherited the island when Beveridge died in 1920, but struggled with living in such isolation and is said to have sold off much of the family silver to fund his alcoholism. He drowned crossing the strand in 1944 and the island was abandoned soon afterwards.

As you enter **Malacleit**, Struan Ruadh, a traditional stone cottage with overhanging marram thatch, sits between the road and Traigh Bhalaigh.

> Overhanging thatch is a distinguishing characteristic of **whitehouses** in the southern Hebrides; the thatch sitting on the inside edge of the blackhouse walls in Harris and Lewis. This is an excellent spot for a photograph as I know of nowhere else where you can get a shot of a cyclist in front of a Hebridean whitehouse with the perfect backdrop of sand and sea. You may even be lucky enough to get a peat stack in the garden.

There is a supermarket at **Solas**, good views out into the Sound of Harris and the uninhabited islands of Boreray and Pabbay – and beyond to the Harris Hills on a clear day. At the junction with the B893, turn left for **Berneray**, following Route 4C.

DAY ROUTES

ROUTE 5.1
Circuit of Barra and Vatersay

Start/Finish	Castlebay
Distance	29 miles (46km)
Total Ascent	2660ft (810m)
Grade	Hard
Time	3hrs 10mins
Map	OS Landranger 1:50,000 31
Ferries	None on route

During the 19th century Castlebay was a bustling herring port, but don't be fooled into thinking it is now just a sleepy ferry terminal. The predominantly Catholic Barra folk have a reputation for knowing how to enjoy themselves and at weekends the bars are bursting with music and laughter. So don't stay up too late if you have a long ride ahead of you next day.

This ride is a complete circuit of Barra and its two main peninsulas.

Sneaking the opportunity to ride on Traigh Mhor beach, where the planes usually land

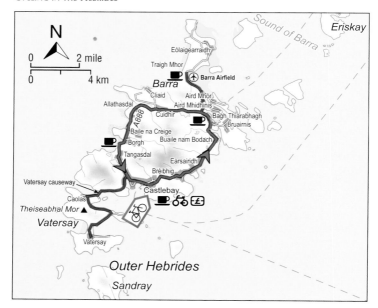

Follow Route 5A east out of **Castlebay** and through **Bagh Thiarabhagh** ('Northbay') to the turn for the ferry, then continue to **Traigh Mhor**.

> This is the only airport in the UK where planes land on the sand. Immediately behind the airport building, which has toilets and a cafe, is the building that was the home of **Compton MacKenzie**, who found fame as the author of *Whisky Galore* – the book based on how the SS Politician foundered in the Sound of Barra, leaving a cargo of whisky as easy pickings for the locals. He is buried in the cemetery just up the road at Eolaigearraidh.

Retrace your route to the main A888, then just keep heading anti-clockwise around the beautiful west side of the island where there are some enticing sandy beaches and a hotel. Pass through **Tangasdal**, then, just before re-entering **Castlebay**, turn right, climb over the the shoulder of Beinn Tangabhal and follow the road across the causeway, which was opened in 1991. Bear right at the road junction and follow the road around the flank of Theiseabhal Mor to **Bhatarsaigh** township at the road end. There is a toilet in the community centre.

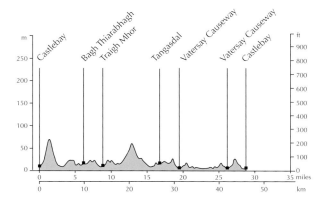

Just above the shoreline on the stretch of road above Bagh Bhatarsaigh is the remains of a **WWII Catalina** aircraft that crashed in May 1944, killing three of its nine-man crew. Further on there is a monument out on the dunes that commemorates the 350 emigrants bound for a new life in Canada who perished out in Bagh Siar in 1853 when the sailing ship, the **Annie Jane**, was wrecked.

On a clear day, a short walk up the hill beyond Bhatarsaigh burial ground gives fine views of the Bishops Isles – Sandray, Pabbay, Mingulay and Berneray – the most southerly point of the Western Isles, with Barra Head lighthouse set dramatically above 190m-high cliffs. Linger over the view before returning to **Castlebay**.

ROUTE 5.2

South Uist machair from Tobha Mor

Start/Finish	Tobha Mor (Howmore)
Distance	12 miles (19km)
Total Ascent	360ft (110m)
Grade	Easy
Time	1hr 15mins
Map	OS Landranger 1:50,000 22
Ferries	Sconser to Raasay

This route, which is one of the few loops possible in the Western Isles, is thoroughly enjoyable at any time of year but is at its best from June through to August when the machair – the 'shell meadow' behind the dunes – is carpeted with wild flowers. The ride starts amid the remains of the medieval churches and two surviving chapels at Tobha Mor (Howmore), which makes it handy for those who are staying over at the hostel and looking for an easy day. Although you could easily spend a rest day at Howmore hostel wandering through the ruins and out to the beach.

Head east to the main A865 with the prominent, yet modest summits of Hecla, Beinn Choradail and **Beinn Mhor** ahead of you. Ride south towards Dalabrog for nearly 5 miles (8km) taking a detour east to **Taobh a Tuath** – North Side – **Loch Aineort** or **Taobh a Deas** – South Side – **Loch Aineort** if you want to experience the east cost of the Uist, which is rocky and deeply split by sea lochs – a complete contrast to the long sandy beaches on the west coast.

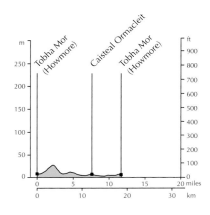

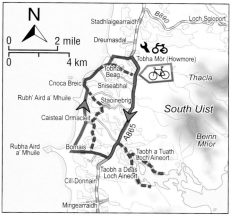

Leave the main road at the telephone box and head west towards **Bornais**. The route continues west using the tracks that take over when the road runs out and leads to the sea and the rocky headland of **Rubh' Aird a'Mhuile**, the most westerly point of the island, where there are the remains of a dun and more recent military installations.

The tracks in this area have been designated and signposted as 'The Machair Way' and provide an acceptable alternative to the tarmac road to head north to Ormacleit, where there is the ruin of the entirely misnamed **Caisteil Ormacleit**.

On the 'quiet' main road through South Uist

This was actually a **rather smart mansion** that included marble in its construction and was destroyed by fire on the day that its owner – Allan Macdonald of Clanranald – was mortally wounded at the battle of Sheriffmuir in 1715.

Route avoiding tracks

If you are not happy riding on the tracks, which are solid enough for anything other than racing tyres, but sometimes perhaps not quite as wide as OS map might lead you to expect, then turn north before **Bornais** and follow the tarmac road through Ormacleit and **Staoinebrig** ('Stoneybridge'), where a left turn leads north to **Cnoca Breic**.

Following the Machair Way north from Ormacleit Castle also leads to **Cnoca Breic** along the western shore of Loch Olaidh an Iar, and then crosses the Howmore River to reach **Tobha Mor**, a pleasant alternative to riding the tarmac road east through **Tobha Beag** and rejoining the main road.

ROUTE 5.3
Circuit of North Uist

Start/Finish	Lochmaddy
Distance	37 miles (60km)
Total Ascent	1280ft (390m)
Grade	Moderate
Time	3hrs
Map	OS Landranger 1:50,000 18
Ferries	None en route

Route 5.3 is a complete circuit of North Uist, starting and finishing in Lochmaddy and following Routes 4C and 4D, with the option of riding out and back to Berneray, which adds 7 miles (11km).

Depending on the wind, either ride clockwise, via **Barpa Langass** and **Clachan** (see Route 5C) then via excursions at **Ceann a'Bhaigh** to **Paibeil**, and **Balranald** to the nature reserve, described in Route 5D, returning through **Scolpaig**, **Malacleit**, **Solas** and **Berneray Junction**: or go anticlockwise, adapting the route descriptions accordingly.

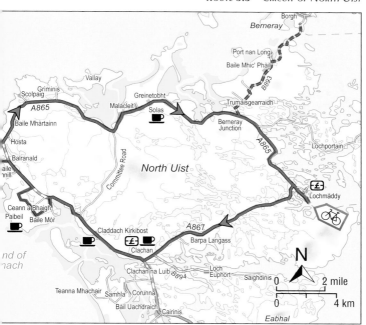

Crossing a causeway on the west side of North Uist

243

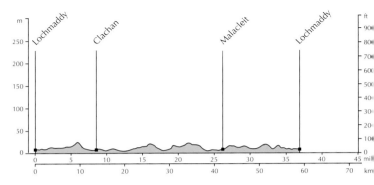

If you want to shorten the route, you can make use of the so-called **'Committee Road'** that crosses the island from south to north.

The name **'Committee Road'** reflects its origins in the 19th century, when the government initiated a number of road building schemes to provide work during periods of famine.

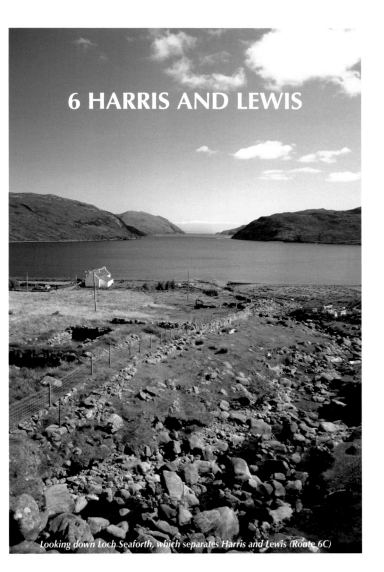

6 HARRIS AND LEWIS

Looking down Loch Seaforth, which separates Harris and Lewis (Route 6C)

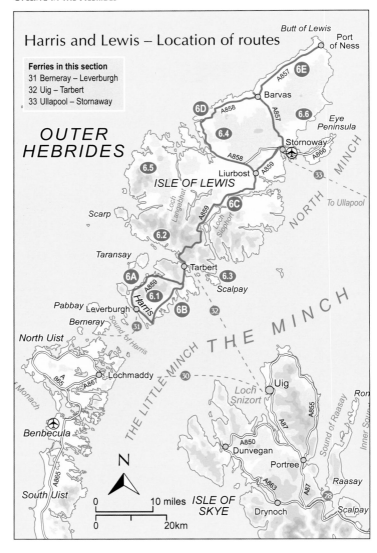

Harris and Lewis – Location of routes

Ferries in this section
31 Berneray – Leverburgh
32 Uig – Tarbert
33 Ullapool – Stornaway

OUTER
HEBRIDES

ISLE OF LEWIS

INTRODUCTION

Harris Hills from the west side of South Harris (Route 6A)

Despite being neighbours on a single landmass which is often referred to as the Long Island, Lewis and Harris are very different. With fish farming, ship building and even software development the economy of Lewis is much less dependent on tourism, although outside Stornoway, the only town in Harris and Lewis, the traditional occupations of crofting, fishing and weaving are still prevalent, with many islanders still having more than one occupation. Having seen parents and grandparents suffering from the boom-and-bust cycles of industries such as herring fishing, rendering seaweed for chemicals and weaving,

Lewis folk are proudly self-reliant and know how to get along. They also know how to enjoy themselves and although the Sabbath is still strictly observed, with no shops open or newspapers, Friday and Saturday nights on the town in Stornoway are just as noisy and boisterous as in any other small town.

Harris is a total contrast: even Lewis people talk about going there as if it was another country. In many ways it is – or at least was. In the past the mountains of Harris formed a substantial natural barrier between Lewis and Harris, and the sea rather than road was the main means of communication and transportation. It's easy to see why, despite being part of the same land mass, they have retained the names Isle of Lewis and Isle of Harris. Everything happened at the periphery where the land meets the sea and even today there are few landlocked villages anywhere on the island.

The division was more than geographic: until 1974 it extended to local government, with Lewis being part of the county of Ross and Cromarty and Harris part of the county of Inverness. Together with the other islands of the Outer Hebrides they are now both parts of *Comhairle nan Eilean Siar* – the Western Isles Council, headquartered in Stornoway.

Compared to Lewis, Harris has far fewer of most things that seem to count in the modern world. It has a smaller population, with barely 2000 people compared to the 18,000 on Lewis. Having little industry other than agriculture, fishing and tourism, it is far less industrialised than its neighbour. And with none of the memorials to the land struggle or the staunch resistance to Lord Leverhulme's ambitions that can be found in Lewis, this suggests that Harris folk are perhaps more tolerant and easier going. It is also said that the Gaelic spoken in Harris has a softer lilt to it than that spoken in Lewis. Certainly everything else about the place seems to have a similar charm. But don't dismiss either. Harris may have higher hills and a greater number of beaches, but Lewis has more prehistory and tourist attractions.

Isle of Harris

Harris neatly divides into two parts at the narrow isthmus of Tarbert. North Harris is characterised by high hills, with An Cliseam (799m/2622 feet) being the highest and the only Corbett – a Scottish peak between 2500 and 3000 feet. For many years, North Harris was owned by private landlords. Although they did not suffer unduly under this arrangement, in 2003 the crofters and tenants established the North Harris Trust and secured funding to buy 58,000 acres of land and effectively become their own landlord.

Since then, further funding has allowed the Trust to purchase the 7,472 acre Loch Seaforth Estate. The Trust has numerous projects for the considered regeneration of North Harris, including providing low-cost housing for rent, tree planting, building a small wind farm to generate electricity for local consumption and restoring the old footpaths and drover roads. In February 2009 the majority of residents in North Harris voted to pursue National Park status. Unfortunately their submission was rejected by the Scottish Parliament possibly due to inadequate funding. The opportunity will come again.

The fertile west side of South Harris, with its fringe of bone white beaches, has been in community ownership since 2010 and there are now initiatives in place to inject life back into the area through the creation of crofts, affordable house sites and renewable energy schemes. The east side of South Harris changes again, with little communities tucked in around the head of each deeply indented sea loch.

Isle of Lewis

Lewis is flatter than Harris, with larger areas of more fertile land that fringe the central peat moor. Consequently it has always been able to support more people and today Lewis accounts for three quarters of the population of the Western Isles, with the majority living on the east coast in and around Stornoway.

Lewis has a strong Presbyterian tradition with many in the community wanting to maintain strict Sabbath observance. Others are not so sure, and in recent years there have been many well-publicised showdowns over the introduction of the Sunday ferry and the issuing of a license for the Sunday opening of the golf club bar.

But even without the religious aspect, life can seem very different from elsewhere in the Hebrides, with the Gaelic language and even peat cutting retaining more importance than elsewhere.

Uigen, at typical settlement in West Lewis (Route 6.5)

LEVERHULME AND THE LONG ISLAND

Lord Leverhulme bought Lewis in 1918 and immediately initiated and personally funded a series of ambitious schemes designed to transform it into a vibrant economy based on fishing and chemicals. But faced with a population whose steadfast desire to be self-sufficient subsistence crofters was stronger than his drive to turn them into waged factory workers, his plans came to nothing. In 1923, when he abandoned Lewis to concentrate on Harris, which he had bought in 1919, he offered the land to the populace to be held in local trusts. Only the town of Stornoway took up the offer and established the Stornoway Trust to administer the land. The trust was a unique institution until fairly recently, when other highland and island communities, such as the North Harris Trust, have taken land into communal ownership.

When he died in 1925 Leverhulme's estate quickly sold off both Harris and the rest of Lewis at knock-down prices. It is easy to point to the relics and follies that mark his time here, such as the Bridge to Nowhere (Route 6.6), and silently gloat. But while he may not have shown sufficient empathy with the people whose lives he wanted to change, the islanders may have been better off by embracing some of Leverhulme's ideas. He was adamant that small scale crofting would not result in wide-spread prosperity and, for the most part, history has proved him right.

LINK ROUTES

ROUTE 6A
Leverburgh to Tarbert (west)

Start	Leverburgh
Finish	Tarbert
Distance	21 miles (34km)
Total Ascent	1280ft (390m)
Grade	Moderate
Time	2hrs 10mins
Map	OS Landranger 1:50,000 14, 18

As soon as you arrive at Leverburgh, after the dog-leg ferry ride across the Sound of Harris, you are presented with a choice – to go up the west side of South Harris or the east? Both have their appeal. The more fertile west coast has good views out across sandy beaches to Taransay and the North Harris Hills, but there is more traffic on the road. On the other hand the switchback ride up the east coast (Route 6B) is more exhilarating and will appeal to the more committed rider.

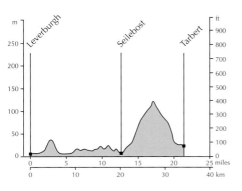

Link Route 6A starts with dreary ascent up Gleann Choiseleitir, hemmed in by low hills on both sides, but as you approach the summit you are rewarded with a view of Ceapabhal and Taransay across Traigh Sgarasta, the first of a number of wide sandy bays along the west coast.

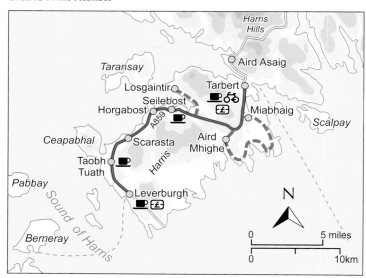

Killegray – one of the many islands in the Sound of Harris

There is a **luxury bird hide** (with toilets and café) – marked as a visitor centre on the map – at the far end of **Taobh Tuath**. This is both a good place to watch the many species of waders that collect out on the saltings and to shelter from inclement weather.

After a stretch of single track skirting around Maodal, there are two lanes all the way through the small townships of **Scarasta**, Na Buirgh, **Horgabost** and **Seilebost**. There are plenty of places to get down onto the beaches, but if you turn off the main road and ride down to **Losgaintir** you will come to Traigh Rosamul, which is perhaps the most magical Hebridean beach of all with fine views – and equally fine toilets.

The next part of the route consists of a steady climb into the interior of South Harris. It looks so 'lunar' that it stood in as the planet Jupiter for the filming of the sci-fi movie *2001: A Space Odyssey* back in 1968. If you are beginning to regret not sampling the east coast, you can drop down either of the minor roads that lead down to the Bays – the first that sweeps sharply down to **Aird Mhighe** is by far the best – and ride into **Tarbert** (✈6B, 6C) along the final stretches of Route 6B. Otherwise keep on the main road and enjoy the unfolding views across East Loch Tarbert.

ROUTE 6B
Leverburgh to Tarbert (east)

Start	Leverburgh
Finish	Tarbert
Distance	26 miles (42km)
Total Ascent	2030ft (620m)
Grade	Hard
Time	2hrs 15mins
Map	OS Landranger 1:50,000 14, 18

Route 6B – the 'Golden Road' – so called because of the cost involved in its construction in the 1930s – which links the little fishing villages of the Bays on the east coast of Harris, is a more exhilarating, yet harder ride than that on the west coast (Route 6A) and comes more highly recommended here. The community café at Geocrab and the nearby Skoon Art Café are the only places for food along the way so you are advised to top up there.

The route starts inauspiciously with a steady climb up Gleann Shranndabhal, but once over the summit you are rewarded with a fast descent down to **Roghadal**.

> **St Clement's Church**, which dates from the first part of the 16th century, is a handsome building, but it's the interior that is the real jewel, with a number of wall tombs and grave slabs judged to be the finest late-medieval sculpture to survive in the Western Isles. The intricate carvings depict a mixture of religious themes and scenes reflecting the status of Alasdair Crotach ('Hunchback') MacLeod, the 8th chief of the clan who commissioned the tomb and saw it completed in 1528, well in advance of his death 19 years later. He was clearly vain despite his injury.
>
> Before you leave Roghadal, ride round to see the **quay and outbuildings** which were built by Captain Alexander MacLeod, a descendant of the Berneray MacLeods, in 1779. His intention was to establish a viable fishing industry, but local rivalry from Lewis and the unpredictability of herring put paid to MacLeod's plans. Today the basin at Roghadal remains a safe harbour for passing yachts and MacLeod's house is a hotel.

As soon as you head north on the minor road, you are immediately into the Bays.

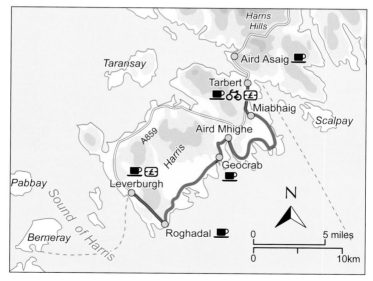

Abandoned blackhouses at Ob Leasaid on the 'Golden Road'

During the **clearances** of the 19th century, those families that didn't choose to emigrate were displaced to the barren rock of the east coast leaving the rich grazing of the western machair for the sheep. But rather than perish, these hardy people flourished, fishing both the sea and the many trout lochs of the hinterland and building up layers of peat and seaweed to create lazybeds to grow potatoes and oats.

Today there is a small township at the head of almost every inlet and many people are still involved in inshore fishing, fish farming and occasionally knitting or weaving. Over the years, they have been joined by a growing number of artists and craftspeople, making the Bays the creative corner of Harris.

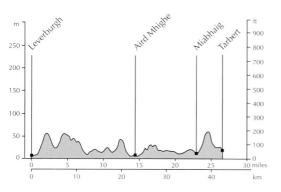

The Golden Road continues its switchback course for the best part of 12½ miles (20km), dipping down to cross the little bridges at the head of each bay before climbing across the shoulder of a small hill to drop into the next – with fine views out across the Minch to the Cuillin of Skye on a clear day. There are opportunities to curtail the ride and head for Tarbert at **Geocrab** and **Aird Mhighe** – and at both junctions you need to ensure you take the right hand turn to keep following the Golden Road.

The final few miles through the villages on the south side of East Loch Tarbert go easily enough, with views north to Scalpay and the hills of southeast Lewis, but the 70m climb from **Miabhaig** to the main road requires some reserves of energy. After that it's easy pedalling into **Tarbert** (✗ 6A, 6C), which has all the facilities you are likely to need.

ROUTE 6C
Tarbert to Stornoway

Start	Tarbert
Finish	Stornoway
Distance	36 miles (57km)
Total Ascent	2590ft (790m)
Grade	Hard to Liurbost, then Easy
Time	4hrs
Map	OS Landranger 1:50,000 8

Despite being part of the same mass, Harris and Lewis are still referred to as 'isles' recalling a time before the arrival of the motor vehicle, when boats were the main form of transport. Route 6C climbs through the north Harris Hills, which once formed a near-impenetrable barrier, and then snakes through the undulating moors of southeast Lewis.

Leave **Tarbert** (✗ 6A, 6C) and join the main A859 heading for Stornoway. Stock up with food at **Aird Asaig**, as other than a sub-Post Office at Baile Ailein this is the only shop you'll pass until Liurbost, and you are in for an energy-sapping climb.

In fact the hardest part of the route is soon with you. As soon as you cross the bridge over the Skeaudale River and ascend through the rock cutting, the incline reaches 15% for about 500m. Stick with it, as the angle soon eases and the remainder of the climb onto the **Harris Hills** is surprisingly pleasant. The road surface is a delight and there are good views left up to the summit of An Cliseam, down to the fjord-like **Loch Seaforth** and beyond to the hills of southeast Lewis.

The hairpin bend above **Scaladal** is a good **viewpoint** for a break before the exhilarating descent back down to sea level. It is also a good place for spotting a **Golden Eagle**. Just scan the sky high above the loch or inland towards the hills. If it looks like an ironing board with shirt sleeves hanging over the end, most likely it's an eagle.

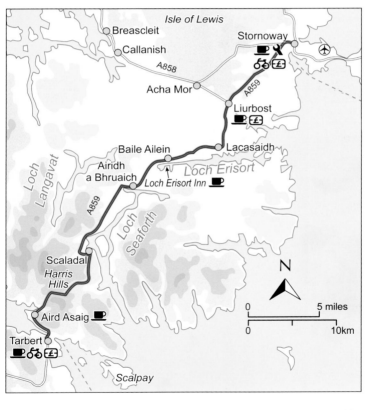

257

Passing Loch Bhaltois in Lewis

The route continues with a steady gradient up through the Loch Aline community woodlands and over the border into Lewis. At **Airidh a Bhruaich**, a roadside monument commemorates Bonnie Prince Charlie passing through in 1745, and further on a cairn at the turn for Eisgein remembers the local men and women who raided the Pairc Deer Park in November 1887 to make a peaceful protest about their conditions. If you are feeling peckish, then a short detour down the B8060 leads to the **Loch Erisort Inn**, which serves food from midday onwards except during winter months. Otherwise, continue through the long, linear township of **Baile Ailein**, making use of a short section of cycle lane, and onwards through **Lacasaidh** to **Liurbost** (29/47). The garage on the Stornoway side of the village has a well-stocked shop and a café.

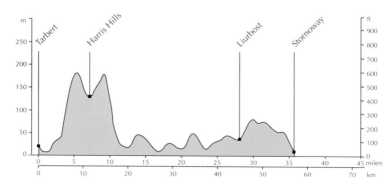

The more interesting and attractive bits of the **Isle of Lewis** are along the coast; the inland area consists of mile after mile of bleak peat moor pitted with lochans and broken only by an occasional, low-lying hill. On a sunny day, you will perhaps discover some beauty in the empty landscape of this section of the link route, but if it's grey and you find yourself pedalling into a headwind you will wonder why you ever came.

The stage continues along the A859 into **Stornoway** (36/57), with little of interest until you reach the town, which is the administrative capital and home to more than a third of the 25,000 population of the Western Isles. If you are heading into the town, turn right into Macaulay Road at the first roundabout and then look out for Charles Macleod – otherwise know as 'Charley Barley', butcher and maker of the world famous Stornoway black pudding – tucked in alongside the supermarket. If you've had enough of black pudding while staying in bed and breakfasts, let them entice you with some fruit pudding, white pudding or haggis. Otherwise pedal on down Bayhead.

> **Lews Castle**, up above the harbour on the right, was built by Sir James Matheson, who purchased Lewis in 1844 with a fortune gained in opium trading in the Far East. It is now a white elephant in need of major repair and is closed to the public, although you can walk through the extensive woodlands where there is a pleasant café.
>
> **Museum nan Eilean**, on Francis Street, has an extensive collection of archeological and historical artifacts to do with island life.
>
> **An Lanntair**, near the ferry terminal, has changing exhibitions of art and crafts; a busy calendar of theatre, music and cinema and a restaurant and bar that are open from 10am until late every day but the Sabbath.

The introduction of the Sunday ferry looks to be the start of a softening of the traditionally strict observance of the Sabbath, but currently Stornoway is 'closed' on Sundays, although you will actually find a few bars and hotel restaurants open for business.

ROUTE 6D

Liurbost to Barabhas

Start	Liurbost
Finish	Barabhas
Distance	32 miles (51km)
Total Ascent	1410ft (430m)
Grade	Moderate
Time	3hrs 20mins
Map	OS Landranger 1:50,000 8

Route 6D is a ride of two halves. The first half from Liurbost to Gearraidh na h-Aibhne consists of a gentle ascent up through Acha Mor, one of only three inland villages on Harris and Lewis, followed by a series of short blind summits. On a clear day there are good views south to the Harris Hills and over to the Uig Hills in West Lewis in the far distance. But once on the 'west side', there are lots of interesting places to stop off.

Leaving **Liurbost** (✗6C) it's an easy ride on the A858 through **Acha Mor** to **Callanish**, famous for its standing stones.

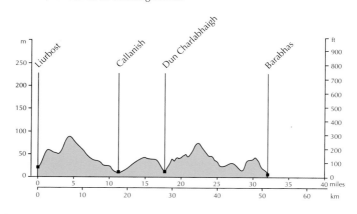

Passing the standing stones at Callanish

Two smaller, well-preserved **stone circles**, Callanish II and Callanish III, are visible on the left as you enter the village, but Callanish I is accessed from the visitor centre, which has a shop and a good café.

There are numerous theories about the **meaning and purpose of stone circles** such as those found at Callanish. Many people believe they were used in rituals relating to the moon, stars and the position of the distant hills. Whatever inspired their construction; all agree that the experience of visiting the Standing Stones of Callanish is not to be missed, especially during sunrises, sunsets and at times when the moon is full.

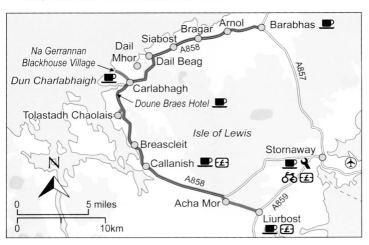

As you leave the visitor centre, turn immediately left and cycle right past the stones. It's a steep little climb, but it's an iconic spot for a photograph before the road leads on to **Breascleit**.

> The red-paint of the **fish oil processing plant** at Breascleit gives it a Nordic look. But look right to the prominent white building with heavy stone lintels and crow-stepped gables. It was newly built to house the families of the keepers of the lighthouse on The Flannan Isles which lie 21 miles northwest of Gallan Head off the Atlantic coast of North Lewis.
>
> The light was first lit on 7 December 1899, but just a year later three lighthouse keepers disappeared in strange circumstances, presumably swept away during a storm. No wonder it became such a famous event, encountered in many an English lesson in the famous poem by WW Gibson.

If you want a break from the main road, take a detour through the village of **Tolastadh Chaolais**, which is on a short loop on the left. Otherwise carry on past the **Doune Braes Hotel** to **Dun Charlabhaigh**.

> This imposing **broch** is thought to date from the last century BC. Two thousand years later and much the worse for being stormed by raiders and pillaged for building materials, it still looks an imposing structure and a visible statement of status and power. It is thought to have been a defensible refuge that could house an extended family and their animals if they came under threat, much like a modern day air-raid shelter.
>
> It is not known how long it remained in use or when it fell into disrepair. It seems to have been still largely complete in the 1500s, when some of the Morrison clan used it as a refuge from the MacAulays, from whom they had been stealing cattle. The story goes that Donald Cam MacAulay climbed the broch by inserting dirks into the exterior wall and threw in burning heather, suffocating the Morrisons.
>
> The broch is next mentioned in a report by the local Minister in 1797. Dun Carlobhagh featured prominently in reports on Western Isles brochs in the latter part of the 19th century and as a result it was one of the very first ancient monuments in Scotland to be taken into state care. But by then a large amount of material had been removed, probably for building blackhouses such as the one whose walls still stand below the access path.

At Carlabhagh, turn left to **Na Gearrannan Blackhouse Village**, where there is a museum, shop, café and hostel, the latter sadly closed at the time of writing.

Dun Charlabhaigh

Don't be fooled into thinking that what you see inside the blackhouses today accurately portrays how it was when people lived there.

On the way back to the main road, stop off at the Blue Pig Gallery and say hello to Jane, who specialises in long, stream-of-consciousness paintings of the local landscape. Further along the main road, the narrow beaches of **Dail Mhor** – much loved by surfers – and **Dail Beag** lie a short detour off on the left. Then comes a series of typical 'west side' villages: **Siabost**, where the tweed mill is leading the renaissance of Harris Tweed; **Bragar**, with it famous whalebone arch; and **Arnol**, with its blackhouse museum. Finally the route arrives at **Barabhas** (✗6E).

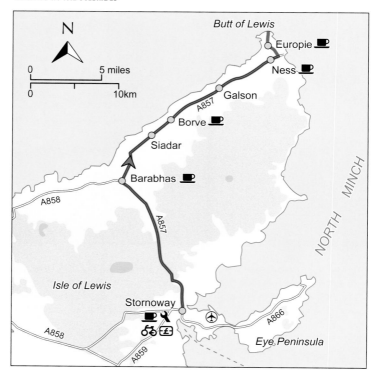

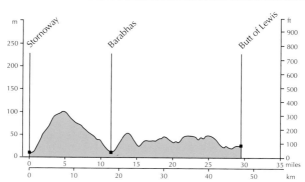

ROUTE 6E
Stornoway to Butt of Lewis

Start	Stornoway
Finish	Butt of Lewis
Distance	29 miles (47km)
Total Ascent	1480ft (450m)
Grade	Easy
Time	3hrs 10mins
Map	OS Landranger 1:50,000 8

Route 6E leads from Stornoway across Lewis to Barabhas on the island's west coast, after which it's not really a link route but a glorious dead end, included here because the Butt of Lewis is the goal for many cyclists touring the Hebrides. Some folk will have had poor weather; others may have developed sore unmentionables and struggled up the Western Isles wondering whether they have set themselves an objective beyond their capabilities. No matter, you're here now with only 17 miles (27km) remaining and no matter how tired you may feel, the prospect of arriving at this extreme outpost of Europe will lift the spirit and help you find new reserves of energy. The miles will fly by. Enjoy them.

The route begins following the A857 out of **Stornoway** (✗ 6C) and north to **Barabhas** (✗ 6D). But as there is little of interest beyond the town until the route has crossed the island, from the ferry terminal follow the A866 along James Street for half a mile, before turning left into Matheson Road to follow the B8027. For ¾ of a mile, before Matheson Road joins the main A857, enjoy this fine avenue of late Victorian and Edwardian villas, particularly the cast iron railings that many still retain. Most of these were made in the Saracen Foundry in Glasgow, which had a catalogue full of moulds, so patterns can still be reproduced. The Town Council provides grant aid to encourage householders to restore missing pieces.

At the end of Matheson Road, turn right at the roundabout and head north to Barabhas. Initially there are good views out across Broad Bay, but eventually all you are left with is the moor and the sky until you reach **Barabhas** (12/19) and

On the quay at Stornoway

get views of the Atlantic. The garage has a well-stocked shop and does takeaway curries on Friday evenings.

From here it's 17 miles (27km) to the Butt of Lewis, the end of the complete cycle tour through the Hebrides.

> The **Morven Gallery** – www.morvengallery.com – just north of Barabhas is open from April to October and has changing exhibitions of some of the leading artists from across the region. They also do an irresistible coffee and walnut cake in their café.

After a stretch of open moor with wide views of the Atlantic out beyond the croft land comes **Siadar**.

> Just as you enter the village, a short detour on the left leads to **Clach an Truiseil**, 'The Thrushel Stone', which is the tallest standing stone in Scotland. Further on, on the opposite side of the road, is **Steinacleit**, which has the remains of either a chambered cairn or some kind of domestic settlement in the middle of a 16m oval of upright slabs.

After passing through **Borve** and **Galson** another section of open moor brings you to the final string of villages that are collectively known as **Ness**.

This is a surprising **buoyant community** for such an isolated place. The inn at Cros has local seafood on the menu: the volunteers who run the community heritage centre in Tabost bake exceedingly good cakes, and the local football club is apparently thriving, although I cannot envisage what tactics are called into play to make the most of a force 8 cross wind.

Turn left at Lionel and follow the signs for the Butt of Lewis. There is another tearoom at **Europie** and then it's out through the back of the crofts and past the isolated St Moluag's church to the lighthouse at the **Butt of Lewis**.

The red-brick **lighthouse** was built by brothers David and Thomas Stevenson in 1862 and remains an important beacon for shipping. The brothers were members of the third generation of the famous Stevenson family who designed and built 97 lighthouses around the Scottish coastline over a span of 126 years that ended in 1937. Thomas's son, Robert Louis Stevenson, was a great disappointment to his father in that he chose not to enter the family profession, instead finding fame as the author of classics including *Treasure Island* and *Strange Case of Dr Jekyll and Mr Hyde*.

If this remote place has been your goal for the last week or so, no doubt you will be feeling slightly strange too. Now all you have to do is cycle back to Barabhas (17/27) and either retrace the route back to Stornoway or join route 6D back towards Callanish.

Stormy weather near the Butt of Lewis

DAY ROUTES

ROUTE 6.1

Circuit of south Harris

Start/Finish	Tarbert
Distance	47 miles (74km)
Total Ascent	3640ft (1110m)
Grade	Hard
Time	4hrs 30mins
Map	OS Landranger 1:50,000 14, 18
Ferries	None on route

Route 6.1 is a complete circuit of south Harris, taking in the sweeping main road on the west coast – Route 6A —and the big-dipper experience of the 'Golden Road' on the east side – Route 6B.

Leverburgh

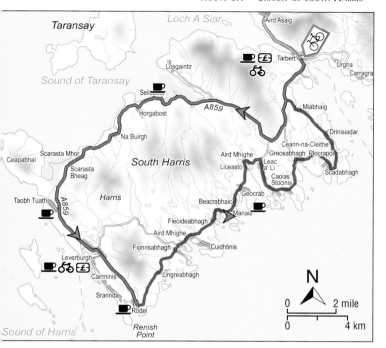

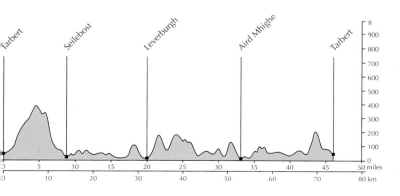

If you start at **Tarbert** then, having gone through **Seilebost**, **Leverburgh** is the obvious spot for lunch, with two places to eat, The Anchorage restaurant near the ferry terminal and the An Clachan café above the community shop. If you start at Leverburgh, then you will find plenty of choice in Tarbert, which has everything from fine dining to fish and chips.

Should you wish to, you can shorten the ride by taking a short cut along one of the minor roads that run between **Aird Mhighe** or **Greosabhagh** and the main A859. But this would be madness unless it was blowing a gale or you were in distress: this is Hebridean cycling at its finest.

ROUTE 6.2
Huisinis from Tarbert

Start/Finish	Tarbert
Distance	33 miles (53km)
Total Ascent	3540ft (1080m)
Grade	Hard
Time	4hrs 30mins
Map	OS Landranger 1:50,000 14, 18
Ferries	None on route

There are no circular rides in North Harris, only out-and-back trips to road ends. All are fine rides, but this one is perhaps the pick of the bunch, in that it takes you close to the North Harris Hills before ending at a small township with a pristine beach and views to the uninhabited island of Scarp.

Leave **Tarbert** and join the A859 main road heading towards Stornoway, steadily climbing alongside West Loch Tarbert to reach Aird Asaig. Past here there is nowhere to eat on the route so stock up at the shop if you need to.

As you set off again, **An Cliseam**, the highest summit in the Western Isles at 799m (2621ft) stands proud immediately in front of you.

Turn left onto the B887, following signs for Huisinis, and keep going pass the old whaling station and the entirely unexpected all-weather tennis court at **Bun Abhainn Eadarra**, to climb the hardest hill of the route to **Miabhaig**, where there

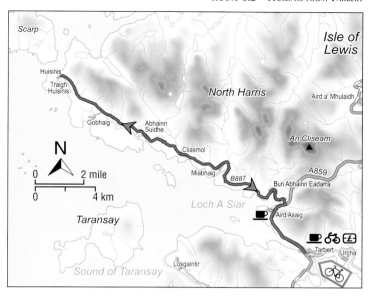

are good views up the glen to the prominent nose of Sron Scourst. The next climb takes you through **Cliasmol** before a gentle descent to Loch Leosavay, where the road passes in front of Amhuinnsuidhe Castle – a Victorian retreat that is now a sporting lodge.

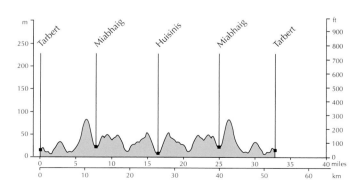

271

Traigh Huisinis at the end of the road in North Harris

After this the road cuts inland until you reach **Huisinis**.

The township has the most beautifully situated **public conveniences** in the UK. You would happily leave the door open to enjoy the view!

When it's washed by turquoise waves coming in from the Atlantic, many people would rank the silver beach of **Traigh Huisinis** as one of the most enchanting places there is anywhere in the world. A walk over the machair to the jetty gives a view of the village on Scarp – which lost its last permanent residents in 1971 – and further north to the remote Uig hills of West Lewis.

When you can finally tear yourself away, return the way you came.

ROUTE 6.3
Scalpay from Tarbert

Start/Finish	Tarbert
Distance	16 miles (26km)
Total Ascent	2030ft (620m)
Grade	Moderate
Time	1hr 45mins
Map	OS Landranger 1:50,000 14
Ferries	None on route

The island of Scalpay is riddled with sea lochs, many of which face into East Loch Tarbert and have right angle turns in them. This makes them ideal harbours for the small boats whose crews earn their living today fishing for shellfish. Until recently, this business was so lucrative that the people of Harris are said to refer to Scalpay as 'Treasure Island'.

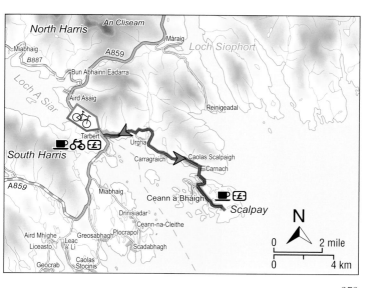

Head east out of **Tarbert** and follow signs for Scalpay. There is no time for relaxing as there is a succession of short climbs all the way to the bridge, first up around Little Urgha Bay and then up around Urgha Bay and through **Urgha** – followed by a nasty little sting in the tail just before the string of crofts that line the road before the bridge at **Caolas Scalpaigh**.

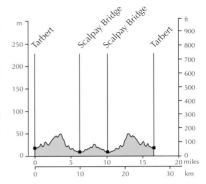

In 1996 Prime Minister Tony Blair formally opened the £6.4m **Scalpay Bridge**, replacing the ferry that previously shuttled back and forth. Not only was it a significant event for Scalpay and Harris, helping to secure investment and jobs at a new seafood processing plant, it was the fist time that a serving prime minister had ever been to the Outer Hebrides. Sadly the seafood processing plant failed. But the Scalpaichs are resilient and will live to fight another day. At the time of writing they are debating whether to take up the current landlord's generous offer of taking the island into community ownership and are re-opening the island's only shop.

Once on **Scalpay**, the road twists and turns past North Harbour, then South Harbour before coming to an end at **Ceann a Bhaigh**.

Bridge over Caolas Scalpaigh

Out to sea there are **islands and skerries** everywhere, with the northern peninsulas of Skye prominent on the other side of The Minch.

From here an occasionally waymarked path leads around the coast to Eilean Glas Lighthouse – built by Thomas Smith, stepfather to Robert Stevenson, the first of the famous Lighthouse Stevensons – and first lit in 1789. It is an interesting spot with the remains of the keeper's gardens and substantial quays where supplies were delivered. But it is 1¼ miles (2km) away and it is not the type of path you would want to negotiate in cleats. So unless you have some suitable walking shoe, perhaps it's best to head back to **Tarbert**.

ROUTE 6.4
Callanish by the Pentland Road

Start/Finish	Stornoway
Distance	39 miles (63m)
Total Ascent	1740ft (530m)
Grade	Moderate
Time	4hrs 30mins
Map	OS Landranger 1:50,000 18
Ferries	None on route

This is a circular ride that starts and finishes in Stornoway and takes in the best heritage sites while keeping off the main roads as much as possible.

As you head south out of **Stornoway** on the A859 towards Tarbert you will have the Lewis war memorial on the skyline to your right. Turn right at a minor road signposted for the Waste Recycling site, then immediately left at a telephone box onto Rathad a' Phentland ('The Pentland Road').

The straightness of this road betrays its origins as the proposed route of a railway that **Lord Leverhulme** planned to carry fish from Carlabhagh on the west side across the island to Stornoway for processing. The scheme was abandoned in 1919, when Leverhulme relinquished his plans for Lewis and turned his attention to Harris.

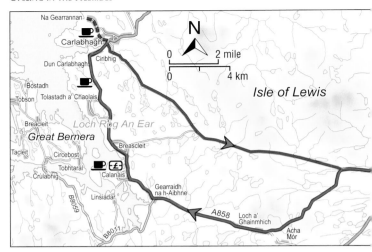

Turn left at the fork in the road down to **Acha Mor**, to join Route 6D. Follow it to **Carlabhagh**, visiting the stones at **Calanais**, **Dun Carlabhagh** and **Na Gearrannan Blackhouse Village**.

On returning to **Carlabhagh**, drop down to the minor road that goes under the main A858, using a bridge intended to carry the road over Leverhulme's railway, and follow it up alongside Abhainn Charlabhaigh and onto the moor. This is the western end of The Pentland Road and will take you all the way back to **Stornoway**.

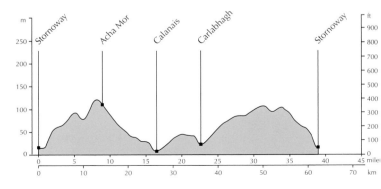

The Callanish stones

ROUTE 6.5

West Lewis from Gearraidh na h-Aibhne

Start/Finish	Gearraidh na h-Aibhne
Distance	56 miles (90km)
Total Ascent	4000ft (1220m)
Grade	Moderate
Time	6hrs
Map	OS Landranger 1:50,000 8, 13
Ferries	None on route

This ride, which goes out and around the Uig Hills of West Lewis, could rightly claim to be the last dead end in Europe. We may think it leads nowhere, but step back 200 years to the time when people had to grow their own food and this road would have lead to a thriving population making a living on the fertile soils of the western seaboard. The road has been considerably improved in recent years and although there is still a fair amount of climbing, all of it is mercifully short and fairly gentle.

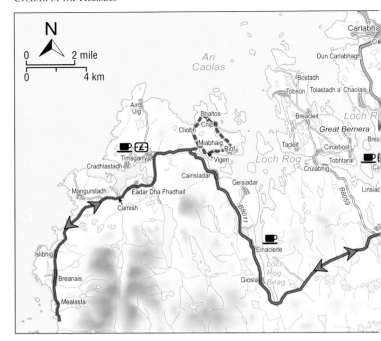

Mealaisbhal – the highest summit in Lewis – from Mangurstadh

Leave **Gearraigh na h-Aibhne**, home of one of the island's sporting estates, and head west along the B8011.

Initially, it is a watery and bleak landscape. The standing stones of **Calanais I** can briefly be seen across Loch Ceann Hulabhig and nearby on the north side of the road sits the smaller circle of Callanish IV.

Further on the Grimersta River looks to be nothing special, but is one of the most productive and expensive **salmon rivers** in Scotland, although these days catches are not what they once were.

There is a military-looking bus shelter clearly built to withstand substantial gales, but not much else until the road swings northwards and gives good views down on to **Loch Rog Beag** ('Little Loch Rog'). After **Einacleite** the road moves away from the coast and runs alongside Loch Croistean, before re-emerging at **Cairisiadar**. Once past the little harbour at **Miabhaig** the road cuts through Gleann Bhaltois, a spectacular channel created by glacial meltwater, to emerge at **Timsgarry**, where the community shop has a hot drinks machine.

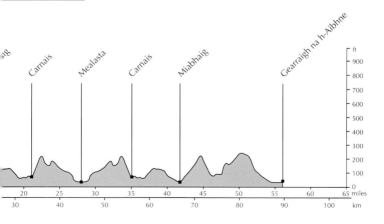

Turn right at Miabhaig for a short detour around the **Riof peninsula**, with its white sands and fine views across to Great Bernera.

The road runs around the back of the magnificent sands of Traighe Uuighe and past the Victorian pile of Uig Lodge, which was built as a sporting retreat by James Matheson and subsequently owned by Lord Leverhulme who gave it to a niece as a wedding present. There is a short sharp ascent at **Carnish** before the road pops out on the wild rocky west coast with the Flannan Isles 20 miles (32km) away in a northeasterly direction and perhaps even sight of St Kilda 40 miles (64km) away in the southwest.

Abhainn Dearg whisky, named after its location beside Abhainn an Ath' Deirg ('the Red River') at Carnish, is the first legal distillery on Lewis for over 170 years.

The road briefly cuts inland through the tiny townships of **Islibhig** and **Breanais** before rejoining at the cliffs at **Mealasta** and coming to an end at the slipway. There is nowhere else to go. On a fine summer's day, there is nowhere else you would want to be and it's difficult to tear yourself away for the return journey.

ROUTE 6.6

The Bridge to Nowhere from Stornoway

Start/Finish	Stornoway
Distance	32 miles (52km)
Total Ascent	2200ft (670m)
Grade	Moderate
Time	3hrs 10mins
Map	OS Landranger 1:50,000 8
Ferries	None on route

The 'Bridge to Nowhere' (OS grid reference NB 531501), which spans Abhainn Ghearadha, is an early example of pre-stressed concrete construction and is all that remains of Lord Leverhulme's scheme to push a road through to Ness. There have been a number of proposals to put a road through ever since, but clearly none met with success. Marvel at the folly of man's desire to change the world. Better still, park up and take a walk on the sands.

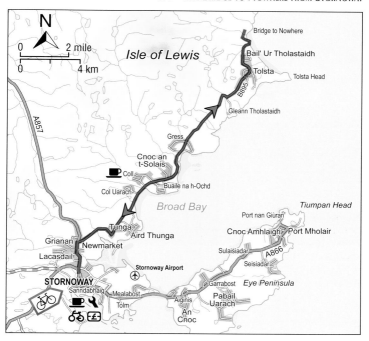

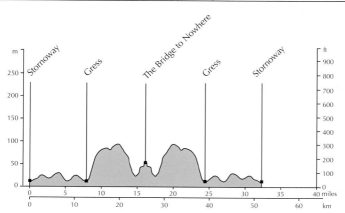

Caisteal a' Mhorair

Pick up the A857 signpost for Barvas and ride through the northern suburbs of **Stornoway** to **Newmarket**, and then turn right on to the B895 signpost for Tolsta. It is easy going around Broad Bay through **Coll** and past the memorial to the land raids in **Gress** before a climb up a new stretch of road leads into **Tolsta**. Carry on through the village to the end of the B895 road, cross the cattle grid and follow the unfenced road northwards, with views down the expanse of Traigh Mhor ('Big Beach'), towards **Tolsta Head** and across The Minch to the prominent peak of Suilven and its neighbours.

> As the road passes below Ben Geiraha, the smaller beach of **Traigh Ghearadha** ('Garry Beach') comes into view, with the remains of Caisteal a' Mhorair precariously perched on one of the prominent rock stacks that tower 21m (70ft) above the sands. It is thought to be the remains of a medieval stronghold or a 'late dun'.

Continue northwards to admire the '**Bridge to Nowhere**' before turning round and heading back into town.

APPENDIX A

Link route summary table

Section 1: Clyde and Kintyre

Ferries are numbered as listed in Appendix C and as on the maps.

No	Location	Route	Distance miles (km)	Time (at 9mph/15kph)	Connecting link routes	Links to ferries
1A	Mainland	Gourock – Wemyss Bay – Largs – Ardrossan	28 (45)	3hrs		1a, 1b, 2, 3, 4
1B	Mainland	Dunoon – Auchenbreck – Portavadie	29 (46)	3hrs 10mins	1C	4, 6
1C	Bute	Rothesay – Colintraive – Auchenbreck	14 (23)	1hr 40mins	1B	3, 5
1D	Arran	Brodick – Lochranza	14 (23)	1hr 40mins		1a, 1b, 1c, 7
1E	Mainland	Claonaig – Kennacraig – Tayinloan	19 (31)	2hrs 15mins	1F	7, 8, 9, 11
1F	Mainland	Kennacraig – Oban	57 (92)	6hrs 20mins	1E	6, 9, 11, 12, 15, 16, 17, 23, 28
Stage 1		Kennacraig – Tarbet	5 (8)	40mins		
Stage 2		Tarbet – Bellanoch	18 (30)	2hrs		
Stage 3		Bellanoch – Oban	34 (54)	3hrs 40mins		

Section 2: Colonsay, Islay and Jura

No	Location	Route	Distance miles (km)	Time (at 9mph/15kph)	Connecting link routes	Links to ferries
2A	Islay	Port Ellen – Port Askaig	18 (30)	2hrs		9, 10, 11

283

Section 3: Mull, Tiree and Coll

No	Location	Route	Distance miles (km)	Time (at 9mph/15kph)	Connecting link routes	Links to ferries
3A	Mull	Craignure – Fishnish – Tobermory	17 (27)	2hrs 30mins		16, 20, 21
3B	Mainland	Lochaline – Salen	30 (48)	3hrs 30mins	3C, 3D	20
3C	Mainland	Salen – Laga – Kilchoan	20 (32)	2hrs 20mins	3B, 3D	21
3D	Mainland	Salen – Mallaig	38 (60)	4hrs 25mins	3B, 3C	24, 25

Section 4: Skye and Raasay

No	Location	Route	Distance miles (km)	Time (at 9mph/15kph)	Connecting link routes	Links to ferries
4A	Skye	Ullapool – Armadale	151 (242); alternative: 179 (286)	16hrs 50mins; 19hrs 40mins	4B	25, 33
	Stage 1	Ullapool – Braemore Junction	12.5 (20)	1hr 20mins		
	Stage 2	Braemore Junction – Gairloch	43 (69)	4hrs 40mins		
	Stage 3	Gairloch – Shieldaig	37 (59)	4hrs 40mins		
	Stage 4	Shieldaig – Stromeferry	26 (42)	2hrs 50mins		
	Alt Stage 4	Shieldaig – Stromeferry	54 (87)	5hrs 40mins		
	Stage 5	Stromeferry – Armadale	32.5 (52)	4hrs		
4B	Skye	Stromeferry – Uig	81 (130)	8hrs 35mins	4A	26, 27, 30, 32
	Stage 1	Stromeferry – Glenelg Ferry	27.5 (44)	2hrs 50mins		
	Stage 2	Kylerhea – Broadford	11.5 (18)	2hrs 50mins		
	Stage 3	Broadford – Portree	25 (40)	2hrs 45mins		
	Stage 4	Portree – Uig	17 (27)	1hr 45mins		

Section 5: Barra and the Uists

No	Location	Route	Distance miles (km)	Time (at 9mph/15kph)	Connecting link routes	Links to ferries
5A	Barra/South Uist	Castlebay – Eriskay – Dalabrog – Lochboisdale	26 (42)	3hrs 5mins	5B	28, 29
5B	South Uist/ Benbecula	Dalabrog – Clachan	31 (50)	3hrs 20mins	5A, 5C, 5D	
5C	North Uist	Clachan – Lochmaddy – Berneray	19 (30)	1hrs 55mins	5B, 5B	30, 31
5D	North Uist	Clachan – Paibeil – Berneray Junction	20 (32)	2hrs 10mins	5B, 5C	31

Section 6: Harris and Lewis

No	Location	Route	Distance miles (km)	Time (at 9mph/15kph)	Connecting link routes	Links to ferries
6A	Harris	Leverburgh – Tarbert (west)	21 (34)	2hrs 10mins	6B, 6C	31, 32
6B	Harris	Leverburgh – Tarbert (east)	26 (42)	2hrs 15mins	6A, 6V	31, 32
6C	Harris/Lewis	Tarbert – Liurbost – Stornoway	36 (57)	4hrs	6A, 6B	32, 33
6D	Lewis	Liurbost – Gearraidh na h'Aibhne – Barabhas	32 (51)	3hrs 20mins	6C, 6E	
6E	Lewis	Stornoway – Barabhas – Butt of Ness	29 (47)	3hrs 10mins	6A, 6D	33

APPENDIX B

Day route summary table

Section 1: Clyde and Kintyre

No	Location	Route	Distance miles (km)	Time (at 9mph/15kph)	Grade
1.1	Arran	Circuit of south Arran	35 (56)	3hrs 50mins	Hard
1.2	Arran	Circuit of north Arran	37 (60)	3hrs 40mins	Hard
1.3	Cumbrae	Circuit of Great Cumbrae	13 (21)	1hr 30mins	Easy
1.4	Bute	Circuit of Bute	27 (43)	3hrs 30mins	Moderate
1.5	Gigha	Gigha	12 (19)	1hr 15mins	Easy

Section 2: Colonsay, Islay and Jura

No	Location	Route	Distance miles (km)	Time (at 9mph/15kph)	Grade
2.1	Islay	South coast of Islay	28 (45)	3hrs 30mins	Moderate
2.2	Islay	Circuit of northwest Islay from Bridgend	26 (42)	3hrs	Moderate
2.3	Islay	Circuit of central Islay from Bowmore	20 (31)	2hrs 30mins	Easy
2.4	Islay	Circuit of southwest Islay (the Rhinns)	21 (34)	2hrs 30mins	Moderate
2.5	Jura	Craighouse and back from Feolin Ferry	17 (27)	2hrs 10mins	Moderate
2.6	Colonsay	Circuit of Colonsay	15 (24)	1hr 45mins	Moderate

Section 3: Mull, Tiree and Coll

No	Location	Route	Distance miles (km)	Time (at 9mph/15kph)	Grade
3.1	Slate Islands	Slate Islands	33 (53)	3hrs 40mins	Moderate
3.2	Kerrera	Kerrera	13 (21)	2–3hrs	Moderate
3.3	Lismore	Lismore	42 (67)	4–5hrs	Moderate
3.4	Mull	Circuit of central Mull	48 (78)	5hrs 20mins	Hard
3.5	Mull	Circuit of northern Mull	43 (70)	4hrs 45mins	Very hard
3.6	Iona	Out to Iona	70 (112)	7hrs 40mins	Hard
3.7	Coll	Coll	27 (43)	3hrs	Moderate

3.8	Tiree	Circuit of west Tiree	23 (37)	2hrs 30mins	Easy
3.9	Tiree	Fishbone Ride in east Tiree	20 (32)	2hrs 30mins	Easy

Section 4: Skye and Raasay

No	Location	Route	Distance miles (km)	Time (at 9mph/15kph)	Grade
4.1	Skye	Across the Sleat Peninsula from Armadale	21 (34)	2hrs 15mins	Hard
4.2	Skye	Elgol and back from Broadford	30 (48)	3hrs 15mins	Hard
4.3	Skye	Three-legged ride from Carbost	38 (57)	4hrs 15mins	Hard
4.4	Skye	Around the Duirinish Peninsula	25 (41)	3hrs 15mins	Moderate
4.5	Skye	Circuit of the Trotternish Peninsula	49 (78)	5hrs 15mins	Hard
4.6	Skye	Circuit of central Skye	53 (85)	5hrs 45mins	Hard
4.7	Skye	Skye Bridge/Glenelg circuit	39 (62)	4hrs 10mins	Very hard
4.8	Raasay	Raasay	23 (37)	2hrs 15mins	Hard

Section 5: Barra and the Uists

No	Location	Route	Distance miles (km)	Time (at 9mph/15kph)	Grade
5.1	Barra	Circuit of Barra and Vatersay	29 (46)	3hrs 10mins	Hard
5.2	South Uist	South Uist machair from Tobha Mor	12 (19)	1hr 15mins	Easy
5.3	North Uist	Circuit of North Uist	37 (60)	3hrs	Moderate

Section 6: Harris and Lewis

No	Location	Route	Distance miles (km)	Time (at 9mph/15kph)	Grade
6.1	Harris	Circuit of south Harris	47 (74)	4hrs 30mins	Hard
6.2	Harris	Tarbert to Huisinis and back	33 (53)	4hrs 30mins	Hard
6.3	Harris	Tarbert to Scalpay and back	16 (26)	1hr 45mins	Moderate
6.4	Lewis	Callanish by the Pentland Road	39 (63)	4hrs 30mins	Moderate
6.5	Lewis	West Lewis from Gearraidh na h'Aibhne	56 (90)	6hrs	Moderate
6.6	Lewis	The Bridge to Nowhere and back from Stornoway	32 (52)	3hrs 10mins	Moderate

APPENDIX C
Ferry routes

Ferries are numbered as listed in Appendices A and B and as on the maps.

Ferry number	Ferry route	Journey time	Frequency/day in summer
1a	Ardrossan – Brodick	55mins	>5
1b	Ardrossan – Campbeltown	2hrs 40mins	Thur, Fri, Sun
1c	Campbeltown – Brodick	2hrs 20mins	Sat only
2	Largs – Cumbrae	10mins	>20
3	Wemyss Bay – Rothesay	25mins	>10
4	Gourock – Dunoon	23mins	>20
5	Colintraive – Rhubodach	5mins	>20
6	Portavadie – Tarbert	25mins	>10
7	Lochranza – Claonaig (Summer only)	30mins	>5
8	Tayinloan – Gigha	20mins	>5
9	Kennacraig – Port Ellen – Port Askaig	2hrs 20mins	3–4
10	Port Askaig – Jura	5mins	>10
11	Oban – Colonsay – Port Askaig – Kennacraig	2hrs 20mins – 1hr 10mins – 2hrs 5mins	Wed (all) and Sat (not Oban)
12	Oban – Colonsay	2hrs 20mins	Mon, Wed, Thur, Fri, Sun
13	Cuan – Luing	5mins	>20
14	Ellenabeich – Easdale	5mins	>20

Ferry number	Ferry route	Journey time	Frequency/day in summer
15	Oban – Kerrera	5mins	
16	Oban – Craignure	46mins	>5
17	Oban – Lismore	50mins	4
18	Lismore – Port Appin	10mins	>10
19	Corran Ferry	5 mins	>20
20	Lochaline – Fishnish	15mins	>10
21	Tobermory – Kilchoan	35mins	>5
22	Fionnphort – Iona	19mins	>10
23	Oban – Coll – Tiree	2hrs 55mins – 1hr	1
24	Mallaig – Small Isles	7hrs 35mins in total	1
25	Mallaig – Armadale	30mins	>5
26	Glenelg – Kylerhea	10mins	>20
27	Sconser – Raasay	25mins	>5
28	Oban – Castlebay and Lochboisdale (Stops at Tiree and Coll on Thursdays in summer)	5hrs 20mins–1hr 30mins	1
29	Barra – Eriskay	40mins	5
30	Uig – Lochmaddy	1hr 45mins	1–2
31	Berneray – Leverburgh	1hr	4
32	Uig –Tarbert	1hr 40mins	1–2 (not Sun)
33	Stornoway – Ullapool	2hrs 45mins	2

APPENDIX D
Day trips to islands

By going out on an early ferry it is possible to make a day trip to many islands and complete one or more of the rides before returning on a later ferry.

The table below lists the islands where day trips are practical during the summer months, showing the origin port and the maximum length of stay rounded down to whole hours. Note that day trips to some islands are only practical on certain days.

Island	From	Longest stay
Arran	Ardrossan	11hrs
	Claonaig	9hrs
Barra	Eriskay	8hrs
Berneray	Leverburgh	7hrs
Bute	Wemyss Bay	13hrs
	Coilintraive	13hrs
Canna	Mallaig	2hrs (Weds only)
Coll	Oban	8hrs (Thurs only)
Colonsay	Islay	7hrs (Weds only in summer)
Great Cumbrae	Largs	15hrs
Eigg	Mallaig	5hrs (Mon)
Eriskay	Barra	10hrs
Gigha	Tayinloan	10hrs
Harris	Uig	8hrs (Mon and Sat only)
	Berneray	10hrs
Iona	Fionnphort	9hrs
Islay	Kennacraig	9hrs
	Jura	16hrs
Jura	Islay	17hrs

Island	From	Longest stay
Kerrera	Oban	9hrs
Lismore	Oban	10hrs
	Port Appin	14hrs
Lewis	Ullapool	6hrs (Weds and Fri only)
Luing	Seil	14hrs
Muck	Mallaig	2hrs (Tues only)
Mull	Oban	11hrs
	Lochaline	11hrs
	Kilchoan	9hrs
North Uist	Uig	5hrs (Sun only)
Raasay	Sconser	9hrs
Rum	Mallaig	2hrs (Mon and Fri), 4hrs (Wed), 10hrs (Sat)
Skye	Mallaig	10hrs
	Lochmaddy	8hrs (Mon and Sat), 4hrs (Tues, Thurs and Fri)
	Tarbert	4hrs
	Glenelg	8hrs
Tiree	Oban	6hrs (Thurs only)

APPENDIX E
Cycle shops and cycle hire

The following is a list, section by section, of cycle shops (🚲) and places where cycles can be hired (🚲🚲). There are other cycle shops in Fort William.

Section 1
Smooth Wheels 🚲
128b Main Street
Largs
KA30 8JN
tel 01475 689385

Phillips Cycles 🚲 🚲🚲
36 Kempock Street
Gourock
PA19 1NA
tel 01475 648223

X Bikes Argyll 🚲🚲
Hunter's Quay Holiday Village
Dunoon
tel 07795 301748
www.xbikesargyll.co.uk

Crinan Cycles 🚲 🚲🚲
34 Argyll Street
Lochgilphead
tel 01546 603511
www.crinancycles.co.uk

The Cycle Shop 🚲
60 Long Row
Campbeltown
tel 01586 554443

Arran Adventure Co 🚲🚲
Shore Road
Brodick
Isle of Arran
tel 01770 302244
www.arranadventure.com

Brodick Cycles 🚲
The Beach
Brodick
Isle of Arran
tel 01770 302460

The Bike Shed 🚲 🚲🚲
23–25 East Princess Street
Rothesay
Isle of Bute
tel 01700 505515
www.thebikeshed.org.uk

Robb Cycles 🚲
19 East Princes Street
Rothesay
Isle of Bute
tel 01700 502333

Bremners Stores 🚲
17 Cardiff Street
Millport
Isle of Cumbrae
tel 01475 530309

FVG Mapes and Son 🚲 🚲🚲
3–5 Guildford Street
Millport
Isle of Cumbrae
tel 01475 530444
www.mapesmillport.co.uk

On Your Bike 🚲 🚲🚲
27–29 Stuart Street
Millport
Isle of Cumbrae
KA28 0AJ
tel 01475 530300
www.onyourbikemillport.com

Gigha Boats Activity Centre 🚲🚲
Gigha
tel 07876 506520
www.gigha.net/gighaboats

Section 2
Islay Bike 🚲
Bowmore
PA43 7JH
tel 01496 810 653

Bowmore Post Office 🚲🚲
Islay
tel 01496 810366

Jim Lutomski 🚲
Port Ellen
tel 07760 196 592

Mick Stuart 🚲🚲
91 Lennox Street
Port Ellen
Islay
tel 01496 302391

Port Ellen Playing Fields Association 🚲🚲
Ellen Brown
Port Ellen
Islay
tel 07831 246911

Persabus Pottery 🚲🚲
Port Askaig
Islay
tel 01496 840753
www.persabuspottery.com

Port Charlotte Bike Hire ⛹
Islay
tel 01496 850488

Jura Bike Hire ⛹
Keils
Craighouse
tel 07092 180747

Section 3
Nevis Cycles ✂ ⛹
87 George Street
Oban
PA34 5NN
tel 01631 566033

Isle of Kerrera Bicycle Hire ⛹
tel 01631 563665

Lismore Bike Hire ⛹
tel 01631 760213

Archibald Brown & Son ✂ ⛹
21 Main Street
Tobermory
Isle of Mull
tel 01688 302 020
www.brownstobermory.co.uk

Finlay Ross Ltd ⛹
Martyrs' Bay
Isle of Iona
tel 01681 700357

Post Office ⛹
Aringour
Coll
tel 01879 230395

Mrs Judith Boyd ⛹
Millhouse
Cornaigmore
Tiree
tel 01879 220435

MacLennan Motors ⛹
Pierhead
Scarinish
Tiree
tel 01879 220555

Tiree Fitness Solutions ⛹
Sandaig
Tiree
tel 01879 220 421
www.tireefitness.co.uk

A McConnell ⛹
Kilchattan
Isle of Colonsay
PA61 7YR
tel 01951 200355

Section 4
Scotpackers Bike Hire ⛹
West House
West Argyle Street
Ullapool
tel 01854 61312

Island Cycles ✂ ⛹
The Green
Portree
Isle of Skye
tel 01478 613 121

Skye Bicycle Hire ⛹
Uig Campsite
Isle of Skye
IV51 9XU
tel 01470 542 714

S S Donaldson ⛹
Fairwinds
Elgol Road
Broadford
Isle of Skye
IV49 9AB
tel 01471 822270
www.isleofskye.net/fairwinds

Section 5
Rothan Cycles ✂ ⛹
9 Howmore
South Uist
HS8 5SH
tel 01870 620283
www.rothan.com

Barra Cycle Hire ⛹
29 St. Brendan's Road
Isle of Barra
HS9 5XJ
tel 01851 810284

Section 6
Alex Dan Cycle Centre ✂ ⛹
67 Kenneth St
Stornoway
Isle of Lewis
HS1 2DS
tel 01851 704 025
www.hebrideancycles.co.uk

Bike Hebrides ⛹
Stornoway and Leverburgh
tel 07522 121414
www.bikehebrides.com

Harris Cycle Hire ⛹
Sorrel Cottage
2 Glen Kyles
Leverburgh
Isle of Harris
HS3 3TY
tel 01859 520319
www.sorrelcottage.co.uk

Harris Outdoor Adventure ⛹
Unit 1
Leverburgh Pier
Isle of Harris
tel 07788 425157
www.harrisoutdoor.co.uk

APPENDIX F
Hostels

Section 1
Inveraray
Inveraray YH
Dalmally Road
Inveraray PA32 8XD
tel 01499 302 454
www.syha.co.uk
April–October

Lochranza
Lochranza YH
Lochranza
Isle of Arran KA27 8HL
tel 01770 830 631
www.syha.org.uk
April–October only

Rothesay
Bute Backpackers
The Pier View
36 Argyle Street
Rothesay
Isle of Bute PA20 0AX
tel 01700 501876
www.butebackpackers.co.uk

Section 2
Port Charlotte
Port Charlotte YH
Port Charlotte
Isle of Islay PA48 7TX
tel 01496 850 385
www.syha.org.uk
April–October only

Colonsay
Colonsay Keepers Lodge
Colonsay Estate Cottages
Isle of Colonsay
Argyll PA61 7YU
tel 01951 200312
www.colonsayestate.co.uk

Section 3
Dervaig
Dervaig Bunkrooms
Dervaig Village Hall
Dervaig
Isle of Mull PA75 6QN
tel 01688 400 491
www.bunkrooms.mull-
scotland.co.uk

Glenfinnan
Glenfinnan Sleeping Car
Railway Station
Glenfinnan
Inverness-shire PH37 4LT
tel 01397 722295/722334
www.glenfinnanstation
museum.co.uk

Iona
Iona Hostel
Lagandorain
Iona
Argyll PA76 6SW
tel 01681 700 781
www.ionahostel.co.uk

Kerrera
Kerrera Bunkhouse
Lower Gylen
Isle of Kerrera
By Oban PA34 4SX
tel 01631 570223
www.kerrerabunkhouse.co.uk

Mallaig
Sheena's Backpackers Lodge
Harbour View, Mallaig
Inverness-shire PH41 4PU
tel 01687 462764
www.mallaigbackpackers.
co.uk

Oban
Corran House
1 Victoria Crescent
Oban
Argyll PA34 5PN
tel 01631 566040
www.hostel-scotland.co.uk

Jeremy Inglis Hostel
21 Airds Crescent
Oban
Argyll PA34 5SJ
tel 01631 565065/563064
www.hostel-scotland.co.uk

Oban Backpackers
Breadalbane Street
Oban
Argyll PA34 5NZ
tel 01631 562107
www.obanbackpackers.com

Oban YH
Esplanade
Oban PA34 5AF
tel 01631 562025
www.syha.org.uk

Salen
Glenaros Lodge
Aros, Salen
Isle of Mull PA72 6JP
tel 01680 300301/
07796 886899
www.glenaroslodge.net

Strontian
Ariundle Centre
Strontian
North Argyll PH36 4JA
tel 01967 402279
www.ariundle.co.uk

Tiree
Millhouse Hostel
Cornaigmore
Isle of Tiree
Argyll PA77 6XA
tel 01879 220435
www.tireemillhouse.co.uk

Tobermory
Tobermory YH
Main Street
Tobermory PA75 6NU
tel 01688 302481
www.syha.org.uk
April–October only

Section 4
Achiltibuie
Achininver YH
Achiltibuie
Ullapool IV26 2YL
tel 01854 622482
www.syha.org.uk
May–August only

Achnashellach
Gerry's Hostel
Craig, Achnashellach
Strathcarron
Wester Ross IV54 8YU
tel 01520 766232
www.gerryshostel-
achnashellach.co.uk

Broadford
Broadford YH
Broadford
Isle of Skye IV49 9AA
tel 01471 822442
www.syha.org.uk
February–October only

Carbost
Glenbrittle YH
Glenbrittle
Carbost IV47 8TA
tel 01478 640278
www.syha.org.uk
April–September only

Waterfront Bunkhouse
Old Inn, Carbost
Isle of Skye IV47 8SR
tel 01478 640205
www.carbost.f9.co.uk

Dundonnell
Badrallach Bothy
Croft 9, Badrallach
Dundonnell
Ross-shire IV23 2QP
tel 01854 633281
www.badrallach.com
Need your own sleeping bag

Sailmhor Croft Hostel
Camusnagaul, Dundonnell
Ross-shire IV23 2QT
tel 01854 633224
www.sailmhor.co.uk

Eigg
Glebe Barn
Cleadale
Isle of Eigg PH42 4RL
tel 01687 482417/
01687 482417
www.glebebarn.co.uk

Gairloch
Gairloch Carn Dearg YH
Gairloch
Ross-shire IV21 2DJ
tel 01445 712219
www.syha.org.uk
April–September

Kyleakin
Dun Caan Hostel
Castle View, Pier Road
Kyleakin
Isle of Skye IV41 8PL
tel 01599 534087
www.skyerover.co.uk

Skye Backpackers
Benmhor
Kyleakin
Isle of Skye IV41 8PH
tel 01599 534 510
www.scotlandstophostels.com

Melvaig
Rua Reidh Lighthouse
Melvaig
Gairloch
Ross-shire IV21 2EA
tel 01445 771263
www.ruareidh.co.uk

Plockton
Plockton Station Bunkhouse
Nessun Dorma
Burnside, Plockton
Ross-shire IV52 8TF
tel 01599 544235
www.plockton.com

Portnalong
Croft Bunkhouse
Portnalong
Isle of Skye IV47 8SL
tel 01478 640254/07841
206157
www.skyehostels.com

Skye Walker Hostel
The Old School
Portnalong
Isle of Skye IV47 8SL
tel 01478 640250
www.skyewalkerhostel.com

Portree
Bayfield Backpackers
Bayfield, Portree
Isle of Skye IV51 9EW
tel 01478 612231
www.skyehostel.co.uk

Portree Independent Hostel
Old Post Office
The Green, Portree
Isle of Skye IV51 9BT
tel 01478 613737
www.hostelskye.co.uk

Raasay
Raasay YH
Creachan Cottage
Raasay IV40 8NT
tel 01478 660240
www.syha.org.uk

Ratagan
Ratagan YH
Glenshiel, Kyle IV40 8HP
tel 01599 511243
www.syha.org.uk
March–October

Sleat
Flora Macdonald Hostel
The Glebe, Kilmore, Sleat
Isle of Skye IV44 8RG
tel 01471 8444272/
07834 476378
www.isle-of-skye-tour-guide.
co.uk

Sligachan
Sligachan Bunkhouse
Sligachan Hotel
Isle of Skye IV47 8SW
tel 01478 650204
www.sligachan.co.uk

Staffin
Dun Flodigarry Hostel
Flodigarry, Staffin
Isle of Skye IV51 9HZ
tel 01470 552212
www.hostelflodigarry.co.uk

Uig
Uig YH
Uig, Isle of Skye IV51 9YD
tel 01470 542746
www.syha.org.uk
April–September

Ullapool
Ullapool YH
Shore Street
Ullapool IV26 2UJ
tel 01854 612254
www.syha.org.uk
April–October

Section 5
Berneray
Berneray Hostel
www.gatliff.co.uk

Castlebay
Dunard Hostel
Castlebay, Barra HS9 5XD
tel 01871 810443
www.dunardhostel.co.uk

Daliburgh
South Uist Bunkhouse
Daliburgh
South Uist HS8 5SS
tel 01878 700566
www.uistbunkhouse.co.uk

Glendale
Glendale Hostel
North Glendale
South Uist HS8 5UD
tel 01878 700545
www.southuisthostel.co.uk

Howmore
Howmore Hostel
Tobha Mhor, South Uist
(Grid Ref NF757365)
www.gatliff.org.uk

Nunton
Nunton House Hostel
Benbecula
HS7 5LU
www.nuntonhousehostel.com

Section 6
Galson
Galson Farm Bunkhouse
South Galson
Isle of Lewis HS2 0SH
tel 01851 850492
www.galsonfarm.co.uk

Kershader
Kershader SYHA
Ravenspoint, Kershader
South Lochs

Isle of Lewis HS2 9QA
tel 01851 880236
www.syha.org.uk

Leverburgh
Am Bothan Bunkhouse
Ferry Road, Leverburgh
Isle of Harris HS5 3UA
www.ambothan.com

Rhenigidale
Rhenigidale Hostel
Rhenigidale
Isle of Harris HS3 3BD
www.gatliff.org.uk

Stornoway
Fairhaven Hostel
28 Francis Street, Stornoway
Isle of Lewis HS1 2ND
tel 01851 705862

Heb Hostel
25 Kenneth Street, Stornoway
Isle of Lewis HS1 2DR
tel 01851 709889
www.hebhostel.com

Laxdale Bunkhouse Hostel
6 Laxdale Lane
Isle of Lewis HS2 0DR
tel 01851 703234
www.laxdaleholidaypark.com

Stornoway Backpackers
47 Keith Street, Stornoway
Isle of Lewis HS1 2JG
tel 01851 703628

Tarbert
Drinishader Hostel
Golden Road
Drinishader, Tarbert
Isle of Harris HS3 3DX
tel 01859 511255

Rockcliff Hostel
Main Street, Tarbert
Isle of Harris HS3 3DJ
tel 01859 502081

APPENDIX G
Tourist information

Section 1
For general information and
all types of accommodation
the official tourist
board website is www.
visitscottishheartlands.com.

Brodick
The Pier
Brodick
Isle of Arran
tel 0845 22 55 121

Dunoon
7 Alexandra Parade
Dunoon
PA23 8AB
tel 08707 200 629

Inveraray
Front Street
Inveraray
PA32 8UY
tel 08707 200 616

Lochgilphead
Lochnell Street
Lochgilphead
PA30 8JN
tel 08707 200 618
April–October

Rothesay
Isle of Bute Discovery Centre
Winter Gardens
Victoria Street
Rothesay
Isle of Bute
PA20 0AT
tel 08707 200 619

Tarbert
Harbour Street
Tarbert
PA29 6UD
tel 08707 200 624
April–October

Section 2
For general information and
all types of accommodation
the official tourist board
websites are www.
visitscottishheartlands.com
and www.visithighlands.com.

Bowmore
The Square
Bowmore
Isle of Islay
PA43 7JP
tel 08707 200617

Section 3
For general information and
all types of accommodation
the official tourist board
websites are www.
visitscottishheartlands.com
and www.visithighlands.com.

Craignure
The Pier
Craignure
Isle of Mull
PA65 6AY
tel 08707 200 610

Kilchoan
Pier Road
Kilchoan
Acharacle
PH36 4LJ
tel 01845 22 55 121

Mallaig
The Pier
Mallaig
PH41 4SQ
tel 01845 22 55 121

Oban
Argyll Square
Oban
PA34 4AN
tel 08707 200 630

Tobermory
Main Street
Tobermory
Isle of Mull
PA75 6NU
tel 08707 200625
April–October

Section 4
For general information and
all types of accommodation
the official tourist board
website is
www.visithighlands.com.

Broadford
The Car Park
Broadford
Isle of Skye
IV49 9AB
tel 01471 822361
April–October

Dunvegan
2 Lochside
Dunvegan
Isle of Skye
IV55 8WB
tel 01470 521581
April–October

Gairloch
Achtercairn
Gairloch
IV22 2DN
tel 01445 712071
April–October

Kyle of Lochalsh
Car park
Kyle of Lochalsh
IV40 8AQ
tel 01599 534390
April–October

Lochcarron
Visitor Centre
Lochcarron
IV54 8YB
tel 01520 722 357

Portree
Bayfield House
Bayfield Road
Portree
Isle of Skye
IV51 9EL
tel 01599 534390
April–October

Ullapool
20 Argyle Street
Ullapool
IV26 2UB
tel 01854 612488
April–October

Section 5

For general information and all types of accommodation the official tourist board website is www.visithebrides.com.

Castlebay
Main Street
Castlebay
Isle of Barra
HS9 5XD
tel 01871 810336
April–October

Lochboisdale
Pier Road
Lochboisdale
Isle of South Uist
HS8 5TH
tel 01878 700286
April–October

Lochmaddy
Pier Road
Lochmaddy
Isle of North Uist
HS6 5AA
tel 01876 500321
April–October

Section 6

For general information and all types of accommodation the official tourist board website is www.visithebrides.com.

Stornoway
26 Cromwell Street
Stornoway
Isle of Lewis
HS1 2DD
tel 01851 703088

Tarbert
Pier Road
Tarbert
Isle of Harris
HS3 3DJ
tel 01859 502011
April–October

APPENDIX H
Further reading

Travel guides

Arran, Robert McLellan, David & Charles, 2008

Bute, Norman Newton, David & Charles, 2009

Islay, Norman Newton, David & Charles, 2009

Kintyre, Norman S Newton, David & Charles, 2008

Lewis and Harris, Francis Thompson, David & Charles, 2007

Mull and Iona, PA Macnab, David & Charles, 2008

Skye, Norman S Newton, David & Charles, 2007

Uists and Barra, Francis Thompson, David & Charles, 2007
A series of souvenir guides that have excellent colour photography but little practical information.

Exploring the Islands of Scotland – The Ultimate Practical Guide, Julian Holland, Francis Lincoln, 2008
Not that useful as a guidebook, but a good introduction to the 42 inhabited islands off the Scottish mainland.

Scottish Islands: Western Isles Book 1, James and Deborah Penrith, Vacation Work Publications, 2004
A thoroughly comprehensive tourist guidebook, somewhat spoilt by the lack of photographs.

Scotland Highlands and Islands, Colin Hutchison and Alan Murphy, Footprint, 2009
Yet another comprehensive tourist guidebook: perhaps not as detailed, but more attractively presented.

The Magic of the Scottish Islands, Terry Marsh and Jon Sparks, David & Charles, 2008
Another excellent introduction to the Scottish Islands by two Cicerone authors.

The Outer Hebrides, Malcolm MacGregor, Francis Lincoln, 2007
Simply the best collection of photographs of the Western Isles

The Outer Hebrides Handbook and Guide, David Perrott, Kittiwake, 1995
Continually revised, this is a good overview of the islands.

The Scottish Islands, Hamish Haswell-Smith, Canongate, 2008
The definitive guide to even the smallest islands complete with wonderful hand-drawn maps and illustrations.

The Hebrides: An Aerial View of a Cultural Landscape, Angus and Patricia Macdonald, Birlinn, 2010
A cultural history of the Hebrides making use of stunning aerial photography.

Cycling

A man, a bike, alone through Scotland, Eugene Cantin, World Publications, 1977
This American journal of a trouble-ridden, but ultimate successful, six week tour around the coast of Scotland shows that you need to ensure your bike is up to the job.

From the Mull to the Cape, Richard Guise, Summersdale, 2008
One man's wry account of a slow journey up the west coast that is never quite as funny as the blurb promises.

Full Cycle, Stuart Craig, Lindsay, 2001
Glaswegian dentist Stuart Craig's write-up of two separate one week tours where island bagging and ferry spotting occasionally take precedent over the cycling.

Riddoch on the Outer Hebrides, Lesley Riddoch, Luarth Press, 2007
Broadcaster Lesley Riddoch's thought-provoking commentary on the Outer Hebrides based on her cycle journey through the island chain.

The Fragile Islands: A Journey through the Outer Hebrides, Bettina Selby, Mountain House, 2003
One woman's account of a slow and thoughtful journey up the Western Isles.

The Isles and Highlands of Western Scotland, Phil Horsley, Cordee, 1997
A gazetteer of the main routes and points of interest with hand drawn maps and illustrations.

Travel writing

Peat Smoke and Spirit: A Portrait of Islay and its Whiskies, Andrew Jefford, Headline, 2005
Wonderful writing of the kind that every island deserves by a professional drinks writer.

The Discovery of the Hebrides, Elizabeth Bray, Collins, 1986
Based on the documented journals of the early travellers to the Hebrides.

Walking guides

The Isle of Mull, Terry Marsh, Cicerone, 2011

The Isle of Skye, Terry Marsh, Cicerone, 2009

Walking in the Hebrides, Roger Redfern, Cicerone, 2003

Walking on Harris and Lewis, Richard Barrett, Cicerone, 2010

Walking on Jura, Islay and Colonsay, Peter Edwards, Cicerone, 2010

Walking on Rum and the Small Isles, Peter Edwards, Cicerone 2012

Walking on the Isle of Arran, Paddy Dillon, Cicerone, 2008

Walking on Uist and Barra, Mike Townsend, Cicerone 2012

Definitive guidebooks from the UK's pre-eminent outdoor publisher.

LISTING OF CICERONE GUIDES

Walking – Trekking – Mountaineering – Climbing – Cycling

Over 40 years, Cicerone have built up an outstanding collection of 300 guides, inspiring all sorts of amazing adventures.

Every guide comes from extensive exploration and research by our expert authors, all with a passion for their subjects. They are frequently praised, endorsed and used by clubs, instructors and outdoor organisations.

All our titles can now be bought as **e-books** and many as iPad and Kindle files and we will continue to make all our guides available for these and many other devices.

Our website shows any **new information** we've received since a book was published. Please do let us know if you find anything has changed, so that we can pass on the latest details. On our **website** you'll also find some great ideas and lots of information, including sample chapters, contents lists, reviews, articles and a photo gallery.

It's easy to keep in touch with what's going on at Cicerone, by getting our monthly **free e-newsletter**, which is full of offers, competitions, up-to-date information and topical articles. You can subscribe on our home page and also follow us on **Facebook** and **Twitter**, as well as our **blog**.

Cicerone – the very best guides for exploring the world.

CICERONE

2 Police Square Milnthorpe Cumbria LA7 7PY
Tel: 015395 62069 info@cicerone.co.uk
www.cicerone.co.uk